D0734588

A Grave for

Bobby

OTHER BOOKS BY JAMES DEAKIN

The Lobbyists

Lyndon Johnson's Credibility Gap

Straight Stuff

The White House Press on the Presidency
   (with Helen Thomas and Frank Cormier)

A Grave for

Bobby

The Greenlease Slaying

James Deakin

William Morrow and Company, Inc.
New York

Library of Congress Cataloging-in-Publication Data

Deakin, James. 1929–
    A grave for Bobby / James Deakin.
        p.   cm.
    ISBN 0-688-06730-1
    1. Greenlease, Robert Cosgrove. 2. Kidnapping—Missouri—St.
Louis—Case studies. 3. Murder—Missouri—St. Louis—Case studies.
4. Hall, Carl Austin. 5. Heady, Bonnie Emily. I. Title.
HV6603.G74D43   1990
364.1'54'092—dc20
[B]   898-37576
                                                                      CIP

Printed in the United States of America

    2   3   4   5   6   7   8   9   10

BOOK DESIGN BY KARIN BATTEN

*To Doris and David, always, and to the memory
of my sister, Carol Reynolds, of St. Louis*

Chapter **1**

A large midwestern city: smug and sooty. It lies in the curve of a great river which was once very important to the city but which now, in the year 1953, is generally ignored. The river, being old to the point of immortality, is a taunt to man's pretensions and has other philosophic aspects, but philosophers are in a minority here as elsewhere. The city is devotedly commercial; it produces beer, shoes, chemicals, warplanes and dog food, and it gave the world T. S. Eliot and the ice-cream cone, after which it rested. It has a population of more than 850,000 persons, and it has universities, parks, museums, a famous zoo, and other fine things of which it is justly proud. But the evidences of decline are unmistakable; decay glows sickly in the city. The downtown buildings that rise immediately west of the river—if buildings so weary can be said to rise—are implacably grimy. A city ordinance against industrial smoke was enacted a few years ago, but it was too late for these blackened Calibans of buildings.

Beyond the downtown section, there is a vast and noisome slum. Here live—in the customary wretched circumstances—the city's poor. Occasionally they riot. On the edges of the slum, waiting to be overtaken, are deteriorating working-class districts of small houses, apartment buildings and shops. These are worn neighborhoods, mile after mile of them, featureless, in which shabby respectability is jostled by disrepute and crime.

In the city's "west end" are wealthy old families, ravaged by money to a condition of intellectual harelip. They dwell (rather than live) in frowning mansions on private streets girded round by walls and entered through fantastical, crenellated gates that appear to have been designed by minor Bavarian artists gone mad. On the "South Side," entrenched as if to repel invaders, which is precisely the case, are the city's burghers, a couple of hundred thousand of them, mostly of German descent, thrifty, clean, respectable and remarkably hard of head: the despair of others and the admiration of themselves. But except for these stubborn folk, the middle class of this old city is fleeing to the suburbs with the speed of debt.

Elsewhere: a big brutish war lately over, a nasty small war coming to an end, Roosevelt dead, Hitler dead, millions dead, nothing new in that, an abstraction. A famous general in the White House eight hundred miles away, money to be made, much money, and unpleasant problems—social justice and the like—to be avoided: Welcome to the Prophetic Fifties.

And on a highway leading to the city, a drunken man and woman, frightened, oh God they are so frightened, are fleeing from the enormity of their crime. They have with them a duffel bag containing a $600,000 ransom. When they reach the city, they will be caught, and less than three months later they will be executed.

At 2:00 A.M. on October 7, 1953, a man sat moaning and vomiting in a room at the Newstead Avenue police station in St. Louis, Missouri. His name was Carl Austin Hall. Earlier that night, Hall had confessed that he and his mistress, Bonnie Emily Heady, had kidnapped a six-year-old boy named Robert Cosgrove Greenlease, Jr., known as Bobby. The boy was still missing, and the FBI agents and St. Louis policemen who stood around Hall, trying to question him, strongly suspected that Hall and Mrs. Heady had murdered Bobby Greenlease. But Hall's responses to questions were confused and indistinct. It was hard to get anything coherent out of him. He began to retch.

"Get something for him to puke in," someone said. A wastebasket was put in front of Hall, and he vomited into it, his heavy body slumped over, his face glistening with sweat. Several times he slipped out of his chair, groaning, his body slack, and had to be hoisted up so the questioning could continue. But it was a one-sided interrogation; most of Hall's answers, an

FBI agent said later, were "mumbled and inarticulate words." Hall, the agent said, was "in a miserable physical condition . . . it could not be determined whether he was suffering from the effects of alcohol or whether the morphine [he had taken] was wearing off." Shortly before three in the morning, he lost consciousness.

Hall thought of himself as a master criminal. He told some of his colleagues at the Missouri penitentiary that he had a plan for a perfect crime. It would be perfect, he explained, because he would make so much money from it that he would never have to commit another crime. He would retire. He outlined glamorous plans to Bonnie Heady. With half of the $600,000, they would build a house at La Jolla, California, on a cliff overlooking the Pacific, where they would live part of the year. They would invest the other half, and on the income they would travel to exotic places. He talked of Mexico; they all talk of Mexico. And Florida. They would go to the races in Florida in the winter. And Europe. They would travel in Europe. He would be like those guys in the movies, Cary Grant and David Niven, suave international types wearing scarves instead of ties, smiling those slight, mocking smiles, beautiful women aching to get into bed with them, although he didn't tell Bonnie about the women.

His total income from crime, prior to the kidnapping of Bobby Greenlease, had been thirty-three dollars, which he obtained from some cab drivers in Kansas City, Missouri, in a series of nervous, sweaty robberies: Okay motherstickers, this is a fuckup. All he had to show for them, other than the thirty-three dollars, was a fifteen-month stretch in the state prison at Jefferson City. However, he would be a master criminal.

But he didn't look like Cary Grant or David Niven. With his fleshy face and bad complexion, his thinning hair brushed straight back from bald spots on each side, his loose body, he looked more like Hermann Goering at the Nuremberg trial. So here was the master criminal, a fat, untidy man in a dingy room in a police station in the middle of the night, whimpering, blubbering and swooning, feeling profoundly sorry for himself, and frightened out of his mind.

They took him to the city hospital, where he was examined by Dr. Cecil Auner. The physician's diagnosis was acute alcoholism. Auner said the patient was "semi-comatose [and] crying and mumbling for water." He described Hall as "very depressed" and unable to answer questions about his condition until the doctor administered caffeine sodium benzoate as a stimulant. Then, Auner said, Hall told him he was a morphine addict and had taken one fourth of a grain of the drug by mouth, but he denied ever taking more than that at any time. Auner said he found "no definite needle

9

puncture[s]'' and no evidence of drug addiction other than what Hall told him.

As the doctor was examining him, Hall "repeated over and over again, in a mumbling voice, 'I don't want the money.' '' Never mind Acapulco.

The FBI put together a physical description of the kidnapper: a white male, five feet ten inches tall, stockily built and weighing 171 pounds. His hair was medium brown, coarse and receding, his eyes light blue, his nose short and wide at the base, his lips thick and the upper lip prominent, his throat flabby. His upper body, the FBI said, "was inclined to slump,'' and his legs were short and stocky. His voice was described as low and husky, and his expression was said to be "dull.'' The dull expression was as close as anyone ever got to assessing Hall's mentality; as far as can be determined, he was never given a psychiatric examination. Under "peculiarities,'' the FBI said Hall "chain-smokes cigarettes; drinks fifth of whiskey per day; uses narcotics of Benzedrine type.'' He was thirty-four years old when he kidnapped Bobby Greenlease.

Bonnie Heady was forty-one. The FBI described her as a white female, five feet one inch tall, and "plump.'' Her weight was not given; perhaps she was unwilling to step on the scales for posterity. However, she was not fat, just heavy-breasted and pudgy. Her hair was dark brown with a reddish tint, and she wore it brushed up in a pompadour effect. Her eyes were brown; her nose was slightly bulbous. The FBI described her complexion as "pale,'' but Mrs. June Michael of St. Louis, who was the receptionist in the FBI office at the time, remembers that Bonnie's skin "was a little slick, like a woman who gets facials all the time. It seemed oily, as if she was nervous and sweating.'' In the period immediately after the kidnappers were arrested, Bonnie was seen to have a rather large bruise on her forehead, above her right eye, and a small abrasion on the bridge of her nose. It turned out that Hall had batted her around a little, shortly before they were arrested, during an exchange of opinions. Under Bonnie's "peculiarities,'' the FBI stated: "Drinks fifth of whiskey per day, sometimes goes without food for period of days.''

Hall was the first to confess the kidnapping. Mrs. Heady held out for a few hours longer, then admitted her part. But both of them insisted the boy was alive. They said he was in the custody of another man—a third kidnapper. The FBI and the St. Louis police were intensely skeptical about this; it had now been ten days since Bobby Greenlease had been abducted from a private school in Kansas City, and the FBI's experience in kidnapping cases was that each day lessened the chances that the victim was alive. So the questioning continued, after Hall was brought back from the hospital on a stretcher. A few hours later he changed his story. He said the boy was dead.

But "I didn't do it, I didn't do it, I didn't do it," Hall sobbed. He admitted that he and Mrs. Heady had kidnapped Bobby, but he still claimed another man was involved as well, and he insisted the "other man" had done the actual killing.

This was the first mystery. Was there another kidnapper, and had he killed Bobby Greenlease? If so, where was this "other man"? Bobby's body was quickly found, buried in Mrs. Heady's back yard as Hall had said. Ten days of terrible anxiety ended for the Greenlease family, to be succeeded by tragedy. But if someone else had killed their son, who was this someone else and where was he?

The first mystery was cleared up a few days later, when Hall and Heady changed their stories again. There was no "other man." Hall and his mistress had killed Bobby—killed him coldly and premeditatedly. They had never intended to return Bobby alive to his parents, because Hall feared the boy might be able to identify his abductors. Instead, they took him to a lonely field in Kansas and shot him.

Then, in another act of unfathomable cruelty, Hall made a series of telephone calls to the Greenlease family, to arrange the payment of the ransom—and each time he assured them that Bobby was alive and well. There were fifteen of these calls altogether, extending over a period of six days from September 30 to October 5, 1953. In each of them, Hall identified himself only as "M."

Bobby had been murdered on September 28, but in the calls "M" said repeatedly: "The boy is fine." In one of the telephone calls, just after midnight on October 4, Hall ("M") talked with Bobby's mother, Mrs. Virginia Greenlease:

Mrs. Greenlease: We have the money, but we must know our boy is alive and well. Can you give me that? Can you give me anything that will make me know that? . . .

M: A reasonable request, but to be frank with you, the boy has been just about to drive us crazy. We couldn't risk taking him to a phone.

Mrs. Greenlease: Well, I can imagine that. Would you do this? Would you ask him two questions? Give me the answer of two questions.

M: Speaking.

11

Mrs. Greenlease: —and we could follow instructions and have everything ready if I had the answer to these two questions. I would know my boy is alive.

M: All right.

Mrs. Greenlease: Ask him what is the name of our driver in Europe this summer.

M: All right.

Mrs. Greenlease: Do you have that?

M: Yes.

Mrs. Greenlease: And the second question—what did you build with your monkey blocks . . .

M: All right.

Mrs. Greenlease: . . . in your playroom the last night you were home. Now, one reason I'm asking you this is because we have other people who claim they have Bobby, and if I can get these answers from you, I'll know you have him and he is alive, which is the thing you know that I want.

M: We have the boy. He is alive. Believe me. He's been driving us nuts.

Mrs. Greenlease: Well, I can imagine that. He's such an active youngster.

M: He's been driving us nuts.

Mrs. Greenlease: Could you get those answers?

M: All right. . . .

At 1:35 A.M., ''M'' called again:

M: Lady, I called them and he wouldn't say anything. He just dummied up and he wouldn't say anything.

Mrs. Greenlease: We need to know that you have the boy and he is alive.

M: Lady, he is very much alive to date. He almost beat me over the head with a ball bat.

Mrs. Greenlease: I know he is a very active boy.

M: I know he comes from a good family. We have treated him well. We didn't beat the information out of him.

Mrs. Greenlease: Well, can you tell me how soon he will be released?

M: As soon as we have the money, he will be released in 24 hours in another town.

Mrs. Greenlease: We are anxious to see him. Can you tell me when he will be released?

M: In another city in 24 hours. Believe me, he's driving us crazy. I couldn't get the information. Did my best—believe me. He talks about a parrot, Polly [Hall and Heady had found out before the kidnapping that Bobby had a parrot], and said he whistled.

Mrs. Greenlease: We are ready to make the payoff, if you can assure me my boy is all right.

M: The boy is well; I saw him this afternoon.

Mrs. Greenlease: We are ready to make the payoff. . . .

M: We'll carry out our bargain if you carry yours out. I assure you your boy is safe—he is a hell-cat—lady, we have earned this money. . . .

When these conversations took place, Bobby had been dead for a week.

Downtown, at police headquarters on Twelfth Street (now Tucker Boulevard), the police reporter for the *St. Louis Post-Dispatch* came to work at about 4:30 A.M. on October 7, his usual time. His name was John Kinsella. He was an experienced reporter, and his experience told him something unusual was going on. There was an atmosphere. Kinsella quickly found out that it involved the Newstead Avenue station and it had people at headquarters very excited. The chief of police and the head of the FBI's St. Louis office had gone to the Newstead station in the middle of the night, Kinsella learned, and were still there. That made it something special—and so did the fact that no one at headquarters would tell him what it was. Kinsella was a big, friendly Irishman; normally the cops would talk to him pretty freely. But this time the lid was on.

He called the *Post-Dispatch*'s city editor, Sam Armstrong, a courtly man with a fine mustache and a bad stomach, an unusual city editor in that he was one of the best-liked persons on the newspaper. Kinsella told Armstrong about the mystery at the Newstead station, and after a moment's meditation on the forces available, the city editor decided to send reporter James A. Kearns, Jr. (The story that resulted, written by Selwyn Pepper from information obtained by Kearns and other reporters, was more than one hundred paragraphs long in its final version, some six columns of newsprint, and was a masterpiece.)

Arriving at the Newstead station, Kearns found more atmosphere. Clearly, something big was going on, but the door to the captain's office was closed, and everyone was strongly disinclined to talk. Then Kearns saw a lieutenant he knew, and asked him what was up. "I can't tell you a thing, not a thing," the policeman said.

"So I sat down on a chair in the outer room, and waited," Kearns recalls. "Then a strange thing happened. This lieutenant—I can't remember his name for the life of me—started walking around the room. He was pacing the floor in a sort of circle, and when he passed my chair he looked at me.'' The first time he passed, he said nothing. Kearns waited.

Another turn around the room. Then, as he passed Kearns a second time, the lieutenant muttered: ''They got the boy.''

He did another turn around the room. Passing Kearns again, he said: ''The Greenlease boy. They got the boy.'' It was now becoming very difficult to wait, but Kearns waited.

Another tour of the room, and then: ''They got the kidnappers, too.''

Kearns was done with waiting. ''I made a dash for the phone.''

He gave his office a bulletin. Then he ran back to the room. The lieutenant was still there, and now he was willing to answer questions. There wasn't another reporter in the police station. Kearns had the story all to himself.

''Then, after about forty-five minutes, a whole bunch of other reporters and TV people rushed in. The police had called them. They took us into the captain's office—and there were Hall and Mrs. Heady.''

And a second mystery, too.

Half of the ransom was missing.

Three hundred thousand dollars.

Chapter 2

I n the year 1894, a boy named Robert Cosgrove Greenlease came to live in Kansas City, Missouri. He was twelve years old; he had been born in 1882 on a farm in Saline County in west-central Missouri. He had little formal education, but that did not hold him back in a time before people had MBAs and interfaced; he was smart, ambitious and willing to work hard. And like many another youth in those bustling, hopeful days, he was drawn irresistibly to that noisy new thing, the automobile; the exhilarating gas buggy that was frightening horses and fascinating people all across the land; the flivver that was launching an enduring national obsession and, as later writers never tired of pointing out, changing the face of America. Lungs, too.

He wanted to make automobiles. In 1903, a few months before his twenty-first birthday, Greenlease and a partner found a small shop at 217 East Fifteenth Street in Kansas City and began manufacturing a sporty, three-cylinder car with "a copper water jacket" and no top. They made it by hand, and they called it the Kansas City Hummer, presumably because it hummed along. It sold for $3,300, and four of the cars were built before the venture had to be abandoned as unprofitable.

Greenlease's second venture was an automobile repair shop, with a livery service attached, just in case. Livery involved the care and feeding of horses, as commemorated in "Livery Stable Blues," with Mr. Rappolo or Mr. Shields doing neighs and whinnies. This enterprise was more successful, but horses were dull. As quickly as he could, Greenlease got back to automobiles exclusively, selling the legendary Thomas Flyer—the car that crossed Siberia to win an epic New York-to-Paris race. However, the Flyer was short-lived.

Greenlease's next try made him an American success story. In 1908, he got a franchise to sell Cadillacs. Shortly thereafter, Cadillac became part of General Motors. If Greenlease could not make cars, he could sell them; his business grew and grew. At its height, in addition to Cadillac and Oldsmobile dealerships in Kansas City, Greenlease was the wholesale distributor for Cadillacs from the Texas panhandle to the Dakotas and from Missouri to Colorado, and was a partner in Cadillac dealerships in Tulsa, Oklahoma City, Omaha, Topeka and other cities. By the 1950's, he was reputed to be one of the ten wealthiest men in Kansas City. And later he was said to be one of the largest individual stockholders in General Motors. Carl Austin Hall claimed that when he was considering the kidnapping he checked Greenlease in Dun and Bradstreet and found he was worth $24 million.

Greenlease and his first wife had no children, but they adopted a son, Paul Robert Greenlease. When Paul reached high-school age, it was decided to send him to a military school. The decision must have caused Greenlease untold grief in later years: One of Paul's classmates at the military academy was Carl Austin Hall. Although the two boys were not close friends, they knew each other, and Hall inevitably found out that Paul's father was a wealthy man.

In 1939, after his first marriage had ended in divorce, Robert Greenlease married Virginia Pollock, a woman considerably younger than himself, and they had two children. A daughter, Virginia Sue, was born in 1942. Then in 1947, when Greenlease was sixty-five years old, they had a son. They named him Robert Cosgrove Greenlease, Jr., and they called him Bobby.

He was the adored and cherished son of devoted parents who were rich enough to give him everything. The family home was a large, Tudor-style house, virtually a mansion, at 2920 Verona Road in affluent Mission Hills, which is a suburb of Kansas City but is located in Kansas, just across the state line from Missouri. The Greenleases had several servants, including a housekeeper, a gardener-handyman, a Swedish maid and a governess for Bobby. They traveled to Europe (Bobby and his governess went with them in the summer of 1953, a few months before the kidnapping), and their neighbors and friends were the elite of Kansas City. Bobby had a miniature, motor-driven Cadillac of his own, and two dogs and a parrot. His sister attended Sunset Hill, a fashionable girls' school, and Bobby went to the French Institute of Notre Dame de Sion. This exclusive private elementary school was then and still is located at 3823 Locust Avenue in Kansas City. It is operated by an order of nuns, the Sisters of Sion.

Most mornings Carl and Bonnie slept late, because almost always they had been drunk the night before. But on the morning of Monday, September 28, 1953, at Bonnie's home in St. Joseph, Missouri, they got up earlier than usual. At 7:30 A.M., they left the house in Bonnie's 1951 Plymouth station wagon, taking with them her dog "Doc," a boxer. They thought that if someone saw them with Bobby Greenlease after the kidnapping, it would look more natural for a small boy to have a dog with him.

They took Highway 71 to Kansas City, a short drive. Bonnie recalled that they made one stop, at Lynn's Inn, a tavern at 1209 West Platte Road in north Kansas City, where they had one or two drinks. But, she said, she was absolutely sober, her mind was clear, and she remembered her instructions "very clearly." Carl had been worried about this; he knew her problem, and he used to say she was a swell gal except she drank too much. So, because he was concerned that she might get drunk and forget her lines, they had rehearsed the previous afternoon and evening at her house, going over what she was to say the next morning. At Lynn's Inn, also, Carl bought a pack of chlorophyll tablets for her to chew, so that the nuns at Notre Dame de Sion would not smell the liquor on her breath. Then they drove into Kansas City.

Arriving at the school, they parked where they could see the front door. At 8:50 A.M., they saw the elder Greenlease drive up in a blue Cadillac and let Bobby out. Then Carl and Bonnie drove to the vicinity of Fortieth and Main streets, parked and waited a while. At about 10:30 or 10:45, Bonnie got out of the station wagon and walked to the office of the Toedman Cab Company at 3834 Main. She got into a cab driven by Willard P. Creech and told him to go to Notre Dame de Sion. Bonnie had taken pains with her appearance; she was wearing a beige nylon blouse with rows of gathered material across the front, a dark gabardine skirt, a brown hat and white gloves. She was trying to look respectable. "It's very hot today," she said primly.

They got to the school at 10:55 A.M., and Bonnie asked Creech to wait

17

for her; she would only be a couple of minutes. She rang the doorbell and was admitted by one of the nuns, Sister Morand.

Bonnie told Sister Morand she was Bobby Greenlease's aunt. She said the boy's mother had suffered a heart attack while shopping, had been taken to St. Mary's Hospital, and wanted to see her children. Bonnie described it as a serious heart attack. Sister Morand said later that the "aunt" (Bonnie implied that she was Mrs. Greenlease's sister) appeared to be very upset and apologized for her agitation. Carl need not have worried; whether from nervousness or talent, Bonnie was playing her role perfectly. She even identified the shopping center where Mrs. Greenlease supposedly had been stricken; it was, she said, the Country Club Plaza in south Kansas City.

The nun said she would get Bobby from class. Meanwhile, she suggested, his "aunt" might want to go into the school chapel and pray. She took Bonnie into the chapel, although Bonnie told her: "I'm not a Catholic. I don't know if God will answer my prayers."

Two other nuns saw Bonnie Heady as she waited for Sister Morand to bring Bobby. One of them, who had been cleaning the hallway leading to the chapel, noted that the woman seemed entirely unfamiliar with the school. But because this nun spoke only French, she said nothing to Bonnie. The other nun, Sister Alphonsina, came into the hallway, saw Bonnie, and thought she did not resemble Mrs. Greenlease at all; the nun wondered if she actually was a sister-in-law. "Are you Miss Greenlease?" Sister Alphonsina asked. "I don't understand you," Bonnie replied. No more was said.

Sister Morand, meanwhile, went to Bobby's second-floor classroom, told the boy his aunt had come to get him, and took him downstairs. Bobby asked his teacher if he could take with him a Jerusalem cross of which he was very proud; only two students had received them so far that year. The teacher said yes, and Bobby left wearing the cross on a red ribbon pinned to his shirt. He also took with him a plastic pencil with the name of the Greenlease-O'Neill Oldsmobile dealership on it.

Bonnie, who had come out of the chapel, met Sister Morand and Bobby at the foot of the stairs. An FBI summary of the case said later that "Bobby walked directly to the unknown woman without hesitation, and there was nothing in [his] actions or behavior to indicate to [Sister Morand] any doubt on his part that this woman was his aunt. . . . As the unknown woman left the school, she had an arm around Bobby's shoulder and was holding his hand."

Later, reporters asked the school authorities why they had allowed the woman to take Bobby away. Sister Marthanna, speaking for the Mother

18

Superior, said the school was always careful about visitors and the double front doors were kept locked. "But there was nothing to make us suspicious about [Bonnie]," she added. "One does not look for trouble."

Why did Bobby go with the woman? He had never seen her before. Why did he accept her unhesitatingly as his aunt? He was six years old, and to a six-year-old the adult world is an incomprehensible place that he is powerless to challenge or change. The difference between six-year-olds and adults is that six-year-olds know it. Or, if you prefer, he was a sheltered and much-loved child and therefore a trusting child. June Michael, the receptionist in the FBI's St. Louis office in 1953, recalls an episode after Carl and Bonnie were arrested. "Mrs. Heady had to go to the bathroom, and one of the agents asked me to go with her. She was weeping and mumbling. When we got to the bathroom, she said: 'You know, he put his little hand in mine, and he was so *trusting*.' "

Bonnie had arrived at the school just before 11:00 A.M. The whole business had taken only a few minutes. At about 11:30, another nun telephoned the Greenlease home to ask about Mrs. Greenlease's condition. To her astonishment, the maid replied that Mrs. Greenlease was at home. Did the nun want to talk to her? Bobby's mother came to the phone. No, she had not had a heart attack. No, she had not sent anyone to pick up Bobby. My God, what is going on here? *Where is my child?*

Leaving the school, Bonnie and the boy got into the cab, and Bonnie told Creech to take them to the Katz Drugstore at Fortieth and Main streets. During the trip, Creech heard the woman ask the boy: "Bobby, what are the names of your two dogs?" And then: "Bobby, what is the name of your black parrot?" (The parrot was green, and no one ever knew why Bonnie thought it was black.) Creech did not hear the boy's replies, but Bonnie said in her confession that Bobby told her the names of his dogs and said his parrot could talk to people. He also told her that his family had two Cadillacs—a little boy chattering away eagerly about his world. Bonnie told him that she was taking him to see his daddy and that they were going to get some ice cream first.

At the drugstore, Bonnie and the boy walked over to the station wagon, where Hall was waiting. "Hello, Bobby, how are you?" asked Hall. "Fine," said Bobby. They drove away from the drugstore, all three in the front seat with Bobby between Carl and Bonnie.

They went west on Westport Road and crossed into Kansas. Now they were traveling south, through the outskirts of Overland Park, Kansas, past

19

farms and fields. They were in Johnson County, about four and three-quarters miles west of the Kansas-Missouri line. Bobby was unaware of any danger; Hall said later that the boy seemed interested in the ride and did not cry or complain.

At the intersection of Highway 69 and Ninety-fifth Street (also known as Lenexa East Road), Hall turned into Ninety-fifth and then into a lane that ran through a field on the Dorothy Belle Moody farm. He drove the station wagon into the field.

Hall got out, went around to the back, and let down the tailgate. On it, he carefully spread out a piece of blue plastic sheeting that he had bought at the Western Auto Supply store in St. Joseph. While Hall was doing this, the boxer dog, Doc, jumped out of the rear of the station wagon. Bonnie got out, called the dog, and then she and her pet walked away from the station wagon, along one of the hedgerows. She said later that the dog was excited by the unusual activity, and she was afraid that he would run away and somehow attract attention to them. Bonnie was about one hundred feet away from the station wagon when she heard two shots. At the sounds, Doc began jumping around and barking loudly. Bonnie grabbed his collar and tried to quiet him. In the struggle with the dog, she lost her hat. She did not realize until later that it was gone.

When he had arranged the plastic sheeting on the tailgate, Hall went around to the passenger side of the station wagon, got in and sat down beside Bobby. In a sudden, quick move, he slipped a piece of clothesline over the boy's head and tightened it around his neck. Bobby screamed and kicked as Hall tried to strangle him—the two figures writhing and struggling on the front seat, the man cursing and straining as he tried to pull the rope tighter, the boy twisting and crying. But the rope was too short; Hall could not get enough of the ends in his hands to strangle Bobby.

Throwing away the rope, Hall pushed the boy down on the floor of the station wagon. Holding Bobby down with his feet, the sweating, cursing man drew his gun, a .38 revolver, and tried to pin the boy down long enough to get a shot. But Bobby was struggling wildly. Leaning over, Hall smashed him in the head with the gun or with his fist, knocking out three of Bobby's front teeth. That stunned the boy long enough for Hall to aim and fire, but the first shot missed, the bullet ricocheting off the floor and burying itself in the left front door panel. Hall fired again, and the second shot killed Bobby. The bullet entered the boy's head about one and a half inches behind the right ear, came out two inches above the left ear and embedded itself in the floor mat.

There was blood everywhere. Bobby's head and body were covered with blood, and there were splashes of blood, splotches and gouts of blood, on the front seat and floor of the station wagon, on Hall's face and hands, and on his blue sharkskin suit.

Hall pulled the body out of the station wagon and laid it on the ground for a moment. Then he picked it up, carried it around to the rear and wrapped it in the plastic sheeting. Pushing the bundle into the back of the station wagon, he concealed it under an old comforter used by Bonnie's dog. Then he and Bonnie got in the car and drove back to Kansas City. Although they were intensely nervous, they must have talked during the trip, but only one scrap of conversation, related by Bonnie, has survived:

"Why did you shoot him? I thought you were going to strangle him."

"I tried to, but the goddamned rope was too short," Carl replied. "Goddamn it, he was fighting and kicking. I had to shoot him."

On the drive back, the reaction hit. Hall was sweating and trembling, his nerves were screaming, he had to have a drink. They stopped again at Lynn's Inn in north Kansas City and parked in a lot at the rear. The day before the kidnapping, Hall had stolen a pair of license plates in St. Joe and had put them on the station wagon; in the parking lot he took them off and put the original plates back on. Then he wanted to go into the tavern for a drink, but he was afraid someone would notice the blood on his face and clothes. His Lady Macbeth tried to wipe it off with Kleenex: Yet here's a spot. . . . Out, damned spot! Out, I say. But it was no use; there was too much of it. So Bonnie went into the tavern instead, got a couple of drinks herself and brought a couple out to Carl. While she was doing this, Hall walked anxiously around the station wagon and squatted down to look under it. He wanted to see whether any blood was dripping out.

Finished with their drinks, they drove back to St. Joseph. Arriving at Bonnie's home, a six-room frame house at 1201 South Thirty-eighth Street, Hall carried Bobby's body into the basement. At this point, he remembered that Bobby had been wearing a Jerusalem cross. He fumbled open the plastic sheeting and removed the little emblem; he had suddenly realized he could make use of it. Then he carried the body upstairs, through the kitchen and out the back door into the yard, where the grave was waiting.

Hall had begun his preparations early. On September 10, eighteen days before the kidnapping, he purchased a fifty-pound bag of "Ash Grove Veri-Fat" lime from the Sawyer Material Company in Kansas City and stored it in Bonnie's basement. He said he had read somewhere that "hot" lime would dissolve human flesh and bone. On September 26, at the

Hatfield Hardware Company in St. Joseph, he bought a long-handled "True Temper" shovel. Mrs. Grace Hatfield remembered Hall. When she asked him what kind of shovel he wanted, he said: "It don't make any difference what kind of shovel. I'm only going to use it once anyway."

Carl and Bonnie had discussed the disposal of the body. First they thought they might put it in the river, but they decided it might float to the surface and be found before they had collected the ransom; their plan depended on persuading the Greenlease family that the boy was still alive. Then they thought of burying Bobby in a wooded area on the Kansas side of the state line, not far from the Greenlease home. But on one of their pre-kidnap drives they saw bulldozers in the wooded area, apparently preparing it for a subdivision. So they decided on Bonnie's back yard.

On Sunday, September 27, the day before the kidnapping, Hall dug a hole near the back porch. It took him almost all day; he would dig for an hour, then go in the house and rest for a while—which meant drinking—and then go out and dig some more. When he had finished, he had a hole about three feet deep and five feet long.

Hall put the body in the grave and covered it with lime. He started to fill in the hole with dirt, but before he got very far he remembered it was time to send the ransom note. He called to Bonnie to come out and finish filling in the grave while he hurriedly tried to wash the bloodstains out of the station wagon with a garden hose. Then he left for Kansas City to mail the first ransom note to the Greenlease family. Bonnie, who had been in the house drinking—she said she was very nervous and unsteady—came out and took over the shoveling. It was hard work, but she finally got the hole filled to within about six inches of the top. That night, she and Carl stayed home, watching television.

The next morning, Hall tried to clean up the basement, where Bobby's body had lain for a few minutes. Using turpentine and gasoline, he scrubbed at the bloodstains on the floor, and with a wet broom he tried to get the blood off the basement door. He overlooked the bloodstains on a fiber rug on the back porch.

After putting his bloody shirt in the washing machine, Hall threw the empty cartridge cases into the incinerator. He must have known they would not burn, but by now lucidity was losing.

Later that day—Tuesday, September 29—Hall drove to Kansas City again, with Bonnie accompanying him this time, and mailed a second ransom note to the Greenlease family. In this note, he enclosed Bobby's

Jerusalem cross, to convince the Greenleases that they were hearing from the real kidnappers. On the way to Kansas City, they stopped at Lynn's Inn again—they were pushing their luck at Lynn's—and had several drinks, and when they got home they got very drunk.

But before leaving for Kansas City, they did one other thing. They went to the McIninch Floral Company in St. Joseph, where they bought a dozen chrysanthemums from Lee Chesser, one of the gardeners, paying six dollars for them. They took the flowers back to Bonnie's house and planted them on Bobby's grave.

It was not remorse. It wasn't even sentiment. Hall said they planted the flowers to allay suspicion if anyone saw the newly turned dirt. He was that kind of man.

Chapter **3**

*T*hat kind of man? What kind of man? Sandra June O'Day thought at first he might be a homosexual. The word she uses, as she talks about Carl Hall, is "faggot," because Sandy never had advantages. She thought Hall might be a faggot because of his behavior toward the cab driver who had brought them together for a night of bliss. Sandy was supposed to supply the ecstasy, but instead Hall kept putting his arm around the cab driver, doing it constantly, and patting his cheek caressingly while saying in a soft voice, "That's my boy." And, as if to confirm her suspicion, she says Hall did not have sex with her during that night at the Coral Court motel in St. Louis—although the cab driver said she told him they did. Hall also said there was no sex. If there wasn't, it was a shame, because in those days Sandy was an appetizing piece when she was dolled up for the evening. But she said she just lay there on the bed, in her nice cocktail dress, and Hall put no moves on her. He didn't even take his clothes off. Of course, they were both drunk.

He grew up spoiled in Pleasanton, Kansas. He was born on July 1, 1919, the son of John Austin Hall and Zella Cannon Hall of Pleasanton, which is a town of about thirteen hundred people, south of Kansas City and very close to the Missouri-Kansas border. Pleasanton is the largest town in Linn County and it is the center of a good fishing and duck-hunting area. Lying between the Missouri corn belt and the Kansas wheat belt, this part of Kansas grows some of both and has dairy farms as well. Altogether a nice place in which to spend a childhood, especially if you were the only child in one of the town's most prosperous and respected families. (There was an older son, but he was injured at birth, was never mentally normal and died when he was about five years old; there were no other children.)

Hall's father was a successful attorney whose law practice and reputation extended well beyond Linn County, and his mother was the daughter of a judge. They lived in a large house at 311 West Tenth Street in Pleasanton. Samuel Tucker, retired manager of the Pleasanton telephone company, described the house as ''one of the nicest in town'' and said Hall's parents were considered among ''the leading people of our community.''

But Hall's father died unexpectedly of a brain tumor in 1932, just before Carl's thirteenth birthday, and thereafter his mother alternately dominated him, doted on him or ignored him. The customary mixed messages: Much of the time she was busy with her women's clubs and civic activities; then she would jump back into Carl's life to deal hurriedly with adolescence, dictating his behavior or pampering and indulging him. That, at any rate, was the version given by hometown witnesses at Hall's trial, but Hall disagreed with their portrayal and resented it. He told an Episcopal minister, Reverend George L. Evans: ''No one could have a finer mother than I had, and the same goes for my father. I had wonderful parents. Their actions were in no way responsible for my going bad.''

He got through elementary school with average grades and without any problems that anyone remembered. But as he entered his teens, he began to get into trouble. Small things at first; then as he got older, more serious things. He would drive to nearby towns and get drunk; sometimes he ended up in jail for reckless driving or disturbing the peace.

Why was he getting into trouble? Freud was still years away from the small towns of the Midwest; their canon was common sense, and common sense probably told Zella Hall's neighbors that the boy was missing the steadying influence of a father. But it may not have been there even when his father was alive. Mrs. Garnett Travis, who knew the Hall family when Carl was a boy, said his father ''wanted to do the right thing,'' but he was ''awfully stern.'' She said she never saw any display of affection between father and son—a common psychological obituary.

But in any event, Carl was fatherless in his teens, and that left it up to his mother. There were conflicting reports about Zella Hall; there are conflicting reports about everybody. There was Carl's Nixonian statement that "no one could have a finer mother than I had," and this was supported to an extent by Mrs. Travis: "I think she loved him like any mother loves a child." But Mrs. Travis added that Zella always "seemed afraid that the younger generation was not very good, and it was hard to get them to do anything."

And there were the recollections of Mrs. Pansy McDowell. The summer after his father died, Carl stayed for a while with the McDowells. When Zella brought her son to their home, she said he had become "quite a problem," but Mrs. McDowell thought the mother, not the son, was the problem. "From the point of view of understanding a child," she said, Zella was "one of the most cold-blooded persons" she had ever known.

One night, Mrs. McDowell said, "Carl was sobbing in his bed, the type of sobs that tear you to pieces. I took him in my arms, and he told me that although he liked me, his father was dead and now he couldn't be with his mother and his 'two-momma,' his grandmother."

Some of Zella's neighbors thought she had made a mistake in letting Carl run free during summer vacations, because this was when he mostly got into trouble. Other boys his age had to get jobs in the summertime, but Carl's father had left the family "so well off that the boy didn't have to work," Mrs. Travis said.

The neighbors thought Zella made another mistake in not sending Carl to high school in Pleasanton, with the boys he knew. "He wanted to go on with the other boys, but she sent him to military school, because she felt he would learn more along the lines she wanted. . . ." Samuel Tucker said. "The boy had ideas of his own. It was hard for his mother to control him. She thought it was better for him to have this military experience in early life. It was her decision that sent him to the Marines [later]." The impression gains ground that Zella had an authoritarian outlook. Or perhaps she was just afraid. How could she hold her head up, as one of the town's leading citizens, when her son was going bad? Better to send him away.

So in September 1933, when he was fourteen years old, Carl entered a military school. He stayed for three years, compiling a record that was good at first and then not quite so good.

In his file for the first year were these comments: "On honor role one month. Member of rifle team. Member of company basketball team." In his second year: "Dependable, conscientious, promising cadet. Very likeable boy [but] slow developing. Good mind, willing to work, but temperamental. Honest and dependable. Fine youngster, dependable, capable and ambitious. A kid with [a] capacity for affection. Member of company baseball team.''

But in his third year, 1935–36, some of his instructors began to have doubts about Carl: "None too straightforward. Has ability but must be observed constantly. A worthless streak at times. Needs strong discipline. Good boy, will develop into fine man. Not serious in attitude. Tries to bluff; authority must be shown over him. Average student and member of company basketball team.''

There was another notation in the file. It said that Carl, while in the academy's hospital for some illness, "had attempted to have liquor brought into him.''

In 1936, Carl left the military school and returned to his hometown, where he attended the local high school in his senior year. His grades were average, but he was elected vice-president of the senior class, the only school distinction he ever received. He graduated in May 1937.

In September of that year, he enrolled at William Jewell College in Liberty, Missouri, but it was a no-win from the start. He stayed only three months. Under the college's hour system he received one half-hour grade of A, five hours of D's and thirteen hours of F's. So his mother decided he would join the Marines.

He enlisted in January 1938 and served a four-year hitch, being discharged as a private first class. He reenlisted immediately and served another four-year hitch, which took him through World War II. He was discharged in January 1946 "under honorable conditions," less than a full honorable discharge. He was a corporal when he left the Marines for good; he had made sergeant at one point but was busted for being absent without leave.

His second hitch took him to the Pacific with the First Marine Division. He was in the New Britain, Pelelieu and Okinawa campaigns, serving as a telephone-equipment repairman, but there is no record of any wounds, medals or heroism. Instead, his military files show six disciplinary actions, although none were for serious crimes; most of them involved drunken sprees. Hall said later that he had been "an habitual user of liquor" since 1946—the year he got out of the Marines. He said he frequently drank a fifth of whiskey a day.

What else can be said about Carl Hall as he entered civilian life in 1946, at the age of twenty-six? At the height of his young manhood and vigor, with the lottery not absolutely decided either way, dissipation making the prospect not good, not good at all, but the spark not quite extinguished, the outcome not irrevocable? What other features had he?

27

He was a slob. He was a member of the largest identifiable group in the American population, then and now: the slobs. He could read and write, but these activities were not pleasurable to him, so he did them as infrequently as possible; had he lived, he would have watched television. Beyond the rudiments, his education was a mockery; he knew next to nothing of history, literature, music, art, philosophy or science. He had no culture worthy of the name. No Mozart slow movement or *Dove sono i bei momenti,* no *Bleak House* or Monet garden, had awakened him to the miracles that this neotenic ape, this evolutionary failure, can nonetheless accomplish. The human condition, in its agonies, falterings and oppressions, and its hopes and sacrifices and loves, was an enormous unknown to him. So he came out into the world.

With $200,000. In 1944, while Carl was still in the Marines, his mother died. She left $200,000, mostly in stocks, bonds and some real estate, and Hall got it all. After his discharge, he hurried back to Pleasanton and quickly converted his inheritance into cash. The lawyer who handled things for him, Marshall K. Hoag, said Hall sold property and securities "right and left." He told Hoag: "Sentiment doesn't mean a thing to me."

Pleasanton was too small to hold him. He swaggered around town for a while, but there wasn't much town to swagger in. Besides, Hall and Pleasanton were beginning to get on each other's nerves. The townspeople thought he had got too big for his britches, and Hall thought they were just jealous because he had money. "I'll show 'em," he said. "I'll show 'em how money and brains can really get along. . . . I hate little people. I like to be big."

He began to spend most of his time in Kansas City. Now here was a big town, a big go-getting town where he could make more money and add to his stake, a town worthy of big Carl Hall. He took a room at the Phillips Hotel, and back in Pleasanton they heard he was living it up, dressing fancy and eating expensively and . . . well, you know Kansas City. The hotel's employees said later that Hall spent money freely, especially on horses that did not run fast enough. He played the stock market, which also disappointed him, and he tried his hand at several ill-fated business ventures.

Not long after he got out of the Marines, Hall married a woman named Irene. They were married in 1946 in Excelsior Springs, Missouri, and divorced in 1950, in Kansas City. Little is known about the marriage, except that there were no children and that his wife left Hall because of his drinking.

In 1947, he set up a crop-dusting business, in partnership with another man. They rented two small airplanes, hired pilots and got some contracts, but heavy rains hampered crop-spraying that year. Displaying some ingenuity, they then obtained a government contract to spray the mosquitoes in the rain-swollen backwaters. However, one of the planes crashed, and Hall got out of the business. He had invested either $16,000 or $18,000—it is not clear which—and said he lost between $10,000 and $12,000, although another estimate put his loss at only $4,000.

He then tried a canned-music business, piping treacle into hospitals and selling earphones to the sufferers. It is not known how much he lost on this one. Later, he operated two liquor stores in Bates County, Missouri, near Pleasanton, but he was better at drinking it than selling it; one of these ventures lasted two years and the other six months.

After his wife divorced him, Hall went to California for a while. He said he had no steady job at this time; he was "just bumming around the country drinking and gambling until I had lost all my inheritance." He said he knew the money from his mother would have kept him "in a comfortable situation for a good number of years," if he had lived "frugally." But he said this after the good times had come to an end—traditionally the moment of contrition. While the champagne was flowing, he did not want to be prudent.

So he spent and spent. He went through the entire $200,000 in less than five years. When it was gone, he did not change his ways. He did not resolve to be provident. He resolved to get more money.

In 1951, he became a master criminal. On May 14 of that year, he was arrested in Milwaukee on a charge of vagrancy by reason of selling an automobile, a 1948 Oldsmobile, without revealing that there was a loan on it. The charge was dismissed when he returned the money. Then he apparently committed a robbery in Kingman, Kansas. There is a reference to this charge being dropped later, because in the meantime he had been arrested in Kansas City.

On September 16, the Kansas City police dropped on him for robbing eight cab drivers. They were strange little robberies. The victims said Hall was very polite. He had a revolver and he showed it to them, but he assured them he would not hurt them. The robberies produced, as previously noted, a total of thirty-three dollars.

He pleaded guilty to two of the holdups and was sentenced to five years in prison. He entered the Missouri penitentiary on January 21, 1952, and

29

was released on parole on April 24, 1953, having served a year and three months.

One of his cellmates said Hall boasted that when he got out, he was going to pull off a perfect crime and then ''laugh in their faces.'' He said Carl told him it would be a perfect crime because it would bring him so much money that he would never have to commit another one. And he asked about the use of quicklime—''he wanted to know how long it would take to consume a body.'' When the cellmate couldn't tell him, Hall began reading medical books in the prison hospital, where he was working as a nurse.

Another inmate said Hall invited him to take part in a ''big deal'' after their release. He said it involved a rich man in Kansas City. When the inmate refused, Hall grew scornful, saying: ''I'll be driving Cadillacs when you're carrying a lunch basket.''

When he was paroled, he went to St. Joseph, Missouri, a city on the Missouri River in the northwest part of the state. St. Joe—no one in Missouri calls it St. Joseph—is best known as the starting point from which the Pony Express riders set off for the West, and as the place where Jesse James was killed (''the dirty little coward who shot Mr. Howard''). A St. Joe attorney, Bernard Patton, had found the paroled convict a job with an automobile agency. Patton had known Carl for several years and had done some legal work for him in connection with his business ventures.

Hall was not successful as an automobile salesman. He worked for two St. Joe agencies at different times, but one of the jobs lasted only a month and the other was also short-lived. He then tried selling insurance, working for a company in St. Joe and another in Kansas City, but he apparently sold only one policy. It was purchased by a woman named Bonnie Heady.

He told a fellow employee that he was living with Bonnie—referring to her as ''Baby Doll.'' He showed this man a pearl-handled automatic and said he had awakened the night before to find Baby Doll pointing the gun at him. Hall said he took it away from her and beat her up. On another occasion he said he was going to try to get Bonnie sobered up long enough for them to get married. Then, he said, he would let her drink herself to death, because she had a lot of money and he would inherit it.

Finally he summed up the way things were with him. He told a co-worker that society had no use for Carl Hall. He said he was ''a misfit,'' because of his criminal record. And, he added, Bonnie was a misfit, too, because she was a prostitute.

She was born Bonnie Emily Brown on July 15, 1912, on her family's farm near Clearmont, Missouri, in Nodaway County, the daughter of

30

French P. Brown and Mabel Clutter Brown. Nodaway County is in the far northwestern part of the state, between the Platte and Nodaway rivers and very close to the border with Iowa. It is thinly populated, bitterly cold in winter, a hard place to live.

Her mother died in 1914, when Bonnie was two years old, but this did not entirely deprive her of affection. She was raised by an aunt—from all indications a good and supportive woman—and she apparently was on good terms with her father. The aunt, Mrs. Troy R. Baker, said Bonnie "was a happy, carefree, normal child. . . . She was a very sweet little girl and was brought up in a good Christian home. She attended Sunday school and church and was like any normal child."

Bonnie graduated from Clearmont High School in 1930. Her overall academic rating was "superior or above," and school records indicate no disciplinary problems. In September 1930, she enrolled in Northwest Missouri State Teachers College at Maryville, Missouri, but she dropped out after one semester. After working for a while as a beautician and saleswoman, she went back to college in December 1931. Again she attended only one semester. This time she left because she was planning to get married.

On June 8, 1932, just before her twentieth birthday, she married Vernon Ellis Heady, a livestock merchant in St. Joe. The marriage lasted twenty years, and during most of that time Bonnie and her husband were thought of as a happy and pleasant, even fashionable couple. V. Ellis Heady, as he was known, bought and sold cattle at the St. Joe stockyards and was prosperous and reputable. Bonnie raised pedigreed boxers, some of which won prizes, and was known as a good horsewoman—a skill she had acquired on her father's farm. She went horseback riding often, wearing a western shirt and tan riding slacks that were admired by the neighbors. "We thought of her as a good-looking woman," one of them said. "She always dressed beautifully and in the height of fashion." Bonnie, on horseback, was a familiar figure in the parades that were part of St. Joe's annual Pony Express rodeo, and in 1951 she won third prize in a contest for "best-dressed cowgirl." For a time, she and her husband went in for square dancing as well. A normal and respectable couple in a comfortable frame house, white with blue shutters, in a quiet residential neighborhood.

But marriage is the best-kept and worst-kept of secrets. In the early 1950's, the neighbors began to say that the Heady marriage was going bad. They ascribed it to Bonnie's drinking. Her husband said the same thing; he told the FBI later that they had separated in June 1952 and said it was because of Bonnie's problem. But in the divorce suit, Bonnie charged her husband with adultery. When the divorce was granted in October, the judge

31

said Heady had indeed been unfaithful. The decree was granted in Bonnie's favor.

In the settlement, Bonnie got the house on South Thirty-eighth Street. Thereafter, things got worse for her. She drank more and more, and she began entertaining men, a lot of men. One of them, a former convict who had done time for statutory rape, said he lived with Bonnie from October 1952 until May 1953, when he was succeeded by Carl Hall. The ex-convict lover said that during the time he lived with Bonnie, many other men came to the house and had sex with her, both "natural and unnatural" sex. He said Bonnie told him some of the men were sent to her by the manager of a local dance hall, with whom she had an arrangement.

Once, the ex-con said, love turned violent at Bonnie's house: She shot one of her "male callers" in the hand. When Bonnie was arrested in St. Louis after the kidnapping, she had a .25-caliber automatic in her purse—apparently the gun she had pointed at Carl Hall one night. The FBI asked her about the automatic. Bonnie said she had bought it for protection because she was living alone—in a manner of speaking—after her divorce. And then, in a rush, it all came out: the man she had shot, the men who came to her house for sex, the nude photos, the sordidness.

One night, Bonnie said, some friends came to her house, bringing with them a man she did not know. After an evening of heavy drinking, the friends left, but the stranger stayed and they had more drinks. Then they went into the bedroom "for the purpose of sexual intercourse," at which point the stranger "went all to pieces." He pinched and twisted her flesh, mauling her cruelly and bruising her. Then he began burning her breasts and arms with a cigarette.

Later, the man went into the kitchen to get another drink. Bonnie got her gun, followed him into the kitchen and told him to get dressed and get out of the house. He turned and started toward her "in a threatening manner," so she shot him, hitting him in the hand. The wound bled profusely, Bonnie said, and the shock "sobered him up a great deal." She helped him get dressed and called an ambulance. Later she told sheriff's deputies that the man had been showing her how to clean the gun and it had gone off accidentally. Law enforcement hears many such stories.

There were many other visitors. Bonnie told the FBI that after her divorce, she had sexual relations with at least 150 men. Among them, she said, were prominent businessmen, doctors, lawyers and judges. Sometimes, she said, she and a "girl friend" posed nude for obscene photos, wearing Halloween masks to conceal their identities.

It is possible that Bonnie exaggerated her sexual exploits, but probably not. There was confirmation from the statutory-rape man, from two St. Joe cab drivers who said they had brought men to Bonnie's house and had split the money with her, and from a woman who said Bonnie had propositioned her to "turn tricks with male companions in St. Joseph, Missouri." Bonnie had become the town whore.

Why? The FBI files examined by the author contain no psychiatric evaluation of either kidnapper, but in the information Bonnie gave about her sex life there may have been a clue. She told the FBI that her husband had never wanted children. In the twenty years that she was married to V. Ellis Heady, she said, she had eleven abortions. Which, if true, means that at the end she had no self-respect left.

These two entropic figures, Bonnie Heady and Carl Austin Hall—their personalities already disintegrating—met in May 1953 in the Pony Express Bar at the Robidoux Hotel in St. Joseph. Carl told Bonnie he was an insurance salesman. They drank and talked for a while and then went to Bonnie's house, where Carl spent the night.

He did not tell her at first that he was an ex-convict, not that it would have mattered, since she had been living with one before she met Carl. But she found out pretty soon, when Hall mentioned that he was on parole and was living in a basement apartment in St. Joe, for which he paid fifty dollars a month. Bonnie suggested he save money by moving in with her.

It was a nice, Aunt Pittypat house, filled with the acquisitions and mementos of a twenty-year marriage. Bonnie liked to collect things; shelves in the living room displayed dozens of figurines, bric-a-brac and trophies won by her dogs at various shows. There were bookshelves, too, well-stocked with current best sellers and mysteries, some two hundred books in all, and lots of magazines. The dining room furniture was described as antique, and a dresser in one of the two first-floor bedrooms was also said to be antique. Reporters who inspected the house after Bonnie's arrest noted that she had an extensive wardrobe; the closets, they wrote, were "filled with hundreds of dresses." They paid special attention to a bar in an upstairs room. It was, they said, a walnut bar, and it was well-supplied with liquor. They also noted four large pictures of nude women, not so Aunt Pittypatish.

Bonnie said later that she and Carl settled down to "a life of leisure," mostly on her money. Bonnie's father had died in 1949, and she had inherited his $44,000 estate. This included the 360-acre farm in Nodaway County, which was appraised at $32,000. Most of Bonnie's income came

33

from rent paid by a tenant farmer; it cannot have been a lavish amount, but she owned the house in St. Joe as a result of the divorce settlement, and she and Hall got by without working. The arrangement was that Bonnie paid for almost everything—food, gasoline for the station wagon, utilities and other household expenses. Hall furnished the whiskey.

Sometimes, however, Bonnie nagged Carl for not having much money. So he said that if she wanted him to, he would hold up some grocery stores in Kansas City. No, she said, changing her tune, don't do that; I have enough money for both of us. Then, in the summer of 1953, they went to Chicago to visit Bonnie's aunt, Mrs. Baker. Several times during that trip, Carl went out for a few hours. When he returned, he told Bonnie he had been casing some small suburban banks.

But he was still dreaming of the big score, the perfect crime. Sometime in June 1953, he began to talk to Bonnie about it. At first he spoke obliquely. He told Bonnie that he had been married and divorced, and that he had a son. But, he said, his former wife had obtained a court order that prohibited him from seeing the boy. It was very sad. A loving father was being kept from his son. Bonnie fell for it. Hall said later that she was so fuzzy from heavy drinking—a pint of whiskey before breakfast some days—that she would believe anything. He worked on her, he softened her up, and finally he felt confident that his story "was getting through to her [and] she was believing it."

His story was that his son was Bobby Greenlease. He told Bonnie that his beloved Bobby lived with wealthy people in a big house in Kansas City. He never claimed outright that Mrs. Greenlease was the woman from whom he was divorced, the woman who was keeping him from his son, but Bonnie said later this was the impression she got from him. All he wanted to do, Hall told her, was to drive past the Greenlease home occasionally to see if he could get a glimpse of his son, and perhaps talk to him. Bonnie was touched; she agreed with him, drunkenly, that it was a terrible situation.

So she went with him several times to look at the Greenlease house, driving past it slowly. They saw the elder Greenlease take Bobby to school several mornings, with Bonnie thinking the boy was Carl's son and wasn't it sad, and Carl thinking it would be hard to abduct Bobby from his home or his father's car; it had better be from the school.

Earlier, during the summer, Hall had made other preparations. He had called the Greenlease house, spoken to a maid, and had learned that the family was in Europe but would be back in September. In this or another call, he also found out the ages of the Greenlease children, the schools they attended, and other information about them.

Now it was time to get specific with Bonnie. He was more sure of her cooperation now, and Bonnie herself said she was so infatuated with him that she never objected strenuously to his plan. Sometime in late summer or early September, therefore, Hall dropped the pretense that Bobby Greenlease was his son and that he only wanted to see him. He told Bonnie it was going to be a kidnapping. And he said he would need her help. But he explained that her only role would be to pick up Bobby at the school. Hall said he would do everything else—she would be only a "minor accessory" and would not be punished severely if they were caught. Of course, they would not be caught. At this point, Hall said nothing about murdering the boy. They would merely keep him someplace until they had collected the ransom, and then return him to his parents.

Bonnie said later she didn't think he was serious. Infatuation aside, another reason she didn't object was that she didn't think Hall had the ability to plan and carry out a kidnapping. They were both drunks, and they sat around a lot, talking drunk talk, and that's all she thought it was. So she was just carried along—but in the meantime, Hall was stepping up his preparations. On September 10, he bought the lime, and on September 26, the shovel. And on September 19, at Sam's Loan Office at 450 Minnesota Avenue in Kansas City, he bought a .38-caliber Smith and Wesson revolver.

In mid-September, Carl and Bonnie almost kidnapped Bobby's eleven-year-old sister, Virginia Sue Greenlease. One afternoon, they followed Mrs. Greenlease and Virginia Sue from Sunset Hill—the school the daughter attended—to the Country Club Plaza in Kansas City. (Later Bonnie told the nuns at Bobby's school that Mrs. Greenlease had suffered a heart attack in this shopping mall.) They saw Mrs. Greenlease park her Cadillac and go into a drugstore. Hall said he got a "sudden urge" to kidnap Virginia Sue, but he decided they could not grab the girl in the parking lot without being noticed and creating excitement, especially since Virginia Sue was older and more aware, so he gave up the idea. However, it crystallized his thinking. Bobby, younger and less aware, would have to be the victim. And later the final decision: Bobby would have to be killed.

Hall said it was on Sunday, September 27, the day before the kidnapping, that he told Bonnie for the first time that they would have to kill the boy. Otherwise, he said, Bobby might be able to identify the station wagon, identify Bonnie's house if he was kept there, and identify them. "He is evidence," Hall said. (Bonnie's recollection was that Hall had begun discussing murder earlier than Sunday, but in any event, she agreed to it.) Hall went into the back yard and dug the grave. And the next morning, they got up early and drove to Kansas City. . . .

Chapter 4

7he first ransom note was received on September 28—the day of the kidnapping. It was a special-delivery letter, addressed to "Robert Greenlease, 2600 [*sic*] Verowa [*sic*] Rd. KC Mo." The Greenleases lived at 2920 Verona Road, Mission Hills, Kansas, but the letter reached them as a result of some quick action by the Kansas City police. The handwritten note said:

Your boy been kiddnapped get $600,000 in $20's—$10's—Fed. Res. notes from all twelve districts we realize it takes a few days to get that amount. Boy will be in good hands—when you have money ready put ad in K.C. Star. M—will meet you in Chicago next Sunday—signed Mr. G.

Do not call police or try to use chemicals on bills or take numbers. Do not try to use any radio to catch us or boy dies. If you try to trap us your wife and your other child and yourself will be killed you will be watched all of the time. You will be told later how to contact us with money. When you get this note let us know by driving up and down main St. between 39 & 29 for twenty minutes with white rag on car aeriel.

Over

On the other side of the letter was this message, also handwritten:

If do exactly as we say an try no tricks, your boy will be back safe withen 24 hrs afer we check money.
Deliver money in army duefel bag. Be ready to deliver at once on contact.
M
$400,000 in 20's
$200,000 in 10's

The letter was written by Bonnie Heady. So much for the "minor accessory." However, Hall collaborated in the wording and made "numerous suggestions to her [about] the spelling." Yes.

The fact that the letter was signed with the initial "M" caused confusion at first, because the last name of the mythical "third kidnapper" happened to start with "M." But after Carl and Bonnie had confessed that there was no third kidnapper, they said the "M" was just a coincidence. They insisted there was no special significance to the signature or to the fact that Hall identified himself as "M" in his telephone calls to the Greenlease home. They said they simply chose "M" at random as their identification.

The ransom letter was written at Bonnie's home a few hours after the kidnapping. Hall took it to Kansas City and mailed it, while Bonnie finished filling in the grave. The letter was received at the Kansas City Post Office at 6:00 P.M. Post-office employees had been alerted by the Kansas City police to watch for letters addressed to Greenlease.

The call from the nun at Notre Dame de Sion school, inquiring about Mrs. Greenlease's "heart attack," had come at about 11:30 that morning. After learning that an unknown woman had taken her son away, Virginia Greenlease sat for a moment in the blank shock that accompanies news too terrifying to be grasped. Then she called her husband at his office. Greenlease rushed home, tried to comfort his wife, and then called Kansas City's chief of police, Bernard C. Brannon. He told Brannon that Bobby apparently had been kidnapped and gave the police chief the few details he had.

Robert Greenlease was then seventy-one years old. For him, nothing in all the world could have been more terrible than the kidnapping of his young son. Later, when the horror overtook him, he broke down, sobbing helplessly, but his initial reactions were calm and strong. After talking to the police chief, he called three old and valued business associates. These men were to be of immense comfort and assistance in the unbearable days ahead. They were Robert L. Ledterman, executive vice-president and general manager of the Greenlease-Ledterman Motor Company of Tulsa, Oklahoma; Norbert S. O'Neill, executive vice-president of the Greenlease Motor Company of Kansas City, and Stewart M. Johnson, general manager of the Kansas City dealership. For the ten days during which Bobby's whereabouts and fate were unknown, the three men virtually lived at the Greenlease home, taking the "M" calls from the kidnapper and playing leading roles in the ransom negotiations and the delivery of the money. The strain on them was enormous, and especially so for Ledterman, who at sixty-nine was almost as old as Greenlease.

At about midnight on September 28, Greenlease and Ledterman carried out the instructions in the ransom letter. In Greenlease's Cadillac, they drove up and down Main Street between Twenty-ninth and Thirty-ninth streets, with a white undershirt tied to the car's aerial. For forty minutes in the middle of the night, the two elderly men drove patiently up and down the street, displaying a silly-looking undershirt, trying to send a signal to the kidnappers, hoping they would see it and be convinced the ransom would be paid, hoping the boy would be returned unharmed, hoping, hoping. They saw nothing to indicate they were observed—and they weren't. Bonnie and Carl, paying no attention to their own instructions, stayed home that night, drinking and watching television. The next morning, Greenlease and Ledterman repeated the procedure, but again they saw nothing.

On that day, Tuesday, Greenlease and Ledterman also went to the Commerce Trust Company, one of Kansas City's largest banks. They talked to the executive vice-president, Arthur B. Eisenhower, who was a neighbor and friend of Greenlease, and whose brother was then president of the United States. They asked Eisenhower to obtain $600,000 in denominations of ten dollars and twenty dollars from the twelve Federal Reserve districts. Eisenhower said he would start assembling the money immediately.

The next day, Ledterman put an ad in the "personals" column of *The Kansas City Star*, also in compliance with the ransom letter. The ad said: "M. Will meet you in Chicago next Sunday. G."

But in the meantime, another note had arrived. Hall said later that he realized the first letter had been misaddressed to "2600 Verowa Rd." Worried that it might not have reached the Greenleases, he and Bonnie wrote another letter on Tuesday. It arrived that night, again by special delivery, and was intercepted by the FBI at the post office. It read:

You must not of got our first letter. Show this to no one. Get $600,000 in 10$ and 20$ federal reserve notes from all distrist 400,000 in 20s—200,000—10s you will not take numbers or treat bills in any way.

When you have money put ad in star personal meet me in Chicago signed G. Call police off and obey instructions Boy is ok but homesick dont try to stop us on pick up or boy dies you will hear from us later. Put money in army duffle bag

M.

In this letter, Hall enclosed the Jerusalem cross that he had taken from Bobby's body, to convince the Greenleases that the message was from the real kidnappers. It accomplished its purpose; Ledterman said later that the family received fifteen phony ransom demands, for amounts ranging from $4,000 to $250,000. "If Mr. Greenlease had complied with all the demands, he would have paid $1,500,000 in ransoms," Ledterman said. "But we knew which of the callers was the right one," because of the Jerusalem medal. The little Jerusalem cross was all the Greenleases had to go on, the only real evidence they ever had that "M" was the actual kidnapper. They clung to this straw for ten agonizing days.

There was never any doubt that Greenlease would pay the ransom, Ledterman said, and he decided to do so even though there was no positive proof that Bobby was alive. Greenlease reasoned that if he demanded definite proof before paying the money, the family might not hear from the kidnappers again and might never know with certainty whether Bobby was alive or dead.

The day after the kidnapping, it was announced that Greenlease would hold a press conference, but it lasted only a few minutes. The reporters remembered the scene for a long time: an elderly man, dignified and erect, of obvious wealth and distinction, standing in front of his imposing house, trying not to cry.

"We think they [the kidnappers] are trying to make contact," Greenlease began. Then his voice broke, and he said: "All I want is my boy back." His eyes filled with tears and he turned to go back into the house, asking the reporters and photographers to leave.

The first telephone call came at 9:00 P.M. on Wednesday, September 30. Stewart Johnson, one of the business associates helping the Greenlease family, answered the phone:

Johnson: What did you say, sir?

39

M: Mr. Greenlease.

Johnson: May I speak for Mr. Greenlease?

M: Have you the money ready?

Johnson: I can't hear you.

M: Have you the money ready?

Johnson: We are making arrangements—

M: This is M.

Johnson: Is this him?

M: Uh-huh.

Johnson: Well—ah—ah—can you identify your—the set-up now—can we get with you on this story?

M: Tomorrow night.

Johnson: Tomorrow night—well, here now, you understand we got to determine that you have the boy—

M: Medal.

Johnson: What did you say, "little"?

M: Medal.

Johnson: I can't hear you.

M: Medal.

Johnson: "Little" or "medal"?

M: Medal.

Johnson: Medal—well, I would like to ask you some further questions—after all, we've got to determine that you do have the boy—

M: Six hundred thousand tomorrow night—

Johnson: Six hundred thousand tomorrow night—all right—can you give me—also can you tell me anything else?

M: (hangs up)

That was on Wednesday night. It gave the Greenleases very little to go on. "M's" reference to the Jerusalem medal was further evidence that they were dealing with the real kidnappers, but the medal itself had arrived the day before, in the second ransom letter. So the telephone call was merely corroboration. As to the ransom money, "M" had seemed to be saying he wanted it delivered Thursday night, but he had given no instructions about the pickup. The money was being assembled at Arthur Eisenhower's bank—but the Greenleases heard nothing at all from "M" on Thursday. All they could do was wait.

The FBI was waiting, too. It had been involved in the case since the afternoon of September 28, but it was not involved all the way. FBI agents had talked to Greenlease and had told him they would stay in close touch with the situation, but they explained that FBI policy in kidnapping cases was that nothing should be done to jeopardize the safe return of the victim.

There were legalities also. Under the Lindbergh Law—the nation's basic statute on kidnapping—the FBI did not have jurisdiction until it was determined that a victim had been taken across a state line—or until seven days had elapsed, at which time there was a legal presumption that a state line had been crossed.

And Greenlease himself asked the FBI to hold off. Ledterman told reporters that the family wanted to give the kidnappers forty-eight hours in which to return Bobby unharmed before bringing either the police or the FBI into the case. Greenlease told the FBI explicitly that he did not want any surveillance of the ransom delivery—no attempt whatsoever to catch the kidnappers when they picked up the money—because of the danger this might pose for his son.

But the FBI was not inactive. It was intercepting Greenlease's mail at the Kansas City Post Office, and it was recording the telephone calls to the Greenlease home. It is possible the agents could have traced Hall through the calls, and captured him—but there was the overriding question of Bobby's safety, so they made no effort to do so.

A description of Bobby was widely circulated in newspapers and on radio and television. He was three feet four inches tall and weighed fifty-three pounds. He was slender but sturdy and had fair skin, light brown hair that had recently been cut, and brown eyes, A lower left front tooth was missing; he was losing his baby teeth. He was wearing a white short-sleeved shirt, short brown linen trousers, brown nylon ankle socks, brown shoes and the bronze Jerusalem medal. A description of the unknown woman who had taken him from the school also was circulated extensively.

In the Greenlease house there was inexpressible horror, unutterable grief. The friends who came to see Bobby's parents, who tried to console and comfort them, if only by being there, by offering the mute warmth of human presence, took refuge afterward in the clichés that serve tragedy. They said Bobby's mother had "collapsed," had been visited by a physician and had been given sedatives. But later they reported that she was up and moving around the house and "doing better." The father was described at various times as "distraught" or "grim-faced" or "in fair spirits." But these were only words—the shorthand of sorrow. Beneath words, the Greenleases had a deep religious faith; when reporters asked their adopted son, Paul, whether the family had any reason to believe Bobby would not be returned unharmed, he replied: "Oh, no, we don't think that. Mother would never think that."

41

Of course, it was all in vain—the descriptions, the drive up and down Main Street in the middle of the night, the ad in *The Kansas City Star,* the waiting, the hoping. Bobby was dead. In the deep place where dread lives, they feared he was dead. But they did not *know.* They could not be *certain.* "We are living on faith and prayer," Ledterman told the reporters. He added: "Faith is eternal."

The second call came at 6:25 P.M. on Friday, October 2. It was taken by another of Greenlease's associates, Norbert O'Neill:

O'Neill: Yes, sir, we have been waiting to hear from you. We are ready and willing to cooperate with you.

M: Later tonight.

O'Neill: Sir?

M: Later tonight.

O'Neill: Will you have any additional evidence that you have Bobby?

M: We have the ribbon, duffel bag, 20's and 10's, 600,000—what more do you want?

O'Neill: Is Bobby all right, sir?

M: He is fine but homesick.

O'Neill: Then you will call later tonight?

M: Yes.

O'Neill: And contact us?

M: Yes.

O'Neill: We are ready. . . .

"Later tonight" turned out to be 1:35 in the morning—Saturday, October 3. O'Neill answered the phone again:

O'Neill: We're sure glad to hear from you.

M: Are you ready?

O'Neill: Would you give me your identification, as you did earlier this evening?

M: We have the ribbon [to which Bobby's Jerusalem medal had been attached], 600,000, 400,000, 20's, 10's, Army duffel bag.

O'Neill: Thank you. We are ready and we are sincere. We're satisfied you're the right party. The money is available.

M: Go to corner of Twenty-ninth and Holmes.

O'Neill: Just a mo— Just a moment please. Go—

M: To corner of Twenty-ninth and Holmes, underneath mailbox, letter.

O'Neill: Go to corner of Twenty-ninth and Holmes.

M: Letter.

O'Neill: Letter underneath mailbox.

M: Yes.

O'Neill: Now, uh, you can understand, M, that we do want some assurance that you are the man that has Bobby. You have given us considerable—

M: We are the people that have Bobby.

O'Neill: You, uh, pardon?

M: The boy is fine.

O'Neill: Uh, uh, well, now of course, if—

M: We ask 400, 200, 20's, 10's, Federal Reserve notes.

O'Neill: That's right.

M: Certainly [this word was not clear].

O'Neill: Oh, ah, there's nowhere we can talk?

M: (hangs up)

The trip to Twenty-ninth and Holmes was the beginning of forty-eight hours of confusion and agony. It was often very difficult to understand what "M" was saying, and the instructions he gave were a mad game of hide-and-seek played by a lunatic schoolboy. He led the intermediaries—Ledterman, O'Neill and Johnson—such a dance that Ledterman finally told him to cut out the kid stuff and act like a grown-up:

"This idea of climbing the tree and looking in a bird's nest for a note, then climbing on your belly somewhere looking for something under a rock with a red, white and blue ribbon around it—that's getting pretty tiresome. You know, you and I don't have to play ball that way. We can deal man to man."

But that came later. Right now, it was two o'clock on Saturday morning, and O'Neill and Johnson drove to Twenty-ninth and Holmes. Under a mailbox, they found a piece of paper. It was a child's spelling exercise, apparently discarded after school and blown under the mailbox by the wind. Disappointed, O'Neill and Johnson returned to the Greenlease house. The piece of paper had nothing to do with the kidnapping: The spelling was too good.

They decided to go back and look again. This time, they found an envelope taped to the bottom of the mailbox, with a message on it: "Go to 42nd—Charlotte, under the mail box."

They drove to Forty-second and Charlotte. Under a mailbox at that intersection, they found another envelope, with a note inside: "Go to 40th—Harrison First Brothern United Church—on corner leave bag on north side of church under 2nd window in alcove. Leave money here drive straight home boy fine if money ok he will be home in 24 hrs."

43

Since O'Neill and Johnson did not have the ransom money, they returned again to the Greenlease house. When they got there, they noticed for the first time that the first envelope—the one that had instructed them to go to Forty-second and Charlotte—also had a message in it. However, this overlooked message did not seem to change the situation:

"Go to your used car lot take money and change to dark used car rember you are being watched—if contact man is picked up boy dies if everything is ok boy will be home in 24 hrs. Go next to adress on envelope—next message will be under mail box. M. Take zigzag route make sure you arnt followed you keep you bargain we will keep ours."

It was getting hard to keep track of things, and they were tired. They had already gone to Forty-second and Charlotte and had found the note about the church. But they had not gone to the church itself because they did not have the money. Now what should they do? They did not want to lose contact with "M," so they decided to leave a message of their own. At 4:45 in the morning, they drove to the church and left a note in the place where Hall had told them to leave the money:

"M, We could not find you note on first try, which delayed us one hour. We don't have the 'bag' at home. It takes an hour or more to get it. Due to these delays it would be daylight before we could comply. Please contact us. We are sincere and there will be no interference. 4:45 A.M. G."

This note did not reach Hall. At 7:45 A.M. Saturday, a person walking past the church saw the message, read it, and called the Kansas City police. The cops notified the FBI that the note had been inadvertently intercepted.

But while O'Neill and Johnson were on their way to the church, "M" called again. It was 4:06 in the morning. Ledterman took this call. He had been up all night, and the transcript shows frequent tired pauses as Ledterman fought his fatigue and tried to explain the situation to this dangerous man:

Ledterman: There is a note being left to you. . . . It came too late. . . . We sent a note down there . . . we got balled up. We didn't find the first. . . . Then the bag was not here . . . it's in a safe place . . . it would have been daylight before we got there . . . we have asked you . . . we have sent you a note to the place and asked you to contact again.

M: Tonight.

Ledterman: It would have been daylight.

M: Tonight.

Ledterman: OK . . . send your instructions and make them very, very clear please.

44

M: All right . . . the boy is fine.

Ledterman: The boy is fine?

M: Yes.

Ledterman: I see. . . . Is it possible for him to talk to his mother sometime tomorrow?

M: I'll see what they say.

Ledterman: All right, try and do that please. That will make her feel much better.

M: Fine.

Ledterman: In the instruction tomorrow night . . . no interference . . . can you give instructions now?

M: No.

Ledterman: No?

M: Tomorrow night.

That ended a sleepless and tormented night for Greenlease, Ledterman and the others. True to his word, "M" did not call during the day Saturday. However, there was one important development that day: The ransom money was delivered to the Greenlease home. When "M" called again, a mother and father would be ready to pay a fortune to try to save their son.

There were 20,000 twenty-dollar bills and 20,000 ten-dollar bills. Forty thousand bills. Six hundred thousand dollars. It weighed just under eighty-five pounds.

Hall said later that he had read an article somewhere that gave the weight of $1 million in $10 and $20 bills, and he had decided that a million would be too heavy and unwieldy to handle without arousing suspicion. He said he did some figuring and found that $600,000 in tens and twenties would weigh eighty to eighty-five pounds, which he thought would be manageable.

Greenlease and Ledterman had gone to the Commerce Trust Company on the morning of September 29 to ask Arthur Eisenhower to get the money. Eisenhower acted quickly; that same morning he called H. Gavin Leedy, president of the Federal Reserve Bank of Kansas City, and told him in strict secrecy that he needed $600,000 "for use by Robert C. Greenlease as ransom money." That afternoon the reserve bank delivered $400,000 in twenty-dollar bills from all twelve Federal Reserve districts. The next morning, Leedy sent over $200,000 in tens.

At Commerce Trust, the serial numbers were recorded—by hand. Eisenhower assigned about seventy of his employees to this laborious task. Then, to have a second record of the serial numbers, all 40,000 bills were photographed. Later, the money was put into a duffel bag supplied by the FBI. The duffel bag had been "appropriately identified" by the FBI laboratory—apparently meaning that it was marked in some way.

The serial numbers would be the principal means of identifying the ransom money if it was recovered intact from the kidnappers. But as a further identification, an FBI agent pressed his right thumb firmly against the wrapper around each packet of bills, leaving an unseen print. These precautions would work if the money was recovered in one batch, but it would be a different story if it was dispersed and got into general circulation—40,000 bills are a lot of bills, money passes through many hands, and few people look at the serial numbers.

At 5:00 P.M. on Saturday, Eisenhower turned over the money to Ledterman, who took it to the Greenlease house to wait for further instructions from "M."

Chapter 5

*S*even days elapsed between Monday, September 28, when Bobby was kidnapped and murdered, and late Sunday night, October 4, when Carl and Bonnie finally collected the ransom and fled to St. Louis. Seven days in which they moved freely around Kansas City and St. Joe, the murderers among us, unnoticed and unremarked.

Their activities on the day of the kidnapping, and the day after, have been recounted in previous chapters: the murder itself, the burial of the body, the chrysanthemums on the grave, the mailing of the ransom letters. During the rest of the week, Carl and Bonnie went various places and did various things. Some were mundane and some were macabre.

That woman in the grocery store—no, not the sexy one in the tight slacks. Over there in the next aisle: the plump woman with the round face, the one whose eyes look like raisins in a pudding. What do you suppose is on her mind? Thinking about what to give her husband for dinner tonight? He doesn't like macaroni, but that's what he's going to get. Then they'll watch Jackie Gleason on TV. Lord, he's funny. Small, dull thoughts of an ordinary woman. She is a murderess.

The man who just came into the dry cleaner's. Has a suit to be cleaned

47

and can we get this little spot off the pants? Sure, mister. Take the suit, give him the ticket. Did you notice what he looked like? Listen, I'm on my feet all day long in this place, customers coming in and going out, how can I remember? He wasn't good-looking, I can tell you that. Sort of a beefy guy, shiny face like he sweated a lot. Like a thousand guys, very ordinary. He is a murderer.

So, on September 30, Bonnie returned some items to Bruns' Hy-Klas Food Store in St. Joe, receiving a refund of $1.29, and Carl took his bloodstained suit to Hodson Cleaners.

He walked in and said he had had "a little accident." Pointing to a spot on one trouser leg, he asked: "Can you get this spot of blood out?" After he left, employees of the cleaning shop found more blood, a lot of it. There were large bloodstains on both trouser legs, some of which ran down the legs; streaks of blood on the right sleeve of the coat from the shoulder to the wrist; a large splotch of blood on the left lapel and some on the right, and more splotches on the right side of the coat itself.

That night, Carl and Bonnie had dinner at Weiss's Restaurant in Kansas City. The waitress who served them recalled that Bonnie had "numerous cocktails" but said Carl did not drink as much. He may have been trying to stay sober, because at nine o'clock that night he made his first call to the Greenleases.

Hall remembered that a man answered the phone (it was Stewart Johnson), but he said he paid no attention to the questions the man asked him. He said he put his handkerchief over his mouth to disguise his voice, and deliberately kept the conversation short.

On the morning of October 1, Hall saw the "Will meet you in Chicago" ad in *The Kansas City Star*. This, he said, was "the contact he had been waiting for." He implied that he had been noncommittal in his conversation with Johnson the night before because at that point he hadn't seen the ad and therefore didn't know whether the Greenleases were serious about paying the ransom. If they weren't, he didn't want to say too much and risk getting caught for nothing.

Later that morning, Carl and Bonnie went to the McCord-Bell car rental agency in St. Joe. Hall waited outside while Bonnie went in and rented a car, a 1952 Ford sedan, light blue. Hall explained later that he did not want to use Bonnie's station wagon for the ransom pickup because it might be seen and traced. Then they had lunch at the Hoof and Horn Restaurant in St. Joe.

On Friday, October 2, Bonnie was in Bruns' Hy-Klas Food Store again, buying groceries this time. Three store employees saw and recognized her;

48

she was a frequent customer. One of them said she wore no makeup that day and had "an unkempt and haggard appearance." Another said she looked "bad."

That evening, Carl and Bonnie drove to Kansas City again—and the first ransom sequence began. At 6:25 P.M., Hall made his second call to the Greenlease home. In this short conversation, with Norbert O'Neill, Hall said several times that he would call back "later tonight."

After the 6:25 call, Hall laid out a route for the delivery of the ransom— but he said later he wasn't serious about this initial route. First he taped the note under a mailbox at Twenty-ninth and Holmes, and then he taped the second note under a rock or mailbox at Forty-second and Charlotte. This was the note that designated the First Brethren Church as the payoff spot—but Hall said later he never intended to pick up the money at the church, even if it had been there. He said he was merely staging a "dummy run" to see whether the Greenleases paid the ransom, and whether the payoff car was shadowed by the FBI.

It is nerve-racking to be interrupted in felonious activities; many persons can testify to that. It happened to Hall that Friday night, as he was laying out the first ransom route. He was seen by a man with whom he had worked at insurance companies in St. Joe and Kansas City. At about 8:00 P.M., the man saw Bonnie's station wagon and honked his horn. Stopping their cars, he and Hall talked for about five minutes. The man told the FBI later that Bonnie, whom he knew, stayed in the station wagon, drinking from a bottle or flask. Hall asked his former colleague to tell the manager of the Kansas City insurance company that he had got "all fouled up" but would be back at work soon. The acquaintance said Hall "acted nervous." This was a fine line in understatement.

The bad state of Hall's nerves may account for his forgetfulness about license plates. He had stolen one set of plates and had put them on the station wagon before the kidnapping, and he planned to do the same thing with the rented Ford before picking up the ransom. On this Friday night, he stole another pair, from a parked car in north Kansas City—but he forgot to put them on the Ford.

Having said he would call back "later tonight," Hall made his next call to the Greenlease residence at 1:35 A.M. Saturday. This time, he gave the instructions to go to the corner of Twenty-ninth and Holmes, where there would be a note under the mailbox.

Then Carl and Bonnie drove around Kansas City for two and a half hours, dark souls on a dark night. They did not go to Twenty-ninth and Holmes to see whether the first note had been picked up; nor did they make any effort to see whether O'Neill and Johnson had switched to a "dark used car." But shortly before 4:00 A.M., they went to Forty-second and Charlotte. There, Hall said, he saw that "the rock under which he had placed the second note was still intact."

He realized something had gone wrong. So, at 4:06 A.M., he called the Greenleases again. In this conversation, Ledterman told him about the mix-up, the delay in reading the first note, the fact that the money was not then available, and the note that O'Neill and Johnson had left at the First Brethren Church. Hall said later that he decided not to pick up this note because he was afraid it might be a trap.

So ended the first ransom sequence—a mad confusion in the night. O'Neill and Johnson had not made the payoff at the church because they couldn't; the money was not delivered to the Greenleases until Saturday evening. And Hall, worried about FBI surveillance, had not intended to pick it up at the church if it *had* been there.

Not much of the night was left. Hall's recollection was that they went back to St. Joe after the 4:06 call, but the records of the Park-A-Nite Motel in north Kansas City showed that he and Bonnie (identified from photographs) checked in at about 6:30 A.M. Saturday. They registered as Mr. and Mrs. V. E. Heady of Boonville, Missouri, and occupied Room 10-B. A woman employee of the motel said Bonnie stayed in the room all day Saturday; once, she said, she opened the door of 10-B by mistake and saw Bonnie asleep. But Hall, according to this witness, left the motel four or five times during the day.

He was laying out the second ransom route, and this time he was serious. First he went to Thirteenth and Summit streets, where he drew a cross on a rock, with a piece of red chalk or a crayon, and left a message under the rock. Then he drew another red cross on a rock near a subdivision called Oak View, and put another message under that rock.

Saturday night started off with a drink at the old reliable—Lynn's Inn in north Kansas City. They were at Lynn's for twenty or thirty minutes in the early part of the evening, and then nothing is known until "M" called the Greenlease home at 12:14 A.M. Sunday, and again at 1:35 A.M. This time he talked to Bobby's mother.

Norbert O'Neill answered both calls but quickly handed the phone to Mrs. Greenlease. The texts of the two conversations between Virginia Greenlease and Carl Hall were given in Chapter 1. The second conversation ended with these words:

50

M: Are you ready to make the payoff?

Mrs. Greenlease: Yes.

M: Go to 13 West Summit—on corner—rock with red crayon cross on it—letter underneath, will tell you what to do.

At 2:00 A.M., Ledterman and O'Neill took the duffel bag with the $600,000 in it and drove to Thirteenth and Summit. There, without too much trouble, they found a rock with a red cross on it. Under the rock was this message:

"If everthing OK, tie small white rag on car aerial. Go north to US 169 on to Oak View Inc. south of Henry's Letter under rock under sign Wait 10 min."

Then the trouble started. It was a dark night, and it had been raining. Visibility was poor, and Hall's directions were worse. Ledterman and O'Neill drove north on Highway 169, looking for a sign saying "Oak View Inc.," which would be "south of Henry's." O'Neill said later that they had "considerable difficulty" finding the sign and had to stop once to inquire. But eventually they found it. They got out of their car and hunted around in the gloom and drizzle. Finally they saw another rock with a red cross on it. Under this rock was another message:

"Go back to Jt. (Viona Rd)—Go West to first rd heading south across from lum reek farm sign. drive in 75 ft leave bag on right side of road. drive home, will call and tell you where you can pick up boy."

This one was even harder to figure out. They drove west on Highway 69, but they missed the "first rd heading south" because it was just a narrow lane, hard to see in the dark. They drove on for a while, with the growing uncertainty of people on a strange road late at night. Finally they decided they had gone too far, and turned back. This time they found the "first rd" and drove down it for 50 or 75 feet. They could not be sure, but they thought this spot fit the description, so they stopped, took the duffel bag out of the car and put it at the side of the road. Then they drove back to the Greenlease house, wondering whether they had left the bag at the right spot. Or had they just dumped six hundred thousand dollars on a country lane to be picked up by anyone who happened by?

Hall saw Ledterman and O'Neill looking for the payoff spot. At least, he thought he did. He and Bonnie were parked near the turnoff from Highway 69, and Hall said he "saw a dark Cadillac sedan go by and assumed it was the payoff car." He said Bonnie saw nothing; she was drunk again and had gone to sleep.

After the dark Cadillac had gone by, Hall drove into what he described later as "a seldom-used lane close to the Lumm Farm off Highway 69 . . ."

51

and looked for the duffel bag. It was never clear whether this was the lane in which Ledterman and O'Neill had left the money—but at any rate, Hall could not find the bag.

So he drove into Kansas City and called the Greenleases again, at 4:32 in the morning. Stewart Johnson answered.

Johnson: Yes, M— We made the delivery.

M: In the side road?

Johnson: Give you what side road—can you—give me some identification, M?

M: We have the other half of the medal.

Johnson: I didn't hear you, M.

M: We have the other half of the medal.

Johnson: Yes—keep going—the medal.

M: Thousand—Army duffel bag.

Johnson: That's right.

M: You've made delivery?

Johnson: That's right. We made delivery.

M: How long ago?

Johnson: It's been—he left here—let's see—about an hour and a half ago.

M: How long has he been back?

Johnson: They haven't been back yet—they are not back yet—they've been gone over an hour and a half—just almost an hour and a half.

M: Delivery hasn't been made—we've checked.

Johnson: Delivery has been made, sir—I promise you. The delivery's been made.

M: It wasn't there.

Johnson: It was made, sir—I promise you the delivery was made—they left right within a short time after they talked with you—that's a promise.

M: They've missed it. . . .

Johnson: Missed the second place.

M: Now listen, when they come back—tell 'em to go back on 169—Oak View, Incorporated, is a big white sign on the right-hand side—a letter is under a rock with the red crayon on it.

Johnson: On the right-hand side with the red crayon on it.

M: When they come, send 'em back immediately.

Johnson: They are on their way back here—I know they have made delivery—I'm just positive.

M: Send them back.

Johnson: Send them back?

M: Yes.

Johnson: All right, sir—M.

M: That's Oak View—look—Oak View, Incorporated, with white sign.

Johnson: Oak View, Inc.

M: It's just a small white sign—underneath of it is the rock.

Johnson: Underneath it is the rock—now, M.

M: Yes.

Johnson: We—everything, the coast is clear, we're going to be there with it—and, my God, we gotta get Bobby back.

M: Bobby will be back when we get the money. . . .

Ledterman and O'Neill got back to the Greenlease house a short time after this call, and learned that the kidnappers had not been able to find the duffel bag. It was exactly what they had worried about on the return drive. Now a bag containing $600,000 was lying at the side of a country road, where anyone might pick it up. They decided to go back immediately and retrieve it before someone else found it. They drove back to the lane, found the bag without difficulty, and brought it back to the Greenlease house.

While Ledterman and O'Neill were gone this second time, Hall made two more calls to the Greenleases. He was very anxious about the money now. Both of these calls were taken by Mrs. Greenlease, the first at 4:58 A.M.:

Mrs. Greenlease: M, this is Mrs. Greenlease.

M: Did you send them back?

Mrs. Greenlease: They are on the way back.

M: Fine.

Mrs. Greenlease: They picked up two letters and left the money where it was instructed to be left.

M: Are you quite positive?

Mrs. Greenlease: I am positive.

M: In the side road?

Mrs. Greenlease: Yes, in the side road, 75 feet . . . down just a little lane. They said it was hardly a road.

M: All right.

Mrs. Greenlease: But I have sent them back. They are on their way. . . . It is there.

M: It is?

Mrs. Greenlease: It is there.

M: If it's there, you get Bobby.

Mrs. Greenlease: Listen, you call me back. . . . Nobody else could have picked it up, could they?

M: I hardly think so.

Mrs. Greenlease: Well, they deposited it there.

M: On the right side?

Mrs. Greenlease: On the right side . . . and they are on the way back.

M: What kind of car was they driving?

Mrs. Greenlease: They were driving a Cadillac four-door sedan, gunmetal.

M: What color?

Mrs. Greenlease: Sort of a gray, maybe a little lighter than a gunmetal . . . kind of a dark gray.

M: They're on their way back?

Mrs. Greenlease: They're on their way back now.

M: When we pick it up we will acknowledge and then we will call you again and tell you where you can get Bobby.

Mrs. Greenlease: All right. . . .

At 5:50 A.M., Hall called again, and Virginia Greenlease again took the call:

M: Did they come back?

Mrs. Greenlease: No, they haven't returned yet. Did you find it?

M: I haven't looked yet.

Mrs. Greenlease: Oh—oh—they came back once and then returned according to your instructions.

M: They haven't come back yet?

Mrs. Greenlease: They have not come back yet—no.

M: I'll call you.

Mrs. Greenlease: All right.

Hall's next call came at 6:17 A.M. By this time, Ledterman and O'Neill had returned with the duffel bag. O'Neill took the call:

O'Neill: M, we just got back.

M: Yes.

O'Neill: From our mission.

M: Yes.

O'Neill: I want to read you your second letter. . . . Go back to junction Viona Road. . . . Go west to first road, heading south across from lum reek farm sign. . . . Drive in 75 feet . . . leave bag on right side of road. . . . We did exactly that.

M: How far did you leave the bag up?

O'Neill: It's a lane.

54

M: Yes.

O'Neill: We pulled it . . . far enough. . . . We could see it just as soon as our headlights hit it when we went back. . . . It was right there pulled off to the side of the road.

M: All right.

At 6:46 A.M., Hall called again. This time he talked to Ledterman:

M: You say you left the money?

Ledterman: We left it. . . .We went out and got it again. Now listen—we followed every instruction. We had a little difficulty at Thirteenth and Summit. We looked on one corner and found it on the other—then we followed all the instructions. We went out to Oak View, went up to Henry's—we came back—we found the note—came on down to the farm. We found the lane—we had to pass that two or three times before we could find it. Then we finally found it. I'll tell you how we found it. We drove up as far as the nightclub, west on that Vivion Road or whatever it is—we asked a farmer boy where this farm was.

M: I don't know how we overlooked it.

Ledterman: It [the money] was there almost two hours.

M: Can we contact you again this morning?

Ledterman: You will contact us?

M: Yes, and it will be specific. . . . We trust you implicitly.

Ledterman: M, just a minute now the first time . . . O'Neill and I went out there. The second run we took [an unidentified man] to prove that we didn't miss—so the three of us made the second run and two of us made the first run.

M: We don't know how it happened, but we will tell [call] you again this morning, and this time—

Ledterman: Let's not miss.

M: We won't.

Ledterman: . . . We are anxious, we want Bobby back, we want him back as quick as we can get him. . . .

That ended the second ransom sequence.

Chapter 6

*I*t was about seven o'clock Sunday morning, October 4, when Ledterman finished talking to "M." Both men had been up all night Friday and Saturday, trying to arrange the ransom payoff. Later in the morning, Carl and Bonnie checked into Luper's El Rancho Motel on Highway 40 in Kansas City. Again they registered as Mr. and Mrs. V. E. Heady of Boonville. Hall said Bonnie passed out as soon as they got there, and slept all day, but Carl left several times, to plan the third ransom route. He decided that the payoff location this time would be a bridge over County Road 10-E about a mile from Highway 40.

Before he went out to look for a suitable payoff spot, he called the Greenleases again, at 10:15 A.M.:

M: It will be early this evening.

Ledterman (skeptically): Early?

M: Early—and there will not be any running around. . . .

Ledterman: All right now—who is this speaking? [Several times during this conversation, Ledterman asked questions aimed at making sure he was talking to the real kidnapper; throughout this period, the Greenleases were receiving calls from other persons purporting to be the kidnappers.]

M: M, and you're all ready?

Ledterman: Yes, can we get the boy back tonight?

M: Well . . .

Ledterman: Let's try it. . . .

M: We'll do our best to get him back this evening.

Ledterman: Well . . .

M: That boy has raised so much hell, we are almost afraid to take him out.

Ledterman: He's not my boy but I know what you mean.

M: Just like a young boy like that, but the boy is fine, he naturally wants to get home.

Ledterman: Say, where was the slip-up this morning—it wasn't our fault.

M: No, it was ours.

Ledterman: I thought so—[expletive deleted by FBI], you know that thing weighs 85 pounds.

M: Yes, I know.

Ledterman: Carrying that [expletive] thing around—like to break your back, let's make it this evening and don't make it so [expletive] difficult.

M: It will be very simple this evening. . . .

Ledterman: Give me one or two other identifications, your voice don't sound the same today.

M: We have the ribbon [to which Bobby's Jerusalem medal had been attached], duffel bag.

Ledterman: That's the whole shooting match?

M: All right.

Ledterman: Where will you contact me?

M: Home.

Ledterman: When—about when?—I want to get some sleep. I've not had my clothes off since yesterday morning, and you haven't either.

M: Eight.

Ledterman: Contact [at] eight?

M: Yeah. . . .

For the Greenleases, another day of waiting. For Hall, a day of drinking. He said later that he drank so much on Sunday that he forgot the name of the hotel where he wanted Ledterman to go that night to receive a call. All he could remember was that it ended with "shire." As the third payoff attempt drew near, the master criminal was heavily drunk, and his nerves were shrieking at him. In the next call, the longest and most frustrating of

57

them all, Ledterman tried again and again to get the name of the hotel. The call came at 8:28 Sunday night:

M: . . . This is a perfect plan. It will have to be a little later. I am sorry too but we have to make sure there's no mix-up this time.

Ledterman: Yes. Let's get this thing over—say, by the way, M, did the boy answer any of those questions?

M: No—I couldn't—we didn't get anything from him.

Ledterman: Couldn't get anything from him?

M: He wouldn't talk.

Ledterman: Uh-huh—I wish you had been able to get 'em—say, by the way, are we going to have the boy tonight?

M: No, you can't because they want to check the money— I'll tell you this much. You will get him in Pittsburg, Kansas.

Ledterman: You're not bunking me on that, are you?

M: That's the gospel truth.

Ledterman: That's the gospel truth—well, now, can I start there to-night?

M: As soon as we make the pickup.

Ledterman: Soon as we make the pickup? I can start for Pittsburg, Kansas. And will somebody contact me there?

M: Someone will contact you.

Ledterman: Where will I be—where will I go?

M: The telegraph office.

Ledterman: At the telegraph office?

M: Yes. . . .

Ledterman: I want to go tonight. I don't want to wait until morning to go down there—I want that kid.

M: You'll get him. . . .

M: . . . I'll call you at Valentine 9279, at exactly 11:30 P.M.

Ledterman: Wait a minute—9279?

M: Valentine.

Ledterman: Valentine—well, what is that?

M: That's a hotel.

Ledterman: Is that here in town?

M: Yes. I'll call you exactly at 11:30 and we—will have no mix-up tonight.

Ledterman: I see—in other words, can I come to the hotel there?

M: Yes.

Ledterman: Do I have to make a country drive tonight?

M: Not too far.

58

Ledterman: This idea of climbing the tree and looking in a bird's nest for a note, then climbing on your belly somewhere looking for something under a rock with a red, white and blue ribbon around it—that's getting tiresome. You know, you and I don't have to play ball that way. We can deal man to man.

M: There will be no mix-up tonight—it will go perfectly.

Ledterman: I'd just as soon meet you in the middle of Main Street—out anywhere.

M: I would too but I don't have everything to say about this.

Ledterman: I thought you were running the thing. . . .

M: Well—it will go perfectly tonight—you'll be contacted about the boy in Pittsburg, Kansas, in the morning.

Ledterman: All right, let me understand this so there is no mistake about it. When can I go to Pittsburg?

M: After the pickup.

Ledterman: After the pickup?

M: Yes.

Ledterman: . . . You're not kidding me about that?

M: You—you—you've kept your promise so far—we'll keep ours. . . .

Ledterman: . . . I go to the telegraph office there?

M: Yes.

Ledterman: Will there be a wire for me or a message?

M: There will be one for you.

Ledterman: A wire?

M: Yes. . . .

Ledterman: All right, and then they will tell me—where to pick up the boy?

M: Yes.

Ledterman: All right.

M: I'll call you at 11:30 at Valentine 9279.

Ledterman: Now wait a minute—you'll call me at—

M: Valentine 9279.

Ledterman: What is Valentine 9279?

M: A hotel.

Ledterman: A hotel—where in Kansas City? Where—in Kansas City?

M: Yes.

Ledterman: Well, I will have to find out what that hotel is.

M: I'll call you there.

Ledterman: I don't want to get this confused now.

M: This is—this is final.

Ledterman: All right—let me ask you this—will I be at Valentine 9279?

M: Yes, at 11:30. . . .

Ledterman: And you will call me there?

M: Yes—and then we'll—we'll get this over with.

Ledterman: All right. Can you tell me the name of this hotel?

M: I just have the number.

Ledterman: You just have the number?

M: Yes.

Ledterman: I would be in the lobby?

M: Yes.

Ledterman: And wait for the telephone call

M: Yes. . . .

Ledterman: All right, now—you don't know where this hotel is?

M: It's around—uh, Troost—I'll hafta leave now.

Ledterman: All right—it's around Troost.

M: Yes.

Ledterman: How do I get to the hotel?

M: It's right near La—the Lasalle.

Ledterman: It's near the Lasalle—but you can't tell me the name of the hotel.

M: I don't know it.

Ledterman: All right. If I call this number, will they tell me what hotel it is?

M: Yes—I think it's a pay phone.

Ledterman: It's a pay phone there?

M: You be there by it and I'll call you at 11:30.

Ledterman: Well, if I knew what hotel to go to, M, I'd do it—I don't know, what the [expletive].

M: I don't know the name—it's near the Lasalle Hotel.

Ledterman: Well, there are a lot of hotels around there by the Lasalle Hotel.

M: It's very near there.

Ledterman: Very near?

M: Yes.

Ledterman: Are you trying to tell me that that is the hotel?

M: No it isn't. . . .

Ledterman: Well now, suppose I call Valentine 9279 and I don't get an answer—how am I going to find out what the hotel is?

M: There will always be someone there to answer it. It's the hotel right across the street from the—the -shire of some kind.

60

Ledterman: Some kind of a -shire, right across from the Lasalle?

M: Yes.

Ledterman: All right—[expletive], why didn't you tell me that in the first place?

M: All right.

Ledterman: Now I'll be there.

M: And be ready at 11:30 and we'll clean this up. . . .

At 11:00 P.M. Sunday, Ledterman and O'Neill drove to downtown Kansas City and quickly located the hotel that Hall could not remember—the Berkshire. O'Neill waited in the car with the money, while Ledterman went in and found a pay phone with the number Valentine 9279. At 11:30, "M" called him.

This conversation was not recorded by the FBI; there wasn't enough time to arrange it. Ledterman said later that "M" instructed him to drive east on Highway 40 to its intersection with County Road 10-E. He was to turn south on 10-E and go about a mile until he came to a bridge. The duffel bag was to be placed on the side of the road by the bridge. After dropping off the bag, Ledterman and O'Neill were to drive on. The kidnappers, "M" said, would pick up the money immediately: "We will not be far behind you." If any other cars came by as they were preparing to drop off the bag, Ledterman and O'Neill were to keep going for a while, then turn around and try again.

The conversation ended with Ledterman saying he would like to meet "M" some day. "M" replied: "I hope you never do."

Leaving the hotel, Ledterman and O'Neill drove east on Highway 40, but they missed the junction with 10-E the first time. On the second try, they found it, turned south and soon came to the bridge. They got out, put the duffel bag on the left side of the road, and drove back to the Greenlease home. The ransom had been delivered.

But why should this night be different from all the others? Hall could not find the duffel bag. He and Bonnie were parked near a filling station on Highway 40, with Bonnie asleep as usual, and Hall saw a Cadillac go by with two men in it. He waited a few minutes and then drove to the bridge on 10-E—but he did not see the duffel bag.

Hall said in his confession that he had told Ledterman to put the bag on the *right* side of the road. Ledterman's recollection, which almost certainly was better, was that "M" told him to put it on the *left* side, and that is what he did.

61

Failing to spot the bag, Hall drove on for a couple of miles and then turned around. He parked on the side of the road and waited for five or ten minutes. Then he drove back toward the bridge. As he did so, Hall said, he saw a Cadillac approaching him, and the two cars passed in the night. Was it Ledterman and O'Neill? Hall thought it was, but the timing wasn't right if his recollection of a five- or ten-minute wait was correct. Ledterman and O'Neill did not recall seeing a Ford go by in the other direction.

When Hall got to the bridge the second time, he saw the duffel bag. The master criminal's moment of triumph: *He had the money at last.* The big score that would never have to be repeated. The fortune that would bring him pleasure and ease eternal. The money for which he had kidnapped and murdered a six-year-old boy. He estimated that it was 12:30 A.M. Monday, October 5, when he picked up the duffel bag and put it in his car.

He had decided earlier that he and Bonnie would go to St. Louis as soon as they had collected the ransom, but there were a few odds and ends before they could leave. The first was his promise to call Ledterman. It was the last of the fifteen calls that ''M'' made to the Greenlease home, and it came at 1:00 A.M. Monday:

Ledterman: . . . Everything was all right, was it?

M: Naturally. We haven't been able to check it [the money] yet.

Ledterman: Well, you will find—I didn't neither, but it will be all right.

M: Well, I am sure of that and you can rest assured and you can tell his mother that she will see him as we promised within 24 hours.

Ledterman: Tell his mother what?

M: That she can rest assured that she will see him within 24 hours as we promised.

Ledterman: Well, now how long am I going to have to wait down there [in Pittsburg, Kansas] for instructions, and how soon can I pick him up?

M: You will hear in the morning and you will be told when you can pick him up.

Ledterman: When and where?

M: Yes. We have to be very careful.

Ledterman: I know. Can I get him tomorrow?

M: Definitely. . . .

Ledterman: Ah, can I get him by 11 tomorrow morning?

M: That I can't tell you, but it will be within 24 hours.

Ledterman: I see, now the boy is alive and well?

M: And as full of [expletive] as any kid I've ever seen. . . .

Ledterman: I can quote you on that, can I?

M: Yes, you can quote me. . . .

They never heard from "M" again. As soon as this last conversation had ended, Ledterman and O'Neill drove to Pittsburg, more than one hundred miles south of Kansas City. It was the middle of the night, and they had been without sleep for forty hours. They checked into the Hotel Besse in Pittsburg, and the next morning they began a vigil at the Western Union office. They stayed in Pittsburg two days. No messages came.

On Wednesday, October 7, shortly after he returned to Kansas City, Ledterman got a call from St. Louis: A man and woman had confessed the kidnapping, and Bobby's body had been found.

"It was my duty to inform his parents," Ledterman said.

Carl and Bonnie had checked out of Luper's El Rancho Motel at 6:15 Sunday night, several hours before picking up the ransom. Bonnie knew they were going to St. Louis as soon as they got the money, and during the evening she remembered that she had left her dog Doc at home. She roused herself long enough to call a friend whose husband worked at a kennel in St. Joe. She left a message with this friend that she would not be home for a while and wanted the dog boarded.

There were other odds and ends: drugs and whiskey. Sometime and somewhere on Sunday night, Hall got a quarter grain of morphine and took it, and he and Bonnie had drinks at several bars. By the time they left for St. Louis, Hall said, they were in "quite a drunken condition."

The last item was the damned license plates. Not long after passing the Cadillac on County Road 10-E, Hall said, he realized that he had not put the stolen plates on the rented Ford. He said he "immediately became panicky." His imagination promptly produced a sequence of horrors: Ledterman and O'Neill had seen the Ford and had noted its license number. The car would be quickly traced back to the rental agency. From the rental agency, it would be traced to Bonnie, and from Bonnie to him. He said he became completely convinced that the license had been seen and that "his identity was known" almost as soon as he had picked up the ransom. None of this had happened, of course, but fear raced through his mind, darting now here and now there, pausing to copulate rapidly with guilt and beget new fears, and then racing on.

As soon as they left Kansas City, Hall stopped and put the stolen license plates on the Ford. But in his mind the damage had been done. "If we go back to St. Joe," he told Bonnie, "the police will be waiting for us."

His forgetfulness about the license plates reinforced the decision he had reached earlier: They would go to St. Louis. Bonnie had never been enthusiastic about this; she said later that she believed everything would have been all right if they had just gone back to St. Joe and laid low. But, she said, Hall "got some shots [morphine] and wanted to travel."

Now, in the early hours of Monday, they were on Highway 40, heading for St. Louis, driving all night, drinking the whole way, pursued by ghosts and furies.

Chapter **7**

hey made several stops during the 250-mile trip across the state. The first time, Hall put the stolen license plates on the Ford—too late to do any good—and then he opened the trunk to check the ransom. This was more important. He had not yet looked in the duffel bag. What if the FBI had stuffed it with newspapers or something else of no value to avarice? "I'm going to see whether we've got a bag of money or a bag of paper," he told Bonnie.

It was money. The bag was packed tightly with bundles of currency. Using a flashlight, he inspected his fortune for a long, long moment. Exultantly. Wordlessly. Silent, upon a peak in Jackson County, Missouri. Six hundred thousand dollars. When he got back in the car, Hall told his drowsy mistress: "I've never seen so much money."

Not so much today, of course. We deal in millions now. The big money comes young and fast, and those who miss the grail are more pitied than those who go to jail. In the law offices, each dry line is read, each arid clause debated, to no purpose except money. In the financial offices, the corporate mergers are proposed and the junk bonds are issued, to no purpose except money. In the brokerage offices, the computers spin cold, noiseless dreams—the more impressive for seeming to come from some disembodied oracle—to no purpose except money. In all this, nothing is produced that is of use or benefit to people; so it will end badly. But, hey, what can I tell you? Have a nice day.

Carl drove very fast through the night, encountering little traffic. He stopped at least two more times, once to buy cigarettes and then at a filling station and all-night café in Boonville, where he bought gas. There may have been other stops; he told the FBI that "the condition of his kidneys" required him to urinate every half hour or forty-five minutes. He was thirty-four years old.

They got to St. Louis at about 6:00 A.M. on Monday, October 5. They found a restaurant—neither of them could remember its name or location—and Carl left Bonnie there while he went in search of a telephone. His fears were following him relentlessly; he could not rid himself of the idea that the Ford's original license plates would be traced. At 7:15 A.M., he called Bernard Patton, the St. Joe attorney who had befriended him after his parole.

He told the lawyer that he and Bonnie were in St. Louis, and that Bonnie had had "some trouble in Kansas City." Carl himself never had any trouble. He asked Patton to go to the McCord-Bell car-rental agency in St. Joe and try to get Bonnie's name removed from the rental record for the Ford. Patton said he didn't think the agency would do this, but Hall asked him to try anyway. He told Patton he would call him again later. Then Carl went back to the restaurant, where Bonnie had ordered ham and eggs for both of them. Bonnie ate some of her breakfast, but Hall did not touch his. Leaving the restaurant, they pointed the Ford at a drink.

They found the Sportsman's Bar and Grill at 3500 South Jefferson Avenue. From this point on, their route became easier to trace. They were beginning a day of heavy drinking, a desperate and erratic but sometimes cunning journey through the bars and alleys of St. Louis.

At about 8:00 A.M., George Oberbeck, a driver for the Yellow Cab Company, got a call to pick up a fare at the Sportsman's Bar. It was a man and woman, and thinking about it later, Oberbeck said he hadn't cared much for the looks of them. The man needed a shave and the woman was unkempt; moreover, she had a hard appearance. Oberbeck decided they were not the kind of people "I would like to take home to dinner." However, a fare was a fare.

Hall asked the cab driver to take them to the nearest pawnshop. Then he began to lie. He told Oberbeck they needed to buy some luggage because their car had been broken into and their bags stolen. He volunteered the information that the stolen luggage had contained "samples." Bonnie added her contribution to the lie: "Yeah," she told Oberbeck, "they even took my coat, and I'm cold."

Oberbeck did not know of any pawnshops in that neighborhood, so he stopped twice to inquire. Both persons he asked were policemen. Unaware that the cab contained murderers, the officers lost their chance at fame. Nor did they know of any pawnshops in the vicinity, so Oberbeck headed for the downtown area, well known for pawnshops.

Well known for bars, too. They found a pawnshop at Sixth and Pine streets, but it was closed. However, Slay's Bar, at 114 North Broadway, was open. They went into this tavern, where Bonnie had two shots of Walker's Deluxe whiskey and Hall one shot of the same. They bought Oberbeck a Coca-Cola.

At this point, Hall excused himself. Leaving Bonnie and the cab driver in the bar, he went looking for a place where he could buy some luggage. At 17 North Broadway, he found the Broadway Army Store, where he bought a dark-green footlocker and a black suitcase, both metal.

Then he returned to Slay's Bar, collected Bonnie and Oberbeck and told the cab driver to take them back to the Sportsman's Bar on the South Side. On the way, he suddenly said he wanted to send a telegram—to whom is not known but it might have been Patton. Oberbeck headed for a Western Union office, but before they got there, Hall changed his mind. "Well, she [Bonnie] talked me out of it," he said. "We'll send it later." They continued on to the Sportsman's Bar, where they parted company with Oberbeck.

The cab driver, a little curious about these people, saw Carl and Bonnie get into a blue Ford near the bar and drive away. "I looked to see if any windows in the car had been broken, because they had made the remark about it having been broken into," Oberbeck said, "but all the windows were rolled up and none were broken."

Now that he had the footlocker and suitcase, Hall wanted to transfer the money from the duffel bag. He drove around, looking for a secluded spot, because this was going to be a tricky operation. He did not want another interruption like the one in Kansas City, when the insurance man had seen him as he was laying out the first ransom route. After a while, he found what he thought was a good place: an alley in the rear of the 2200 block of Wyoming Street, near a small park known as Benton Park.

He drove into the alley and took the duffel bag out of the trunk—and then he couldn't get the drawstring untied. It wouldn't come loose. Cursing and sweating, he fumbled with the knot, but it would not yield. *Jesus, someone is going to come into this fucking alley and see us.* Bonnie tried to help, but that only made it twenty thumbs.

"For Christ's sake," she said, "get out your knife and cut it!"

With his pocketknife, Hall finally managed to saw through the drawstring. Then, working very fast, he upended the duffel bag and dumped the bundles of currency into the footlocker and suitcase. Six hundred thousand dollars in tens and twenties filled both of them to the brim. The footlocker had a tray, and Hall had to take it out to get all the money in.

Well, he had *thought* it was a good place. But just as he finished transferring the money, another car came into the alley.

A man and woman were in this car. They saw Carl and Bonnie (whom they identified later from photographs) standing in the alley by a dark blue car, with two large pieces of luggage beside them. The people in the car were afraid they would hit the luggage if they tried to edge by. They indicated this with the gestures that are used on such occasions, and Carl moved one of the bags, then waved to them and said: "It's okay."

It must have taken a tremendous effort for Hall to appear nonchalant, but he managed it. The couple in the other car said he and Bonnie seemed perfectly normal "and not the least bit nervous."

As soon as the other car had gone, Hall tossed the empty duffel bag into a garbage can at the rear of 2202 Wyoming (from which the FBI later recovered it), and then he and Bonnie got out of there fast.

At about 9:30 A.M., they entered the Hi-Nabor Bar at 2801 Wyoming. Mrs. Lenora Hoegemeier, co-owner of the tavern, noticed that Hall was carrying a large suitcase. He put it down, went outside and came back with a footlocker. Then he left again, and this time he was gone five or ten minutes. Bonnie, meanwhile, sat down at a table and kept an eye on the luggage. Apparently she began to feel neglected. "Would it be possible for me to get a drink in this place?" she inquired. Sarcasm at 9:30 in the morning. She ordered a shot of bourbon and drank it, sarcastically.

Where did Hall go? He drove the rented Ford to the 2800 block of Utah Street, parked it and walked away. He abandoned it. He had never felt right about that car. However, it seems he didn't feel right about abandoning it, either, because in his next call to Bernard Patton he told the lawyer that he had left the car in the 2800 block of Wyoming (not Utah) and the Hertz office in St. Louis could pick it up there. But the master criminal got the address wrong. When a Hertz employee went to the 2800 block of Wyoming, he could not find the car. The St. Louis police later recovered it on Utah Street, a block away.

68

Hall's mental processes were not the sort that made this country great. He was running a fearful risk in giving Patton so much information. He had called Patton because he wanted desperately to have Bonnie's name removed from the car rental record—but why tell the lawyer that he and Bonnie were in St. Louis? Suppose Ledterman and O'Neill *had* seen the Ford and had noted its license number? Even if the rental record had been changed (a dubious assumption), did Hall think no one at the McCord-Bell agency would remember Bonnie? Did he think no one would talk? Inevitably, the car would have been traced to Bonnie, and she and Carl would have been identified as the kidnappers—the crucial point. Presumably, Patton would have heard of it and would have notified the FBI that they were in St. Louis.

Of course, this was not the scenario that actually unfolded. Ledterman and O'Neill had *not* seen the Ford. When Carl and Bonnie were arrested in St. Louis, it was for another reason. But the fact that the Ford had not been spotted and traced had great importance for other persons, because it meant that at the time of their arrest, *it was not known that Carl and Bonnie were kidnappers*. It was not known that the money Hall had with him was blood money and was therefore very, very hot. If these things *had* been known, two men—and later, indirectly, a third—might not have gone to prison.

After abandoning the Ford, Hall walked back to the Hi-Nabor Bar, where he ordered a shot of bourbon for himself and a second one for Bonnie. Then they began to talk about the future. They agreed that they needed a place to stay for a few days, while they figured out what to do next, but they disagreed about what kind of place it should be. Bonnie wanted to go to a fancy hotel, now that they could afford the best. She suggested the Chase-Park Plaza, an expensive address in midtown.

Hall thought this was a terrible idea. Bonnie was getting drunk again, and he could see her staggering into the Chase, to be observed and remembered by some snooty desk clerk. But he didn't put it that way to Bonnie. "We're hot," he told her. "We've got to find some nice quiet place and hole up for a while." He urged a low profile, but Bonnie wanted to cha-cha-cha. They started to argue—a low-voiced argument that continued, off and on, for some time.

With the housing dispute unresolved, they had some more drinks, and then Hall called another cab.

Irwin F. Rosa picked up Carl and Bonnie at the Hi-Nabor. Rosa put the footlocker and suitcase in the trunk of his cab and recalled later that they were so heavy he could hardly lift them. Then another argument began. But this one was not really an argument. It was a maneuver to throw pursuit off the trail.

"Take us to used-car row," Hall said.

"Which one?" Rosa asked.

"It don't make any difference—anyplace where there are lots of cars," Hall replied.

As Rosa headed for a used-car lot, Bonnie and Carl began a whispered conversation. A few moments later, Hall spoke to the driver:

"She wants to go to the bus depot. You better take us there."

Rosa turned east and headed for the Greyhound terminal. More low-voiced conversation between Carl and Bonnie, and then Hall said:

"I didn't enjoy that place [the Hi-Nabor Bar]. It was too hot in there. Take us to a cool bar."

Cab-driving is a philosophic occupation. Rosa shrugged his shoulders and waited for his passengers to make up their minds. Meanwhile, he continued in the direction of the Greyhound terminal. Then he heard Bonnie mutter something about being late, and Hall said:

"I know we are driving you crazy, but she wants to go to the bus depot. Let's go there."

There was more whispered conversation. Hall apparently was prioritizing a used-car lot or a drink, while Bonnie rebuttalized with the bus depot. Things had reached interpersonal polarization, until Hall definitionalized the bottom line:

"Shut up and keep quiet," he finalized.

Then he said: "Oh, we've got plenty of time. Take us to a bar."

"When does your bus leave?" Rosa asked.

"We've got about twenty minutes," Hall said.

Rosa let them off at the bus station, unloaded the golden luggage, collected a fare of $1.25, received a tip of 50 cents, chalked up another day's education, and pointed out a bar across the street from the terminal. But as he drove away, he saw Carl and Bonnie walk toward the station instead.

Glenn Hartley, a ticket agent, said later that a woman came up to his counter at 10:30 A.M. He said the woman resembled Bonnie Heady although he was not positive it was her. For one thing, he said he did not see the bruises that other witnesses had observed on Bonnie's face.

Hartley said the woman inquired about a bus to Kansas City. Then she

70

changed her mind and asked about a bus to Tripp, South Dakota. She also wanted to know whether she could go on to Bismarck, North Dakota, if she decided not to stay in Tripp. Hartley told her there was only one bus to Tripp, that it left at 5:15 P.M., that it took twenty-four hours to get there, and that she would have to change buses in Kansas City and Sioux City, Iowa.

The woman thought for a moment and then indicated that, despite the odds, she desired to go to South Dakota.

"Do you want traveler's insurance?" Hartley asked.

"What do I have to do to get that?" the woman replied.

"All I have to have is your name, your address and your age," Hartley told her.

Hearing this, the woman suddenly said she didn't want a ticket after all. She told Hartley to forget the whole thing—"Forget I asked you, I don't want it"—and walked away from the counter. Ticket agent, sang Bessie Smith, ease your window down.

Was it Bonnie at the ticket counter? If it was, it raised the possibility that the kidnappers had an accomplice in Tripp or Bismarck. Did Carl and Bonnie plan to split up in order to confuse pursuit, with Bonnie taking $300,000 of the ransom money and heading for the Dakotas? Or did they plan to send the $300,000 to the third kidnapper? (At this stage, Hall was still claiming there was a confederate in the picture.) Bonnie might have lost her nerve this time, when she was asked for her name and address, but could there have been another time? The investigators had one tangible, tantalizing lead that was dominating the search at this point: Hall's remark to another cab driver, "I feel relieved. I just shipped out a bundle." Had the money been sent on another bus? Or in some other way? To an accomplice out west?

The FBI investigated the Dakota connection painstakingly. It checked not only the Greyhound depot but also the Trailways and Union terminals. Every bus driver who had arrived at or departed from these stations on October 5 was interviewed and shown photographs of Carl and Bonnie. Did either of these persons travel on your bus that day? The results were negative. Fanning out, the agents also questioned ticket sellers, porters, newspaper vendors, cooks, waitresses—virtually everyone who worked at the three bus stations. All negative. In addition, waybills were checked to determine whether Carl or Bonnie had shipped a package or luggage from any of the depots, under their own names or any of their aliases. Negative. Rental lockers and storage areas in the terminals were searched. Negative. No one, with the possible exception of Hartley, had seen Carl or Bonnie in the bus station on October 5, and there was no evidence that the missing money had been shipped anywhere by bus.

Hall said later, in effect, that it had all been a waste of time. There was, he insisted, no Dakota connection. He said he and Bonnie never had any intention of separating permanently, never split up the money, never sent part of it anywhere, never stored it anywhere. The bus station, he said, was just a ruse in case someone was on their trail.

On their trail. That was his obsession. Hall's plerophories would not go away. They arose not from fact but from ignorance, and therefore would not change. That is their nature, as witness fundamentalism. First he had decided that the Ford had been traced. Then he became convinced that the police and FBI would be looking for cab drivers who had picked up people in bars and taken them to hotels or apartments. To throw off pursuit, he decided to go to a used-car lot and buy a car. Then, in the car, he and Bonnie would rent an apartment. Thus there would be no cab driver to remember taking them there, no record of such a trip. You have to pay close attention to a master criminal when he gets cunning. It was Bonnie's idea, Hall said, to go to the bus station first and take a cab from there to a used-car lot. He said he didn't think the bus station was necessary—they should just go directly to a used-car lot—but he did it to "pacify" Bonnie, since she was already giving him hell about the Chase Hotel.

So they went to the Greyhound station; that much is certain. But when Hall was questioned later, he denied that Bonnie had inquired about buying a ticket to the Dakotas or anywhere else. He said they just stayed in the station for a few minutes, as part of their strategy.

Question: "Didn't she go in and check about a bus up to North Dakota?"

Hall: "No, she was right with me."

Question: "She never went up to the window and talked to a ticket seller?"

Hall: "No, definitely. She was with me every second of the time."

Question: "Never made any inquiry on buying insurance on something she wanted to ship?"

Hall: "Never. We weren't in there over three or four minutes. . . ."

Had he rented a locker at the bus station and stored half of the ransom money in it? Was that why they went to the station? No, said Hall, he had the entire $600,000 with him up to the moment he was arrested.

Chapter 8

*B*efore leaving the bus station, Carl and Bonnie argued some more over whether to go to a hotel or an apartment. Then Hall looked in a telephone book for a used-car dealer. Another cab—the driver unknown this time—took them to a used-car lot operated by the Barrett-Weber Ford Company at 3157 South Kingshighway. Across the street was Columbo's Tavern. It drew them like a magnet.

They went into Columbo's, where they had two highballs each. Then Hall left Bonnie in the tavern with the footlocker and suitcase while he went across to Barrett-Weber and inquired about used cars. Without inspecting any, he bought a 1947 Nash sedan. He paid $425 for it, giving the salesman twenty-one $20 bills and one $10 bill—all ransom money. He told the salesman, Lindsay Worley, to keep the extra five dollars as a tip. Hall gave his name as ''Steve Grant'' or possibly ''Stanley Grant'' and said he was from Elgin, Illinois.

At this point, a mysterious stranger entered the scene. Some witnesses described him as being rather thin—about six feet tall and weighing about 165 pounds. Others said he was short and stocky—''kind of heavy-set.'' Between them, they licked the platter clean. There was general agreement that he had a swarthy complexion and perhaps was Italian.

The stranger was sitting in a 1950 Studebaker convertible outside Columbo's, reading a newspaper. While Hall was buying the Nash, Worley told the FBI, he kept looking across the street at Columbo's. He seemed to be more interested in the tavern than in buying a car. To explain what was distracting his attention, Hall pointed to the Studebaker.

"I've got a friend in that Studebaker over there, and he's drunk," he told Worley. "He's passed out. I want to get him home." Later, however, the St. Louis police asked Worley if the man seemed to be drunk.

"Not to me he didn't," the salesman said. "He didn't appear to be intoxicated at all . . . [he was just] sitting there reading the newspaper."

Then there was a development that could have been significant or even sinister. Henry Patchin, another salesman at Barrett-Weber, told investigators that when Carl and Bonnie drove away in the Nash, the Italianate stranger followed them in the Studebaker. Fifteen or twenty minutes later, Patchin said, the stranger came back and again parked near Columbo's.

The newspapers drew attention to this, because newspapers love a mystery man. And the FBI and St. Louis police tried hard to identify the man in the Studebaker, because anyone and everyone who might have had contact with Carl and Bonnie was a suspect in the disappearance of the $300,000.

Worley, however, said the Studebaker had gone before Carl hurried back to Columbo's, collected Bonnie and drove away. If Worley was correct, the stranger drove away before Carl and Bonnie, and could probably be ruled out as a suspect. But Patchin said the Studebaker followed the Nash and "both cars turned right on to Arsenal Street."

Hall himself said later that he didn't know the man in the Studebaker from the man in the moon. He said he lied about the drunken friend, on the spur of the moment, to conceal the fact that he was keeping an anxious eye on Columbo's. He was worried because he had to leave Bonnie in the bar with the suitcase and footlocker while he went across the street to buy a car. He didn't trust her by herself. She was drunk and in an ugly mood about the hotel. He was afraid she might say or do something goddamned foolish while he was gone.

But was it a lie? With Hall, it was never possible to be sure. He might have been trying to draw the FBI's attention away from the stranger in the Studebaker by saying he was actually watching Bonnie. In which case, the stranger could have been an accomplice to whom Hall had given half of the ransom money. Or, conceivably, a criminal who had followed Carl and Bonnie and taken the $300,000 from them by force, threatening to kill them unless they remained silent. But if he was an accomplice or a thief, why had the stranger, like the swallows, come back to Columbo's?

Complication then followed complication. A little later, Patchin went across the street to Columbo's to get a sandwich and watch the World Series on TV. In the bar, he noticed a man about thirty-five years old who had a swarthy complexion and "looked like an Italian." The man was "drinking 10-cent beers" and watching the game. About twenty minutes later, Patchin said, another man came in—this one about fifty and weighing about two hundred pounds—and sat next to the younger man. They did not speak to each other, but when the older man got up to go to the rest room, "the Italian followed right behind him," Patchin said.

Then the key question: Could the Italian-looking man in the bar have been the stranger in the Studebaker? Patchin said he was not sure at all, but "it possibly was the same man."

Trying to sort all this out, the investigators showed Worley and Patchin a number of photographs of well-known St. Louis gangsters and hoodlums, many of them Italians. They got no positive identifications. Worley said one gangster had "some resemblance" to the man in the Studebaker, and Patchin said another gangster was "around the same height and build" as the Italian in the bar who in turn could have been the stranger in the Studebaker. And Shakespeare's plays could have been written by another man with the same name.

The Nash was just an interlude; it was the Ford that Hall was worried about—the Ford with the telltale license plates that Ledterman and O'Neill might have (but hadn't) spotted. Before leaving Columbo's, Hall made a second telephone call to Bernard Patton in St. Joe. He asked the lawyer if he had gone to the McCord-Bell agency to get Bonnie's name removed from the car rental record. Patton said he had not, and Carl again asked him to do it.

Patton told Hall he would like to help him but would need more information before he would agree to do anything. Specifically, he asked whether the Ford had been involved in a hit-and-run or some other serious accident. Hall said it had not, but Patton still held out for more information.

"Please, Barney, don't ask questions—just do it," Hall pleaded. "I'll send you some money, anything, if you'll just do this. I would really appreciate it." Then he collected Bonnie.

She was extremely drunk, but he managed to get her out of Columbo's and into the Nash. They drove for a few blocks, and then Carl parked the car and they took a short walk. He apparently hoped this might sober her up a little. They stopped at a drugstore, where Hall bought a newspaper. Then he needed a place where he could read the ads. So, undoing the benefit of the walk, they went into another tavern—name unknown—and Hall began searching through the apartment-for-rent columns. He wanted, he said later, "a quiet apartment where they could live unpretentiously, not attracting any attention." He found one that seemed okay.

At about noon, Mary Josephine Webb, manager of an apartment building at 4504 Arsenal Street, got a call about a two-room furnished apartment that she had advertised. A few minutes after his call, Hall arrived. He told Mrs. Webb that his name was "John Grant" and that he was from Elgin, Illinois, where he operated a liquor store. He said he and his "wife" were going to be in St. Louis for about two months on an extended vacation. He added that his wife, whose name he said was Esther, was recovering from a serious illness and needed rest. The "serious illness" was an explanation for Mrs. Webb, because one look at Bonnie and she was going to know something was wrong.

After inspecting the apartment and pronouncing it suitable, Hall said he wanted his wife to look at it. He went out and got Bonnie, who had stayed in the car. Sure enough, Mrs. Webb saw a woman who appeared to her to be "quite weak," leaning heavily on her "husband."

Hall paid a week's rent—twenty dollars—and brought in the suitcase and footlocker.

Alone at last. What did they do? According to Bonnie, her lover was ungallant. She said Carl "immediately flopped himself onto the bed" and fell into a sound sleep from which she could not wake him. Hall's version was equally ungallant. As soon as they got into the apartment, he said, he "dropped Bonnie on the bed, and she immediately went to sleep." Hall's memory was obviously more reliable, because he was out and around not long after they arrived.

He wanted to get rid of the Nash, send some money to Bernard Patton, and buy a radio so he could listen to news broadcasts about the kidnapping. Most of all, he explained later, he wanted to find out whether the Ford had been traced. The Ford, the Ford, he could not exorcise the Demon Ford. At about 12:30 or 1:00 P.M., he departed on his errands, leaving Bonnie asleep.

The Nash was first. He drove it away and abandoned it in the 3500 block of Arsenal. He had paid $425 for this car and had used it for about an hour and a half or at the most two hours. That came to more than $200 an hour. Then he took a cab to the Old Shillelagh Bar at 3157 Morganford Road.

The New York Yankees were playing the Brooklyn Dodgers in the World Series, with predictable results, when Hall walked into the Old Shillelagh and ordered a bottle of beer. He watched the game on TV for a few minutes, and then he put $500—twenty-five twenties—into an envelope on which he wrote: "Please pay [name withheld by the FBI]. Please mention nothing." He put the envelope into another one which he addressed to Patton in St. Joe. (The lawyer received it on October 10 and turned the money over to the FBI; name withheld presumably never got it.)

Then Hall asked the bartender to call a cab. A cab driver who was in the bar, watching the series, said he would take him. Hall told the cabbie, Edwin Gorman, that he wanted to go to the Hampton Village shopping center.

When they got to Hampton Village, Hall said: "I don't see the place I'm looking for. Take me back to where we were." They returned to the Old Shillelagh, at which point Gorman asked Hall what he was looking for. "A radio," Hall replied.

If people won't tell other people what is on their minds, they will have wars or get divorced or spend unnecessary money on cab fares. Directly across the street from the Old Shillelagh was a store that sold radios.

The cab driver drew Hall's attention to this. Hall went into the store— Petruso's Appliance Company—and said he wanted to buy a small radio. Something for $12 or $15, he said. The proprietor, Frank Petruso, said the only thing he had was a clock radio at $29.15.

"That's fine," Hall said. "How about putting it in a box?"

The radio's original box had been discarded, but Petruso found another one. It was about thirteen inches long, ten inches wide and seven inches deep—too big for the radio—but Hall seemed pleased and left with the radio and the box.

Later, the FBI became keenly interested in this box. The reason was the same as before: Hall's remark that he had "shipped out a bundle." That clue had sent FBI agents swarming through three bus stations in downtown St. Louis, and now they rushed across the Mississippi River to East St. Louis, Illinois.

A clerk in the East St. Louis Post Office, after reading about the case and seeing newspaper photos of Carl and Bonnie, told the FBI that on Monday, October 5, he had waited on a man who resembled Hall. The man had mailed a package to St. Joseph, Missouri. It was said to have weighed about forty pounds and was about twenty-four by twelve by eight inches. This was larger than the box Petruso had given Hall, but descriptions are often imprecise.

The important thing was that $300,000 in currency would have weighed about forty pounds. And East St. Louis would have been only a few minutes' drive for Hall. Poor East St. Louis, to paraphrase Porfirio Díaz, it is so far from God and so close to St. Louis,

Had Hall sent the $300,000 to someone in St. Joe? He swore he had not. He said the remark about shipping out a bundle merely referred to the $500 he had sent to Barney Patton. It was, he said, an expression of gratitude to the lawyer for helping him get a parole and a job and doing legal work for him for which Patton had never been paid. If this was so, who was the "name withheld" to whom the $500 was supposed to be paid? Was it Patton or someone else?

But the $500 was a minor issue. The more significant points were: (1) Hall had obtained a box, (2) half of the $600,000 would have weighed about forty pounds, and (3) Hall was a world-class liar. Could he be believed when he said the "bundle" remark referred to a letter to Patton and not to a box full of money?

FBI agents questioned twenty-two postal employees in St. Joe, asking them if they had handled a package from East St. Louis a few days after October 5. Negative. The package was never found, and neither was the man who mailed it.

After buying the radio, Hall had Gorman take him to a corner near the Arsenal Street apartment. He got out and walked to the apartment, where he tried to awaken Bonnie. No luck. So he lay down for a while himself and listened to the radio. But he was very restless; he couldn't stay still. After a few minutes, he got up, left the apartment and walked back to the Morganford Road area. However, he did not return to the Old Shillelagh. Instead, he went to a tavern at 3225 Morganford. This one was called the Squeeze Box. Yes. Box.

The owner of the Squeeze Box, Henry Schmidt, said Hall seemed nervous. He paced the floor and kept looking out the window. Then he ordered a shot of whiskey, but before drinking it he went to the men's room. When he came back, he drank some of the whiskey and then called a cab.

Howard A. Lewis, a driver for the Laclede Cab Company, picked up Hall at the Squeeze Box. Lewis said Hall appeared to be pretty drunk. For one thing, he paid lavishly, giving Lewis a twenty-dollar bill to start with and another twenty later.

"Just drive," Hall said. "Just drive around." The liquor was hitting him; he said later that he dozed for a while in the cab.

But then he woke up—and decided he wanted a woman. "I'd like to have a girl, and I don't care about the cost," he told Lewis. "I want a nice girl. I don't want to go to a whorehouse."

"That's not my line," Lewis said, "but we'll take a ride downtown and I'll see if some other driver can fix you up."

They cruised through the downtown area for a while, looking for a cab driver with lax standards, but were unsuccessful. "I don't think I can help you," Lewis said.

"Well, take me to 4504 Arsenal then," Hall told him. "I've got a couple of sample cases back there." To explain the weight of the footlocker and suitcase, he was telling people they contained "samples" of some kind.

On the way, Hall saw a bar—Brownie's Tavern at 3553 Arsenal. Telling Lewis to wait, he ducked in for a quickie. He came out about five minutes later and they went on to the apartment.

Bonnie was still asleep. Hastily, her lover scribbled a note and left it for her, in an envelope addressed to "Mrs. Esther Grant."

The note said: "Had to move bags in a hurry as report came in on radio— Girl next door looked funny— Couldn't wake you— Stay here and I'll call when I can."

That was the last time he saw Bonnie until they were arrested.

When he left the apartment this time, Hall took the luggage with him. Lewis said he seemed concerned about the footlocker and suitcase, testing them to make sure they were locked. The cabbie said they seemed to weigh a total of about seventy-five pounds, and Hall himself said later they weighed the same as they had all along, indicating that no large sum of money had been taken out at this point.

As they drove away, Hall again told Lewis he wanted a woman, so the search began anew. This time, Lewis decided to try the Jefferson Hotel, downtown on Twelfth Street, where there was usually a line of cabs. At the Jefferson, he found a driver who said he would be willing to get a woman for the fat drunk in Lewis's cab.

Hall had used many cabs in St. Louis that day, but this would be the last one. This driver, who worked for the Ace Cab Company, stayed with him the rest of the time.

In this book, he will be called Oliver Johnson, which is not his real name. Three or four months before, in a bar in St. Louis, he had met a young woman named Sandra June O'Day. After some preliminary discussion, they had entered into an arrangement under which Johnson brought men to her and received forty percent of the money they gave her. He would see if Sandy was available for the big spender.

She was available.

Chapter **9**

She was born on April 9, 1931, in Harco, Illinois, the product of a rape. She never knew her father's name—does not know it to this day. Her mother was a whore.

Harco is a very small town in the extreme southern part of Illinois not far from the confluence of the Ohio and Mississippi rivers. It is primarily a coal-mining area, bituminous coal, although there is farming as well.

Oh, it was a hard, harsh, unforgiving and *burdensome* region, this southern Illinois—had been always, would be evermore. Coal was master; man was slave. The people ground away in the mines, and the mines ground away at the people, turning their skins gray and seamy, giving them black lung, maiming them, and then in the Depression years, the terrible 1930's, casting them away. They had never had hope; now they had no work either. They sat on the sagging porches of old frame houses, in faded dungarees, staring into an indefinite distance. They coughed and coughed, and then they died.

John Redd was a miner. He and his wife, Mary, lived in Harco and they had two daughters. One was named Cecilia Ann, but she called herself Ann; she never used her first name. Ann Redd was raped, perhaps by force or perhaps it was a statutory rape because she was young, and she became pregnant from it. In 1931, she gave birth to a daughter, and then she left Harco and went to Du Quoin, Illinois. There, according to her daughter, she became a prostitute and later proprietor of a brothel. Sandra June O'Day, reminiscing, says that while she was growing up in Harco, her mother was "running a whorehouse on Oak Street in Du Quoin."

Ann Redd left her baby with her parents, who raised the child and named her Maryann Redd. It was the first of many names. During much of her childhood, Maryann Redd thought her grandparents were her parents.

In her teens, Maryann went to live with her mother in Du Quoin. At first she says she "went to be a whore with my mom," but then she thinks it over, decides she didn't become a hooker quite as early as that, and says she just lived with her mother in the house on Oak Street. Ann Redd was married at various times. For several years Maryann was known by the last name of one of these men.

On September 2, 1946, when she was fifteen years old, Maryann gave birth to a daughter of her own. She named the child Michelle; her nickname was Mickey. When the baby was about six months old, Maryann developed an inflammation of her uterus or ovaries. It got worse, and she had to have surgery. Before the operation, she says, Ann Redd told the doctor: "Be sure she doesn't have any more children." She was sterilized.

Maryann was not married to the father of her child when the baby was born, but they made it legal soon after, and she took his name. The marriage lasted about two years. After the divorce, Maryann decided she would have a new name—her fourth. She chose it herself: Sandra June O'Day.

Now she was seventeen years old, divorced, and with a young child to support. She went to work as a waitress, earning eighteen dollars a week. The next line writes itself: Then she met a man. And the next one: He said he would take her away from all this. But Sandy laughs and says there was more to it than that: "Yeah, I met him all right—my mother *sold* me to him." His name was Garland E. McGarvey, and he operated a restaurant-tavern in Madison, Illinois.

Sandy moved to Madison and went to work at McGarvey's "restaurant." Five other women were employed there also, and Sandy noticed that they frequently went down into the basement, taking male customers with them. McGarvey explained that the women augmented their income in this subterranean manner. He said he "kept the girls' money and gave it to them when they asked for it." The bookkeeper rules the world.

Sandy began taking men to the basement. She was popular with them because she was becoming a voluptuous woman—not beautiful but plentiful. In the prime of Miss Sandra O'Day, she was five feet ten inches tall, weighed 170 pounds and had other generous measurements. She was soon given "the nicest room in the basement." In 1951 and again in 1952, she was arrested in McGarvey's establishment and charged with vagrancy by reason of prostitution.

Now, McGarvey was an ex-convict, and he kept a pistol and a blackjack with him, and he drank and had a bad temper. Nevertheless, he and Sandy became good friends. She began calling him "Papa," and he in turn said Sandy "became just like a member of my family." Considering that McGarvey testified later that he and his wife had "fought like cats and dogs for 27 years," and considering also that Sandy herself put two bullets into him in 1958, the "member of the family" remark was ambiguous, but there it was: They became friends. So friendly that McGarvey aided her financially when Sandy decided to go into the tavern business herself.

In 1953, after working for McGarvey for about four years, Sandy opened a bar on a highway near Benton, Illinois. She called the tavern Pickle City because, her daughter Mickey says, "everyone got pickled there." However, the tavern closed after a few months, due to burning down. Sandy and her daughter both say it was arson.

The only other thing of note was the Pickle City Shootout. McGarvey got into an argument while drinking at Sandy's place, and when he was in this mood, he would go for his gun. There were a few seconds of rooty-toot-toot. Gunsmoke filled the bar and customers emptied it. However, neither McGarvey nor his opponent was hurt.

After her tavern burned down, Sandy moved to St. Louis, accompanied by her daughter and her aunt, Ann's sister. The aunt is still alive; in this book she will be called Molly Paine, which is not her real name.

They came to St. Louis in mid-1953. Sandy was twenty-two years old and Mickey was six. The arrangement was that Sandy would provide money for their support and Molly would look after Mickey. There wasn't much money; whenever they got some—as when the cab driver, Oliver Johnson, showed up with the big spender that day—Sandy and Molly would rush out and buy some clothes. They rented an apartment at 2023 North Ninth Street, in a very poor neighborhood. Even Carl Austin Hall, as drunk as he was, remembered that Oliver Johnson took him into a "slum" to pick up Sandy.

When—many months later—the FBI finally decided that Sandy did not know what had happened to the missing $300,000 or if she did know was never going to tell about it, when the agents finally let her go after questioning her endlessly, holding her in jail—not very legally—in Kansas City for twenty-three days, taking her before grand juries for more questioning, flying her out to the West Coast at one point in the hope—vain as it turned out—that she would con some information out of Oliver Johnson in a bugged room, when all this was more or less over and she was a marked woman but at least a semi-free one, Sandy went back to Du Quoin.

But there was really no place for her to go. She stayed in Du Quoin for a short time, and then she became a wanderer, one of America's anonymous minor pilgrims. She joined the drifting world of temporary jobs and shabby apartments, the intermediate world between certified criminality and certified respectability, the world in which the cops move you on, like Jo the crossing-sweeper, always move you on.

From Du Quoin, Sandy went to Chicago Heights, Illinois, where she worked as a bartender. Later she lived in New Orleans and Syracuse, New York, but the Syracuse cops found out about her after a while (she was still calling herself Sandra June O'Day), checked with the FBI, and then ran her out of town.

In February 1959, she was back in St. Louis. The cops got word of it and went to her apartment to question her about her "recent activities." They said she resisted them. They said she swore at them and kicked them and tried to bite them. They handcuffed her and took her to headquarters.

There, Sandy says, she was given a shot of penicillin in her buttock and then put in a cell. After a while, she was released, but before they let her go, she was forced to walk down a long cell block, past a line of cops. She still had on the white, low-cut dress she had been wearing when she was arrested. It was crumpled and sweaty from the cell, and her cosmetics were smeared.

When she reached the end of the line, the cop who had organized the event grabbed her arm, turned her around and made her do it again. He told his colleagues to "take a good look at her, and if you ever see her again, arrest her on sight." A bedraggled woman and a line of cops: She terrified 'em.

Sandy had a variety of jobs in those years. She worked in restaurants as a hostess, waitress or cook. She managed a diner for a while, and at other times she worked in bars. There was a period during which she hung out with a "sporting, horse-racing and betting crowd" in Chicago and other cities; she was "a sort of hostess" for these men, fixing drinks for them and serving canapés.

On December 13, 1957, she made a dramatic reappearance in Du Quoin. Accompanied by McGarvey and another man, she swooped down on a theater where Michelle was watching a movie, and took her away. Mickey, who was then eleven years old, was staying with Ann at this time, and relations between Sandy and her mother apparently had reached another low point. The Du Quoin police tried to intercept the car, but Sandy and the others got away. The question of kidnapping was raised, but Ann refused to press charges.

Leaving Du Quoin at high speed, Sandy went to Madison for a short time and then to South Bend, Indiana, where she operated a tavern. Later she went to Los Angeles. And then in April 1958, she came back to Madison and shot Garland McGarvey.

Sandy said it was unintentional. At her trial, the events were described as follows:

During the afternoon and evening of April 3, McGarvey began drinking heavily: It was double Scotches, one after another. He got meaner by the minute. Late that night, a bitter scene developed, with McGarvey cursing his family and proclaiming the grievances of life. When things had reached a certain point, his wife called their son at his home and asked him to come over. The son was twenty-four years old, six feet tall, weighed 190 pounds and was a railroad switchman; perhaps he could handle the situation. He tried to persuade his father to go to bed, but McGarvey testified later, "I was not about to be told what to do."

McGarvey went to the bedroom to get his pistol, but it was missing, so he got his blackjack instead. Seeing her husband with this weapon, his wife gave the younger McGarvey another one so he could defend himself. The father and son were facing each other in a hallway, each with a blackjack in hand—nasty little things that could smash and crack. The scene, McGarvey said later, "was not peaceful."

McGarvey's gun was missing because Sandy had beaten him to the bedroom. She testified that she took the pistol, intending to brandish it at him "so he would leave [his son] alone." As she came into the hall, she heard McGarvey say, "I'll knock your fucking block off," and saw him raise his arm. So she pointed the pistol in the general direction of the two men and fired twice. One bullet hit McGarvey in the right shoulder; the other went through his right arm and lodged in his chest. They were serious wounds, but he recovered.

"Did you point it [the pistol] at McGarvey?" Sandy's lawyer asked.

"Oh no, I didn't want to hurt Papa," she replied.

85

However, the son testified that the quarrel had subsided and his father had begun to weep when Sandy appeared in the hall and fired. And two Madison officers, Chief of Police Barney Fraundorf and Patrolman Frank Dutko, testified that Sandy said after the shooting that she "hated McGarvey and wished she had killed him."

Under our system, juries have to figure out what happened. The jury at Sandy's trial deliberated about three hours and then acquitted her. She left town again.

There is a postscript. It may explain Sandy's statement that she hated McGarvey. What had happened to the close friendship? Many years later, in an interview with the author, Sandy said she didn't shoot McGarvey to break up a family quarrel at all. She said she shot him "because he was trying to get the Greenlease money from me." He was convinced she had the $300,000 or knew where it was, and he was pressuring her to cut him in on it, giving her a very hard time, which McGarvey could do.

In the aftermath of the shooting, as she reflected on the publicity she had received, Sandy decided she should have another name. She began calling herself Patricia Nelson. Then she resumed her married name and used it for about twenty years. Around 1979, she switched to yet another name and was still using it when the author interviewed her in 1986. This name may be the last in a turbulent life that has finally grown quiet. To protect her identity, the two names that she has used since about 1960 are not being disclosed in this book.

In the early sixties, Sandy went to a large city in the East, where for many years she owned and operated a restaurant; she is proud of that. Now she is retired and still living in the eastern city. She is very poor—her only income is a welfare payment of $133 a month—and her health is not good. But since 1979, or thereabouts, she has lived with a man of whom she is very fond—"he is a good man." He is very poor also.

And that is where it has all ended. The FBI agents, the police, the grand juries, the prosecutors, the newspaper reporters, all the people following her and hectoring her, wanting to know about the $300,000. Where did it go? Who had it? Did she have it? *Where was the money?* And the years of wandering, going from city to city to escape her pursuers, to escape her reputation, to escape being Sandra June O'Day—all over now. The FBI no longer keeps track of her, does not know where she is, no longer is interested.

And that is funny, richly funny. Because Sandy *did* try to steal the money.

$\mathcal{W}$ hen Hall got into Oliver Johnson's cab, he told Johnson his name was ''Steve.'' And when they picked up Sandra O'Day at the apartment on North Ninth Street, he introduced himself as ''Steve Strand.''

Hall suggested they get a drink, so Johnson drove to McNamee's Bar at 2500 St. Louis Avenue. Hall and the cabbie drank beer, and Sandy had a highball. Then Johnson noticed something that made him a little anxious about this fare. When ''Steve'' got up to go to the men's room, his coat bulged on one side. The cabbie wondered if it was a gun. It was—but Johnson drew a wildly incorrect supposition from this. He became fearful that ''Steve'' was a plainclothes cop.

His anxiety increased when Hall asked the bartender for a pencil, some paper and an envelope. Then, turning away so Johnson and Sandy could not see, he wrote a note and put it in the envelope, which he carefully sealed.

''We need another cab, Ollie,'' he said. ''I want to have this letter delivered. It's for someone on Arsenal Street.''

''Well, we're going that way,'' Ollie said. ''We can drop it off our-selves.''

''No, we need another cab to deliver it,'' Hall insisted. ''This person it's going to, if she sees me she's gonna be mad as hell." That was the truth, but Ollie did not know it.

His problem was that he was an ex-convict. Things like concealed weapons and mysterious notes made him nervous. He said later, "I thought he [Hall] might be a cop, trying to trap me for getting a girl for him." He decided to put it to "Steve" directly.

"Listen, I'm doing this as a favor," he said. "Are you a cop?"

Hall laughed. "Ollie," he said, "if you knew what I know, you'd realize how funny that is."

That reassured Johnson somewhat—and so did the money that Hall gave him. When the bartender said their tab was two dollars, Hall gave him a twenty and then handed the change to Johnson. Then, when they were back in the cab, he gave Ollie five twenties, saying, "That's just a starter."

"I said to myself, 'What a fare I've got here,'" Ollie recalled. "I decided I was going to stick with this guy."

The predictable next stop was a motel, and predictably Hall said that was where he wanted to go. Johnson had already decided to take the loving couple to the Coral Court, a motel at 7755 Watson Road. As an experienced St. Louis cab driver, he was familiar with the Coral Court's reputation at that time. Its reputation was that it was a place where experienced cab drivers took loving couples.

On their way to the motel, Hall said he wanted to clean up and needed a razor and shaving cream, so they stopped at a drugstore and Johnson went in and made the purchases. As he came out, Hall drew his attention to another cab parked across the street. He asked Johnson to give the driver the letter he had written in McNamee's Bar.

Still wary of a police trap, Ollie asked the other cabbie to open the letter before delivering it. He was to ascertain whether it was a message that detective "Steve" was on his way to an immoral rendezvous arranged by ex-convict Ollie Johnson, who would then be up Shit Creek. If that's what it says, Johnson told the other cabbie, throw it away. If not, go ahead and deliver it.

Since it was not a message to the cops, the driver delivered it. The note was to Bonnie Heady, and it said: "Stay where you are, baby—I'll see you in short order— Tell them you're not well and they'll (landlady) bring you food— Just say your husband was called away unexpectedly."

Then they made another stop. "Steve" wanted cigarettes and whiskey— he already had the wild, wild woman—so they pulled up at a package liquor store and Johnson again made the purchases.

Were they ever going to get to the Coral Court and get down to business?

Well, yes and no. They arrived at the motel at about 5:30 P.M., but it's a mystery whether they got down to business.

Hall registered for himself and Sandy as "Mr. and Mrs. Robert White" of Chicago. He said they would be staying three nights. They were given Room 49-A. Johnson brought in the suitcase and footlocker, again noticing how heavy they were. Hall invited him to stay a while and have a drink, so the three of them settled down for a cocktail hour.

Pretty soon Sandy brought up the subject of money. Hall had taken off his suit coat when they got into the room, and Sandy said later that she saw, in an inside pocket, something that looked like a lot of money. Hall, who was walking around the room, grew boastful and expansive.

"Money doesn't mean anything," Johnson remembered him saying. "All you can do with it is spend it. I trust you two kids. Sometimes I go on a bender for two or three days. I like to have a good time and maybe spend two or three thousand. I hate little people. I want to be big." It was his leitmotif; he had said the same thing upon leaving Pleasanton, Kansas.

He got his coat from the closet, took out a big wad of twenty-dollar bills and began to count them. But he was, according to Johnson, "pretty well intoxicated by that time," and when Sandy said something that distracted him, he lost count. He handed the money to the cab driver: "Here, you count it."

The total was $2,480. Hall produced another twenty to make it an even $2,500. Then he said: "Ollie, I want you to keep this for me."

"I began to think that maybe he was a bank teller who had run off with some funds," Johnson said later. He noticed that "Steve" had hands that were soft and well cared for; to Johnson this meant a white-collar occupation.

(Later, Hall made an oblique remark to Johnson that implied he might have embezzled "some insurance money." Then he added: "Everything would have gone fine if this guy hadn't made one mistake." After Carl and Bonnie confessed the kidnapping, this remark initially seemed to support Hall's story that a "third kidnapper" had done the actual killing of Bobby Greenlease.)

After giving Johnson the $2,500, "Steve" went to the closet again. From another pocket he took out a pistol—the same gun he had used to kill Bobby—and tossed it on the bed.

"Ain't this a beaut?" he asked. He explained that he had the gun for protection "because I carry a lot of valuable stuff with me."

"It's cute," Sandy said. "It's just what I need around the house."

She picked up the revolver and removed the shells. Hall did not like this.

89

"There's no need to do that," he said fretfully. "I've got some more." He produced some spare bullets from his coat pocket, but Sandy took those, too. Later that night, however, Hall retrieved his toys, and she saw him put the reloaded pistol under the nightstand.

Johnson left Room 49-A after a half hour or forty-five minutes and went to a nearby tavern, where he bought three bottles of Budweiser and two cigars. When he returned, he saw $200 in twenty-dollar bills on the bed. It was Sandy's fee for the night.

Sandy had asked Johnson earlier to go to her apartment and pick up some clothes she needed—a dress, shoes, a stole and another purse. Now she handed him the $200 and asked him to give it to Molly Paine when he got the clothing. (He did so, after deducting $80 as his share.) Hall also had an errand for the cab driver. While picking up the stuff for Sandy, he was to buy Hall a white silk shirt, some silk underwear and some socks. Johnson left on the errands, telling the loving couple he would be back around 10:00 P.M.

That gave them three or four hours, he with a new and younger woman, she with a capitalist. But both Hall and Sandy insisted there was no sex. Hall said later that when they got to the motel, he had not had any sleep for more than thirty-six hours—at another point he said it had been five days—and wasn't "physically capable" of intercourse. He said he had been living on "nerve whiskey" and "other drugs" and was "half gone."

After Ollie Johnson left, Hall said, he and Sandy drank and talked. He remembered that Sandy told him she had a daughter. She also said she had a farm somewhere, and she asked him for money to buy a bull for the farm.

"I recall thinking, why would anyone want to spend money for a bull?" Hall said. "Whiskey, yes, but not a bull."

Nevertheless, he promised her that if she would do a favor for him, he would buy her "the biggest bull they could find." He wanted her to go to Los Angeles and mail a letter from there.

Then, Hall said, Sandy grew flirtatious.

"Let's go to bed," she said.

"I paid you your money," Hall replied. "I've got something I want you to do, so relax."

"Come on, baby," Sandy wheedled. She made inviting gestures and patted the bed.

"I told you to relax," said Carl. "I got you here for one reason, and I'll tell you what it is later."

Again Miss O'Day suggested sexual intercourse, but even though the elder Pliny said it was good for physical weariness, hoarseness, pains in the loins, dim eyesight, melancholy and "alienation of the mental faculties," and even though Hall was suffering from some of these ailments, he again refused. Whereupon Sandy got off the bed and began walking angrily around the room. She was, Hall said, "stomping around and raising hell."

"What kind of deal is this?" she yelled. "What's going on here?"

"Don't worry about it. You got your money."

"What's wrong with you anyway? Is something the matter with you? Shit, I don't understand this at all." Sandy was working up to a fine rage. She stood in the middle of the room, five feet ten inches of angry Amazon, glaring at him.

"Listen, goddamn it, I haven't slept for five days," Hall shouted. "The last thing I want is to screw. So just sit down and shut your trap."

"Oh? Well, fuck you, buddy!"

"Fuck you too, you goddamn broad!"

An adaptable work, fuck. An all-purpose word. They were telling each other to fuck each other because they weren't fucking each other.

There was some more of this, and then they cooled down a little. Hall sat drinking in tired and sullen silence, lost in his own thoughts. Sandy wandered around the room, looking unseeingly at motel blankness, and then she turned on the TV. She sat, equally sullenly, watching it.

After a while, Hall roused himself. "Listen, when Ollie gets back we'll go get some dinner, so why don't you get cleaned up?"

Sandy went into the bathroom and took a shower. Carl drank steadily, automatically, staring at the gibbering figures on the TV. From time to time, he got up and peeked through the venetian blinds, apparently anxious for Ollie Johnson to return.

Sandy came out of the bathroom, refreshed and ready for Round Two.

"Well, what about you?" she said.

"Whadda you mean, what about me?"

"Aren't you gonna get cleaned up? God knows you could use it."

"Leave me alone. Just leave me alone."

"Well, for God's sake. Listen to you. I get all cleaned up, and you're gonna go out to dinner looking like a slob. For Christ's sake, I didn't even *need* to get cleaned up, and just look at you."

Then another switch to cajolery. "Come on, honey, go get cleaned up. I want to go to some real nice place for dinner."

"All right, ALL RIGHT! Anything to keep you quiet."

Hall went into the bathroom. While he was splashing around, Sandy came in, flirtatious again.

"Move over," she said. "I want to get in with you."

91

The sex scene at last? Unfortunately, Hall did not say what happened next. This portion of his narrative ended with Sandy proposing to join him in the bath. So the rest of the script can be written two ways:

In the movie version, Sandy slips into the shower, and girlish giggling and masculine arousal ensue, followed by mutual washing of backs and other parts, with appropriate comments. After which, all rancor is washed away in a torrent of lust, explicit or implied depending on the rating.

In the other version, Carl Hall, drunk and exhausted and thinking—to the extent he can think at all—only of the mortal danger he is in, says to Sandy: "Get your ass out of here."

Which was it? Hall can tell no more, but what about Sandy? In an interview with the author many years later, she said she did take a shower, but otherwise her version was demure. She did not invite Hall to bed. At no time did he take off his clothes. There was no bathroom scene. Sandy described Hall as "a nervous wreck." She said he spent most of the time drinking, pacing around the room and peeking through the venetian blinds. "I think he was looking for Ollie Johnson," she said, and then she told of Hall's affectionate behavior toward the cab driver, which was recounted in Chapter 3. While Hall drank, paced and peeked, Sandy lay on the bed, untroubled, as they used to say, by advances.

"He never took his clothes off while I was with him," she told the author. "He just kept walking around the room with jerky movements and peeking through the blinds all the time."

Ollie Johnson's version, however, was less demure. He said that when he got back to the motel, Hall was wearing only his shorts. Then Johnson told of having a few whispered words with Sandy while Hall could not hear them; he may have been in the bathroom.

"He was a terrible lay," Sandy confided, according to Johnson.

"Is that right?"

"You better believe it. He was awful. I almost had to rape him."

They did not argue constantly; they had some ordinary conversation, too. Sandy recalled, for instance, that Hall told her he was "in some kind of research and had samples in his suitcases." Sandy became very interested in the suitcase and footlocker.

As with Richard Nixon, so with Sandra O'Day: What did she know, and when did she know it? In her testimony before the St. Louis Board of Police Commissioners, which conducted its own investigation of the missing

$300,000, Sandy insisted she never saw the contents of Hall's luggage. She said she simply assumed he had a lot of money because he gave her $1,000 to go to Los Angeles and mail a letter.

But in her conversation with the author, she said she left the room for a few minutes the next morning and when she came back the venetian blinds apparently were partly open. At any rate, she said she could see into the room. Curiosity overcame her. She peeked in and saw the footlocker. It was open, she said, and it was full of money.

However, it is virtually certain that she saw the money for the first time at some point during the night, not the next morning. Otherwise it is hard to explain her actions later in the night. And there is confirmation: After she was released from jail in Kansas City, Sandy told part of the story to a person in whom she had confidence. She told him that after Hall passed out that night, she got the keys to the footlocker and suitcase, opened them, and there was "more money than she had ever seen."

Johnson got back to the motel about 10:30 P.M. Hall let him in and "seemed very glad to see me." He thanked the cab driver effusively for bringing the silk shirt and underwear: "You're really on the ball, Ollie." He was clinging hard to Johnson now; he wanted his allegiance. One fear succeeded another—the insurance man in Kansas City who had seen him as he was setting up the ransom route, the rented Ford and telltale license plates, the people in the alley as he was transferring the money, and now the possibility that his new companions might betray him. Johnson, like Sandy, saw a very nervous man; he said Hall was pacing "up and down the floor."

They had some drinks, and then Sandy said she was hungry. "Let's get out of here and get some dinner."

But Hall had changed his mind about going out to dinner. He said he didn't want to leave the motel—meaning he didn't want to leave the suitcase and footlocker.

"Let's just have Ollie go out and get us some sandwiches," he said.

"Oh, no," said Sandy. "You're not gonna give me a damn old sandwich."

After some more bickering, Hall agreed to go out to dinner, but he said it had to be someplace near the motel.

They went to the Harbor Inn at 8520 Watson Road, not far from the Coral Court. Hall and Sandy ordered steaks; Johnson had fried chicken. They talked about this and that, and they played the juke box; a routine evening.

Hall complained that it was taking a long time to bring the food, but when his steak came Ollie noticed that he ate only a few bites of it.

After dinner, they went back to the motel. Now Hall seemed even more "fidgety and worried," Johnson said. Apparently hoping to assuage the demons and furies, he asked Ollie "if I could get him some morphine." He also wanted a syringe and a "number 25 or 26 needle." Johnson said he told Hall he would try to get some morphine but he had no intention of doing so; he was just playing along.

Before Hall and Ollie parted company for the night—if they *did* part company at that point—Hall had some instructions for the next day. He told Ollie to rent a car and bring it to the motel in the morning—he said he wanted to "visit someone." He also asked Ollie to buy him a suitcase and a briefcase—"the best and most expensive" available. Johnson said he left the motel around midnight.

It was then Sandy decided she would try to steal the money. She told the author that sometime after midnight, with Hall "passed out in a chair," she left the Coral Court and took a cab to the home of a friend, from whom she borrowed a car. Then she drove to a cocktail lounge in East St. Louis, looking for another friend "who knew Buster Wortman." If she could get in touch with Wortman, she thought he might be interested in helping her roll a drunk.

Frank Wortman—nicknamed "Buster"—was a criminal. He was an "East Side rackets boss," a "gangland leader" and a "notorious hoodlum." All this according to the St. Louis newspapers, which lavished attention on him. He was not a great criminal mind—not a Capone or Moriarty, a government official or corporate executive—but the local journalists counted it a dull day if there was no story on Wortman.

Some of his income derived from the Plaza Amusement Company, which dealt in pinball machines, slot machines and other coin-operated devices. But he also dominated the gambling scene on the East Side, and no whorehouse operated there without his blessing. He did not look nice—his nose especially was criminal—and he was *not* nice. He had served almost ten years in Alcatraz for assaulting a federal officer, and when he returned to the East Side he eliminated his rivals, notably gangsters Carl and Bernie Shelton, whose murders he was said to have arranged. After that, he had a moat dug around his home near Collinsville, Illinois— yes, a *moat;* it was a source of fascination for years—and reigned over the rackets. Although not a Mafioso, he was reputedly the southern Illinois representative of the Chicago crime syndicate.

This, then, was the man Sandra O'Day went looking for that night. The FBI never found out that she left the motel—although it certainly suspected her of designs on the money—and it never knew she had tried to find Buster Wortman. If it had known that, it would have torn her apart. The mere mention of Wortman, just the possibility that he was involved, would have created a brand-new game. So Sandy kept very quiet about leaving the motel. She told only one person about it at the time, and she gave him only a partial account—nothing about Wortman. Many years later, Sandy yielded the rest of the story:

"I wanted that money. I was human, poor and desperate. I wanted that money for my child. You have no idea how naïve and ignorant a young woman can be."

She did not find the friend who knew Buster Wortman. She did not find Wortman. She went back to the Coral Court, arriving there about three in the morning. It was Tuesday, October 6.

Monday had been a long day, and Tuesday would be just as rich and full. But some loose ends remain before the dawn: Did Carl Hall go somewhere with Oliver Johnson at 2:00 A.M.? Was Sandy's aunt, Molly Paine, at the Coral Court that night? Was Bonnie Heady there also? And if not, what was Bonnie doing while Hall was playing Ulysses in Night-town with his Circe and his Dedalus?

If Hall and Johnson left the motel while Sandy was gone, and then she came back and then they came back, and if Molly Paine came to the room while they were all there, and then she left and Bonnie Heady came in, or if Bonnie came first and then left and Molly came, and if Hall and Johnson left after Bonnie and Molly, then Room 49-A was a Marx Brothers scene, with everyone rushing in and out at top speed, falling over each other and making noise, after which a man in a funny wig plays the harp.

When FBI agents and cops and newspaper reporters are investigating a major crime, they hear a great many rumors, and the preceding paragraph is a summary of the rumors and stories they heard about 49-A, together with some they never heard. The situation has to be considered numerically:

1. Sandy says she left the motel during the night, to look for Buster Wortman.

2. The St. Louis newspapers reported that Molly Paine was at the motel for a while. But Sandy emphatically denies that Molly came to the Coral Court, and there is no evidence that she did.

3. Sandy told her confidant in Kansas City that Bonnie Heady came to the motel that night, got drunk, passed out, and then woke up and left. But

there is no evidence to support this either. Mrs. Mary Webb, the manager of the Arsenal Street apartment where Bonnie was staying, said Bonnie did not leave at any time during the day or night Monday—and Mrs. Webb was a good witness, who accurately described other events involving Carl and Bonnie. So this one, despite Sandy, was apparently a non-starter.

4. The possibility that Hall and Johnson left the Coral Court together is a more important loose end. If it happened, it could have given Hall an opportunity to hide the $300,000, perhaps with Ollie's help.

In his statements to the FBI and the St. Louis police board, Ollie said he left Hall at the Coral Court around midnight and did not see him again until the next day. Hall, in his confession, said he did not leave the motel with Ollie or anyone else. He said he went to sleep around midnight or 1:00 A.M. and that was it until the next morning.

But a woman who operated a tavern on Chestnut Street, in the downtown area, told investigators that Johnson came into her bar at about 2:00 A.M. Tuesday and said he had an ''angel''—a big spender—outside in his cab. He said the angel wanted a drink. The woman said she reminded Ollie that it was after hours. No drink for the angel, but she admitted she gave Ollie one for himself because she knew him. The angel never came into the bar; everyone agreed on that.

Ollie said he went to the bar on Chestnut Street, had three or four after-hours drinks, not one, and then went to his hotel and to bed. In neither of his statements did he say anything about telling the woman in the tavern that he had an angel in his cab. However, he admitted asking her if she knew where he could get some Benzedrine—''I had a guy that wanted some.''

Was Hall the angel in the cab at two in the morning, or was he asleep at the Coral Court? Johnson told the FBI that he picked up a couple of late-night fares after leaving the motel. If that was true, the angel could have been one of them, not Hall. But Phillip King, the FBI agent who worked on the Greenlease case longer than any other investigator, said he believes Hall *was* the angel in Ollie's cab, although he emphasizes he is not sure. So it remains a loose end. Only Johnson could clear it up, but he declined to be interviewed for this book.

5. For Bonnie Heady, Monday was a quiet day. She slept all morning, not waking until midafternoon. When she woke up, she found Hall's first note, telling her, ''Stay here and I'll call when I can.'' She remembered that later in the afternoon a cab driver brought her the second note (written in McNamee's Bar). Bonnie said she tried to find out where her lover had gone, but the cabbie told her that all he knew

was that another driver (Ollie Johnson) had given him the note with instructions to deliver it to her.

Bonnie did not know where Hall was or what was happening. "I was frantic," she said later. "All I found was a note sitting on the dresser." Since there was nothing else to do, she said she spent the rest of the day and night drinking and sleeping.

Chapter 11

*T*uesday, October 6, 1953. St. Louis is preparing for a traditional celebration: the Veiled Prophet's Ball. The city's aristocracy will assemble tonight at Henry W. Kiel Auditorium, a large downtown hall named for a former mayor. There, in finery, the debutantes of the current season will be presented to the Veiled Prophet of Khorassan. One of them has been selected as the Prophet's Queen of Love and Beauty.

Each debutante will approach a throne on which the Prophet sits, his identity concealed by a heavy veil although Daddy probably knows him well. A man will announce her name in a loud voice and proclaim that she has been summoned to the Prophet's "Court of Love and Beauty." The Queen is last. Her name has been a secret until this moment. The suspense is unbearable. The Queen will reign over St. Louis society for a year, opening charity bazaars, cutting ribbons at dedications, visiting hospitals and attending horse shows, where she will bestow prizes on the rear ends. During her reign, she will be expected to remain a virgin, although in the long history of the Veiled Prophet, love sometimes found a way. These lapses were great scandals; however, they rejuvenated the institution.

The Prophet made his first appearance in 1878, as an inducement to farmers to visit the city after the harvest and spend their money. He was said to be the ruler of the mythical kingdom of Khorassan, which dated from "10,842 B.C., some 294 years before the creation of the world." This was six millennia older than Bishop Ussher's 4004 B.C. and should be of interest to fundamentalists, as it has their kind of validity.

Actually, there *was* a Veiled Prophet of Khorassan. His name was Hakim ben Allah. He founded an Arab sect in the eighth century and claimed that he had been Adam, Noah, Abraham and Moses in previous incarnations; he had been busy. Hakim wore a veil to conceal facial scars he had received in battle and was known as Mokanna, or "The Veiled." Ultimately, he poisoned all his followers and threw himself into a cask of acid. Thomas Moore wrote a poem about him. In it, Mokanna lifts his veil and frightens a young maiden; she shrieks.

The night after the ball, there will be a parade. The Prophet, his Queen and his Merrie Krewe of merrie businessmen will lead a procession of floats through midtown St. Louis. Each parade has a theme—children's stories, folk tales, historic events and so on. Because 1953 is the Prophet's seventy-fifth anniversary, tomorrow night's floats will reproduce favorites from the past: "Tom Sawyer," "Cinderella," "The Old Woman Who Lived in a Shoe," "Robin Hood" and other subjects that indicate how the world came to have Disneyland.

But the Veiled Prophet's annual visit is not a Mardi Gras. There is no dancing in the streets, no public revelry. St. Louis is not that kind of city. With the exception of its gilded youth, who occasionally taunt the police or elope with the family chauffeur, its eccentricities are private. The Veiled Prophet is not a Rex or Comus unloosing open bacchanalia. He comes and goes in just two nights, which is not enough time to work up a good, general orgy. St. Louis is not frolicsome. Never has been and never will be, unless a civic miracle occurs, and no known miracle has ever taken place there.

The city was founded in 1794 by Pierre Laclède Liguest, known to history as Laclède, with the assistance of a young companion, Auguste Chouteau. The founder was a fur trader and a cultured man—a graduate of the University of Toulouse. He came up the Mississippi River from New Orleans, looking for a place to establish a fur-trading outpost that would not celebrate Mardi Gras. Laclède chose a location near the confluence of the Mississippi and Missouri rivers, and tradition insists that he named the settlement after King Louis the Ninth of France. This medieval king, who was canonized in 1297 as Saint Louis, built part of Notre Dame de Paris, rebuilt Chartres, constructed hospitals, founded institutions for the needy, the blind and the leprous, encouraged learning, dispensed justice wisely and was one of France's few beloved monarchs.

Tradition may insist, but Chouteau wrote in his diary that Laclède actually intended to honor Louis the *Fifteenth*. This Louis was one of the later Bourbon kings, who were neither learned nor just. He was frolicsome with Jeanne de Pompadour and Marie Du Barry, was associated with the prediction *"Après nous* (or *moi), le déluge,"* which is the motto of modern leaders, too, and was not beloved at all.

As Europe's huddled masses poured into America in the nineteenth century, the French in St. Louis suffered the ancient fate of *anciens régimes*. The newcomers were largely German, Italian and Irish. They divided the city's neighborhoods, occupations, religions and politics among them.

The Germans made beer and prospered greatly. In the year 1857, a soap manufacturer named Eberhard Anheuser took over a bankrupt brewery that owed him money. In 1873, his star salesman and son-in-law, Adolphus Busch, the youngest of twenty-one children of a Rhenish wine merchant, became a full partner in the brewery and soon the dominant figure in American beer. "Prince Busch," President William Howard Taft called him, in tribute to his life-style. Today, Anheuser-Busch's Budweiser and Michelob own the nation's thirst, especially at half-time.

Entrenched on the South Side, the Germans were an Almanach de Gotha of local respectability, heavy on "B's" and "K's" and other hard consonants: Biederman, Brandhorst, Broemmelsieck and Bronfenbrenner, Kindelsperger, Kleinschmidt and Knoernschild. And Deichmiller, Diddledock and Driemeyer, Freyermuth and Friedrich, Gildehaus, Gonsenhauser and Griesedieck, Lautenschlager, Leimkuehler and Lueking, Muckenfuss and Mueller. And Schwerdtman, Schiele, Schneider and Schultz, Von der Ahe, von Gontard, Wiese, Wohlschlager and Ziegenhein. And (among the vowels) Aftergut, Althoff, Orthwein and Uthoff. Frolicsome, all.

The Italians in St. Louis had a difficult time. Clustered in a vigorous midtown area known as "the Hill," they operated produce markets, small businesses and marvelous restaurants. Their dispositions were sunnier, but in the 1950's their efforts to win acceptance were handicapped by the presence of an active local chapter of the Mafia. At this time, FBI Director J. Edgar Hoover was still insisting that La Cosa Nostra did not exist, but the cops and the newspapers did not agree. As a result, the leaders of the St. Louis Mafia, John J. Vitale and Anthony G. "Tony G" Giordano, were the subjects of constant attention, and Vitale was to figure in the Greenlease investigation.

The Irish, per custom, had been allotted law enforcement. They also did much of the city's muscular work, especially in the railroad yards. In the early days, they had lived in a most distressful neighborhood called Kerry Patch, but time and their political abilities rescued them.

The ethnic ferment proceeded, but the power structure remained undisturbed, low-profile and Anglo-Saxon. The city's major corporations and its biggest banks and law firms were securely in the hands of WASPs. While the Germans were getting all the attention, the Princeton crowd just slipped in and took over. By the 1950's, most of them had abandoned the city itself and were living in expensive suburbs—Ladue, Frontenac, Warson Woods, Huntleigh, Creve Coeur—but the commercial heart, in faraway downtown, belonged to them. They were the people of the Veiled Prophet.

At one end of every rainbow is a pot of gold. But consider the other end. In the early and middle decades of this century, millions of blacks left the rural South in search of higher wages and the intensely dubious prospect of better conditions in the cities of the North and East. By the 1950's, most of midtown St. Louis had gone to them by default, but it was a prize not worth having. A vast, infamous central slum had formed and was metastasizing into north St. Louis and the "west end." In response, the great white flight to the suburbs had begun; except for the South Side bastion, the city was being given over to a destitute black population. The core of St. Louis was a Dickensian Tom-all-alone's: a swarm of misery, a foul existence "sowing more evil in its every footprint than Lord Coodle, and Sir Thomas Doodle, and the Duke of Foodle, and all the fine gentlemen in office, down to Zoodle, shall set right in five hundred years. . . ." For Coodle, read the White House; for Doodle, Congress; for Foodle, all the Ladues and Frontenacs; for Zoodle, every one of us, fine gentlemen that we are.

The period after the Civil War was the best time. In 1890, St. Louis was the fourth largest city in the nation, exceeded only by New York, Chicago and Philadelphia, and it held that rank for twenty years. In 1904, it celebrated its eminence with a World's Fair—the Louisiana Purchase Exposition—and proudly invited everyone to "Meet Me in St. Louie, Louie" (although St. Louisans themselves never pronounce it St. Louie). It was a memorable fair, but the sad thing was that it had to be remembered so long.

Because in the 1960's and '70's, the fine old city—the city of T. S. Eliot and Tennessee Williams and Marianne Moore, Sara Teasdale, Kate Chopin, Eugene Field and William Inge, the city of Nobel Prize winners, renowned universities and medical centers, artists, intellectual leaders and crusading journalists, of the Dred Scott trial and Carl Schurz, who helped

101

elect Abraham Lincoln ("We defy the whole slave power and the whole vassalage of hell," Schurz shouted), of Henry Shaw's noble garden and, later, Eero Saarinen's exultant arch, of Dizzy Dean, the Gashouse Gang and Stan Musial, of Helen Traubel, the first Pulitzer and O. K. Bovard, and Scott Joplin, the incomparable Scott Joplin—was a burnt-out case, its midsection a grim desolation known locally as "Hiroshima Flats," its industries fleeing, its suburbanites gone out so far they were falling off the edge of the earth. And yet St. Louis was still there and would always be there, and someday would rebuild itself westward from the river again, with a stubbornness as good as courage.

Tuesday, October 6, 1953. There has been enough suspense. The Veiled Prophet's choice was Julia Terry, an eighteen-year-old debutante. On the night she was crowned Queen of Love and Beauty, in splendor, two St. Louis cops arrested Carl Austin Hall in a nondescript apartment about forty blocks away. The tip that led to his capture was provided by the cab driver, Oliver Johnson.

He was born in 1914 in a working-class suburb. His formal education appears to have ended in high school, but he was a trained machinist and at various times earned his living making precision tools and dies. In the mid-1930's, he worked at an automobile plant in St. Louis, and then from 1938 to 1940 he apparently operated a tavern on Hodiamont Avenue, in a blue-collar neighborhood. In 1940, he went to Los Angeles, possibly attracted by the high wages being paid in defense plants as the nation prepared for war. On the West Coast, he worked for an electric company and then for two precision-tool firms, but in 1943 he was back in St. Louis, sometimes working as a machinist and at other times driving a cab.

In 1949, Ollie got into trouble. The St. Louis police charged him with writing worthless checks and using them to buy twelve or fourteen automobiles, which he then resold. He was convicted and sentenced to two years in the state prison at Jefferson City—the same prison in which Carl Hall did time later, for robbing cab drivers.

The FBI interviewed several felons who had known Ollie in prison, because it had concluded that his day and a half with Hall in St. Louis made him "a logical suspect" in the disappearance of the $300,000. This is what his fellow cons said about Oliver Johnson:

He was garrulous, a big talker who "spent a great deal of time trying to impress the other inmates with his outside connections." He was "the type who would take money if he had the opportunity." He talked about "rolling drunks while driving a cab" (this presumably was of particular interest to the FBI, since Hall was certainly a drunk). He was "basically dishonest." He "talked considerably about making a great deal of money" when he got out of jail; he didn't say how he would do this, but one inmate said he got the impression that Johnson "had in mind pulling a bank robbery." This inmate added that Johnson did not impress him as having enough nerve to rob a bank; he was "more the type that would stand on the sidelines and offer advice . . . while someone else actually did the job." No wonder he was a prime suspect. He sounded like a temptable man.

Gambling was Ollie's central problem. It kept him broke, apparently wrecked his marriage, and rendered him susceptible. As a result, the FBI now had three suspects in the $300,000 theft: Carl Hall, a kidnapper, murderer and congenital liar; Sandra June O'Day, a prostitute with a need for money; and Oliver Johnson, a gambler with the same need.

Ollie was released on parole in 1951, after serving a year of his two-year sentence. In July 1953, he went to work for the Ace Cab Company.

Prison had done his marriage no good, but it had been in difficulty long before that. In 1947, he had been convicted of failing to make support payments for his children—a son and a daughter. He was sentenced to a year in the city workhouse but was paroled after a month. His wife was not yet willing to call it quits altogether, but they were separated (later they were divorced).

At the time of the Greenlease case, then, Ollie Johnson was living apart from his family, in a shabby, cheerless hotel on Olive Street, a heavy man, two hundred pounds on a five-foot-ten-inch frame, his hair receding, several teeth gone, driving his cab heavily, hustling johns for whores, scrounging for a few bucks—Christ, a man crowding forty shouldn't have to scrounge—with which to make his support payments and place his bets, his mind heavy, too, with frustration and failure: adrift in the city.

So "Steve Strand" was a godsend. Ollie pushed his apprehensions as far back in his mental closet as he could and hoped the money would keep coming: the strategy of affluence.

"I was feeling pretty good, because it appeared that Hall . . . had a lot of money, and it seemed that he would be quite generous with me," he said later.

"I told my wife that I had two fellows in a room who had given me $2,500 to keep for them [one of the "fellows" was Sandra O'Day, but Johnson didn't want his wife to know about her], plus $100 for myself to start, and that it looked as though my chances of making $400 or $500 that evening appeared good.

"I told her we might be able to . . . live decently again."

103

$\mathcal{H}$ all and Sandy got up around 8:30 or 9:00 o'clock Tuesday morning. They wanted breakfast, but Hall again was unwilling to leave the suitcase and footlocker in the room, unattended. He told Sandy to find a maid and ask her to bring some food and coffee. But the maids were not allowed to bring food to guests. So, Hall said later, he and Sandy "just sat around and drank and waited." They were waiting for Ollie Johnson.

Ollie arrived a little after ten, in the rented car that Hall had requested the night before; it was a 1952 Plymouth. He also brought the briefcase and suitcase that Hall had asked for. He had told Ollie he wanted the suitcase because he planned to buy some clothes, but the new piece of luggage was to become another complication in the search for the missing $300,000.

Ollie said Hall "appeared to be in a very bad mood" and was pacing the floor again. However, "he seemed happy to see me." Johnson apologized for being late, saying he had overslept.

"That's okay, Ollie," Hall told him. "I knew you would come back. I knew I could count on you." Then he sent him out to get some fried-egg sandwiches and coffee.

Meanwhile, Hall had written another letter to the St. Joe lawyer, Barney

Patton. He had told Sandy the night before that he would buy a bull for her "farm" if she would go to Los Angeles and mail a letter from there, and he had given her $1,000 in ten-dollar bills for the trip. The master criminal said later that he hoped the letter would throw pursuit off the track by making it appear he was on the West Coast. But the only pursuers were demons and furies.

"Dear Barney," Hall wrote, "Things are not so good regardless of what I say. The evidence is all against me so I decided to play it all the way. Please clear out my apartment. I am getting a ship or plane out of the country, but will try and get some money to you. You have been a true friend Barney, and I certainly enjoy all of my associations with you. Perhaps we'll get together again some day. [signed] Carl."

After he and Sandy had eaten, Hall told Johnson to drive Sandy to some place where she could get a cab to the airport.

"Why don't you come with us?" Ollie asked. He didn't want to let Hall out of his sight, but Sandy could have kicked him. She wanted desperately to get away from "Steve Strand" so she could tell Ollie something in private. To her great relief, Hall said: "No, I've got something to do. You go ahead and take her where she can get a cab, and then come back here."

And now things began to fall apart for Carl Hall. As they drove away from the motel, Sandy turned to Johnson and spoke urgently:

"Get going. I've got something big to tell you. This guy is loaded with dough. He opened one of the suitcases and there must be a million dollars in it. I never saw so much money in my life. Don't tell him I told you, because he made me swear I wouldn't tell you."

The words poured out. She didn't think his name was "Steve Strand" at all. Who was he? What had he done? Where had he gotten all that money? She was supposed to go to Los Angeles and mail a letter to some guy named Bernard Patton in St. Joe. Who was Patton? What the hell was this all about? What do you think, Ollie?

Ollie thought they had better open the letter. They did so, and it sounded suspicious, but they didn't know what it meant, except that it was signed "Carl," not "Steve." Then Ollie told her that he had noticed the initials "C.A.H." and the words "St. Joseph" on Steve's hat back at the motel. "C" might stand for "Carl."

Then Sandy had an idea. She would go to St. Joe, not Los Angeles. "We wanted to find out who he really was and what he had done," she said later. "We knew he had done something, but we didn't know what it was, and so I suggested that I go to St. Joseph and find out about Mr. Patton [and try to learn] who this person was that signed his name 'Carl.' . . . And so when I mentioned that, Mr. Johnson thought it over a few minutes and [then] he said he thought it was a brilliant idea. . . ."

A plan of action having been devised, Ollie drove to a cabstand in midtown, let Sandy out and then hightailed it back to the motel.

But according to Sandy, her associate left something out. She told the St. Louis cops that Johnson wanted to steal the money. She said he wanted her to help him do it. When she refused, Sandy said, Ollie gave up the idea.

Sandy: "I said I knew that one of the suitcases contained a lot of money, and so Mr. Johnson suggested that we go back and get it, and I said no, I wouldn't do nothing like that. . . ."

Chief of Detectives James Chapman: "You said that you had mentioned the money in the suitcase to him . . . and that he had answered, 'Let's go back and get it.'"

Sandy: "Oh sure. He wanted to go back right then."

Chapman: ". . . If you [had] consented to go back with him, do you think he would have . . . ?"

Sandy: "Yes, I think he was sincere when he asked me to go back. . . . Mr. Johnson was all for getting the money from him. . . ."

When Ollie got back to the motel, he found Hall "in a stew, very nervous." He reminded Ollie that he had given him $2,500 the night before; now he said he could keep $500 but he wanted the rest back. Johnson counted out $2,000 and handed it over. As he did so, Hall began to talk excitedly about money, and about some unspecified trouble he was in.

"Ollie," he said. "if you have no money, you're nothing."

And then: "This thing would be fine if it wasn't for this man making the one slip. That's why I've got to be like this. You know I trust you and Sandy. You don't have to worry; I'm going to really set you up, but you've got to play it cool. I need a place in a nice, quiet, refined neighborhood where I can stay about a month."

Then he pulled a fistful of money from his pocket and, without counting it, gave it to the cab driver.

"Here," he said, "I want you to go downtown and buy the best suit you can find. Get all fixed up. I'm going to buy you a motel in Florida. I'm going to really set you up good."

Again he reached into his pocket, pulled out another wad of money and gave it to Ollie: "I want you to rent a nice apartment in a nice residential district, something for about $200 or $300 a month. Rent it in your own name; you're legit. Tell them you're a dispatcher with Ace Cab and your uncle will be staying with you for a while."

Ollie was stuffing money into his pockets as fast as he could, but Hall abruptly cut off the philanthropy and said it was time to go. He told Ollie to put the suitcase and footlocker into the trunk of the Plymouth, and he took the briefcase with him as they left the motel, but he left the new suitcase—the one Ollie had bought for him—in the room.

Hall had something he wanted to do, and he didn't want his new pal to know about it. They drove to a supermarket in midtown, where Hall let Ollie off. He told him to meet him later at a bar near the Coral Court.

Hall drove to the Hardware Mart at 5755 Chippewa. Mrs. William Koenig, a clerk at the Hardware Mart, takes up the narrative at this point:

"This man came in by himself about midmorning on Tuesday. He said: 'I'd like to see some garbage cans.'" Mrs Koenig showed him a stack of sixteen-gallon galvanized garbage cans. "These will be fine," Hall told her. "I'll take two."

Next he asked for some large plastic bags. He wanted four of them, but the store had only two in stock. Hall bought them, and then he inquired about a plastic spray "that will protect something." He bought a can of liquid spray, and a shovel. Then he asked Mrs. Koenig to carry the stuff to his car. Hall stood by and watched as the clerk wrestled the garbage cans out of the store and into the Plymouth; he was the kind of customer a salesperson remembers.

Hall intended to bury the ransom money. His plan was to coat the packets of $10 and $20 bills with the plastic spray to protect them, put the entire $600,000 (except for about $20,000 that he had transferred to the briefcase) into the plastic bags, then put the bags into the garbage cans and bury the cans "in some secluded spot." Later, when the heat was off, he would retrieve his fortune.

He drove west, looking for a safe place. The journey took him out of the city and through a succession of suburban communities until he reached the Meramec River, a stream that meanders through St. Louis County and then enters the Mississippi. He ended up on the outskirts of a suburb called Fenton—but he insisted later that he never found a satisfactory place to bury the money.

He was very fuzzy about the route he had followed; he told investigators he had taken some drugs and couldn't remember where he had gone. Later, however, he remembered enough to enable the FBI to find the garbage cans in a shack in Fenton. The shack was on Yarnell Road, which runs along the west bank of the Meramec, and it had a sign on it saying THELMA. The garbage cans were empty.

The rented Plymouth was spattered with mud, indicating that it had been near water. Probably Hall got out several times and tramped befuddledly along the riverbank, only dimly aware of where he was, looking for a suitable place, looking, looking, and not finding.

Unless, of course, he found. He said he didn't bury the money, and the garbage cans were empty when they were recovered, but Hall nevertheless was by himself for several hours Tuesday afternoon. Half of the $600,000 was found in the suitcase and footlocker after he was arrested, but the FBI had to assume he could have hidden the other half, not in the garbage cans but in some other way.

When Ollie let her off, Sandy had the $1,000 that Hall had given her for the trip to Los Angeles, and her aunt, Molly Paine, had another $120—Sandy's fee minus Ollie's percentage. Altogether it was a lot of money. There was only one thing to do: She went shopping.

Around noon, an Ace Cab driver named Herman Joseph Dreste picked up a fare at a bar on Hampton Avenue. The passenger, whom he later identified as Sandra O'Day, told him to take her to the TWA ticket office downtown. But before they got there, Dreste said, Sandy asked him how much he would charge to drive her to St. Joe, which is about three hundred miles from St. Louis. Dreste said he would have to use his own car, and it would cost $100 or $150.

"You'd do better to go by plane," he said.

"No," said Sandy, "I want you to drive me there."

But first, she said, she had a letter to mail and needed some glue to seal the envelope. This was the letter from Hall to Bernard Patton, which Sandy and Ollie had opened. Dreste stopped at a drugstore and bought some glue. Then Sandy told him to take her to 2023 North Ninth Street. When they got there, she told him to wait.

Lady Bountiful swept into the apartment, dispensing largess. She gave Molly $200 to buy some new clothes for herself and for Sandy's daughter, Michelle. Molly was a little surprised by the sudden wealth, and perhaps a little apprehensive too, but Sandy told her: "Don't ask questions, and don't worry."

Then it was Sandy's turn. What the hell, she wasn't going to Los Angeles, so she wouldn't need the $1,000 for that. Let's spend it, lend it, keep it moving along. With Molly in tow, she rushed downstairs, got in Dreste's cab and told him to take them to the Lane Bryant store downtown. She also told Dreste that while they were shopping, she wanted him to go to a luggage store and buy her a small suitcase and an overnight bag. She gave him $80 for this. "Pick me up later at the apartment," she added.

At Lane Bryant, Sandy bought a three-piece suit, a pair of slacks, a blouse, some panties and a girdle. Then she and Molly went to a shoe store, where Sandy bought a pair of black pumps, a pair of black flats and several pairs of stockings.

They took a cab home, and then Sandy told Molly that she was going to go out of town for two or three days. Again she told her aunt not to ask questions and not to worry. "I know what I'm doing," she said. She also wrote a telegram and left it with Molly, telling her to send it at ten o'clock that night: "Steve Strand, care of Western Union Main Office, St. Louis, Mo. Leaving at 2 A.M. Love, Sandy."

Dreste, meanwhile, went to the Ace Cab office, turned in his cab and picked up his own car for the trip to St. Joe. Then he bought a small suitcase and an overnight bag for Sandy. As a result, the investigation had a luggage problem again: Had Sandy transported the missing $300,000 in the suitcase and overnight bag? Had Hall given her the money to take to St. Joe for him? Or had she stolen it from him?

The full $600,000 in ransom money had been in Hall's suitcase and footlocker. Then Oliver Johnson had bought another suitcase (and a brief-case) for Hall, and then Dreste bought a suitcase and overnight bag for Sandy. The FBI now had five pieces of luggage to figure out. Through the Greenlease investigation ran an undercurrent of luggage.

Dreste said that when he got back to Sandy's apartment with the bags, he saw Sandy put "what appeared to be a large amount of money" into one of them. He said he couldn't see how much it was, but it appeared to be a folded wad of bills about the size of a man's fist. That couldn't have been anything like $300,000, but Dreste got only a fleeting glimpse of Sandy's packing. Suppose she put a lot of money into her new luggage and Dreste saw only a little of it?

Sandy said good-bye to Molly and left the apartment with Dreste—for more shopping. They went to Burdie's Millinery Shop, where Sandy bought a pair of gloves and four brassieres, size 38, B cup. Then they headed west.

All whores have dreams, and they are long ones. Sandy sat beside Dreste as he drove, and she began to talk. The first thing Dreste remembered her saying was that she had spent the previous night at the Coral Court Motel with a man she described as "a young jerk." And then:

"I've been on a binge for a couple of days. I lost all my luggage and my money. I had to wire my lawyer in Los Angeles for money. I've got to get to Los Angeles. I have to be there by 8 o'clock tomorrow morning; I have to appear in court. I was supposed to go to St. Joe, but I went to St. Louis by mistake. I've got to meet a guy in St. Joe, and then I have to get a plane back to L.A. I've got two kids, you know. One's seven, and I've got an adopted daughter, too; she's nine. I'm getting a divorce in L.A. I've got enough on my husband so I won't have any trouble getting one. I want custody of the kids. I want child support, too. I'm going to make him set up a trust fund for them; he's loaded. I'm going to get alimony, too; he's got plenty of money. He's a very wealthy man. He's got a big farm in New Jersey.'' Life in America has become one long whore's dream.

When they reached Columbia, Missouri, Sandy said she wanted a drink. They went into a bar and drank some beer. Then Sandy went across the street to a Western Union office, where she sent a telegram to Molly Paine: "Hold wire [to Steve Strand] until I contact you. Will advise later. Plans have changed. Don't worry. Love and kisses, Sandy.''

Sandy asked Dreste to wait for her when they got to St. Joe, but he said he couldn't do that. That's okay, Sandy said, maybe we should just go to Kansas City instead. She said she could call the man in St. Joe (Barney Patton) and ask him to meet her in Kansas City. On the outskirts of K.C., Dreste phoned the Hotel Muehlbach and reserved a room for Sandy. She said it would be better if she arrived at the Muehlbach in a Kansas City cab, so Dreste let her off at a cabstand downtown. That was the last he saw of her.

In Kansas City, she fell into convivial company, "both male and female," and forgot all about the man in St. Joe.

Chief of Police Jeremiah O'Connell: "Did you know these people?''
Sandy: "Oh no.''

O'Connell: "Well, how did you happen to meet them?''

Sandy: "I just went into a bar and met them. How do you meet people in a bar? Gee, I don't know [how I met them]. . . . And then we just made a round of all the bars and we all got drunk.''

In the group, Sandy said, was "some show girl I got tangled up with, I don't know who she was, [and] she said her roommate [had] left, and she suggested that I move to her hotel, and so I moved down there to her hotel.''

She told the author that the "show girl" was a prostitute and that they got very drunk together. They ended up at the other woman's hotel and were in bed—Sandy wearing only bra and panties—when FBI agents burst into the room with guns drawn and arrested her.

"I knew I was going to get in trouble over that damned letter," Sandy said.

110

Chapter 13

*O*llie Johnson was frightened. Everything about "Steve Strand" made him apprehensive: the money, the gun, the likelihood that he was using an alias, the suspicious letter. Ollie might find himself in deep shit with the law again. "I got scared not knowing what it was all about," he said later. The pale cast of thought sicklied o'er the native hue of resolution. He wanted to hang in there, because more money might be forthcoming from Hall, and that was a powerful inducement. He *wanted* to—but the deep shit makes cowards of us all.

After Hall let him off at the supermarket, Ollie took a cab downtown and went into a tavern, thinking he would call a cop from there. But then he decided to "wait a while longer."

Hall had asked him to rent "a nice apartment in a nice residential district," where he could lie low for a month or so. Johnson thought of the Branscombe apartment hotel on Pershing Avenue in the west end. But the clerk at the Branscombe said she had nothing suitable. She suggested the Town House apartments at 5316 Pershing, a few doors away and somewhat less expensive. Ollie went there.

Mrs. Jean Fletcher, manager of the Town House, said a man came in about 2:30 that afternoon, gave his name as Oliver Johnson and inquired about renting an apartment. She showed him several, and he selected Apartment 324 on the third floor. The rent was $185 a month. He paid for a month in advance, with ten-dollar bills.

Then Ollie followed Sandy's example: He went shopping. Hall had told him to get fixed up with some new clothes, so he bought a suit, a hat and a pair of shoes.

The new clothes, Hall had said, were part of his big plans for Ollie Johnson—if Ollie would remain steadfast and loyal, if he would not betray his new friend. "You stick with me and you'll be set for life," Hall told him. "I'm gonna buy you a motel. How about that, huh? A really good motel—forty or fifty thousand bucks."

But there could be a hitch in the plans; he was in a little trouble. "If it hadn't been for another guy making a mistake, I wouldn't have anything to worry about," Hall said.

"Are the cops looking for you?" Ollie asked.

"No, but I think it might be some insurance investigators," Hall replied.

Ollie thought about all this. An insurance embezzler. With a lot of money and a gun. Things were getting too hot for Ollie Johnson, the ex-con who didn't want to go back to jail. It was time to consider the safety of his ass; it was time to cut loose from "Steve Strand." As he was shopping, Ollie thought of a cop he could call—or perhaps someone told him who to call. This time, at any rate, he *did* call.

The cop's name was Louis Ira Shoulders. He was a lieutenant and was night commander of the Newstead Avenue station. He was a tough cop; in the line of duty, as they always said in these instances, he had killed two men, or possibly three.

Ollie did not know Shoulders. He told the St. Louis police board later that he thought of the lieutenant because he had heard other cabbies talk about him. They said he was a heavy.

"I heard he was a pretty rugged man and handy with a pistol," Ollie said. "I was afraid of what I had hold of."

Was that it? Just that he had heard on the grapevine that Shoulders was a hard case, and figured he could handle "Steve Strand"? Or did someone tell Ollie to call Shoulders? Did Ollie tell *someone else* about the "insurance embezzler" with all the money, and did that person say: "Okay, listen, here's what you do—you call Lou Shoulders at the Newstead station. . . ?"

When he finished shopping, Johnson went to the Happy Hollow Tavern at 207 North Ninth Street, had a drink, for courage, and then called Shoulders at the Newstead Avenue station. He told him about "Steve Strand" and the money:

112

"I think he's hot. He's throwing twenty-dollar bills around like confetti. I think he's hot as hell."

Wearing his new suit, Ollie returned to the motel. He said he found Hall "very wild and fidgety" but "very relieved to see me." Hall was working on a fresh fifth of whiskey.

"You really look sharp," he told Ollie. "We're gonna get a lot of new clothes. We'll even be herding a new Cadillac before long. Just take it easy."

Hall wanted to buy some new clothes, too, so they drove to Clayton, a large suburb west of the city. As they got in the car, Ollie noticed a can of plastic spray on the seat.

At Boyd's, a clothing store in Clayton, Hall bought a suit, five shirts, some socks and handkerchiefs and a hat. The suit needed to be altered, so he gave the claim check to Ollie and asked him to pick the suit up later—but it was never picked up.

On the way back to the motel, Hall thought of love and loneliness. "I want another girl tonight," he told Ollie. "I don't want to stay by myself."

"I'll get you a good one," Ollie promised.

As they started to turn into the Coral Court, Hall suddenly told Ollie to keep going. Ollie said he seemed extremely nervous now. They drove on for a while and then stopped at the Villanova Inn for a sandwich, but Ollie noticed that Hall ate very little of his: "I never saw him eat much of anything."

At the restaurant, Hall began talking about a girl again—"tell her I'll give her $200 or $300"—so Ollie went to a phone booth and pretended to call a girl. Then they headed back to the Coral Court. On the way, Ollie said, Hall "got the jitters very bad."

"When I get hunches, I'd better play 'em," he said. "Something's wrong. We've got to move [to the Town House] tonight." But a moment later he decided not to.

They were on the outside stairs, taking the suitcase and footlocker up to Hall's room, when a car pulled in behind the Plymouth and stopped with its lights on. Hall took one look at the car and froze with fear. Then he pounded up the stairs to his room.

Burdened by the heavy luggage, Ollie felt very vulnerable. He looked around frantically for some place out of the line of fire, "in case there was any gunplay."

Hall got the key into the lock somehow, his hands trembling. He ducked into the room and stood behind the door.

113

"Ollie," he whispered, "take the bags downstairs and put them back in the car."

Warily, Johnson carried the suitcase and footlocker back down and put them in the trunk of the Plymouth. As he did so, he noticed there were two persons in the other car. After a few minutes, they drove away.

Ollie went back upstairs and told Hall everything was okay. He said it appeared that two people in a downstairs room had come in for a moment and then gone away again.

But Hall was not reassured; the demons and furies were urgent now. "I got the shakes," he said. "I got a bad hunch. We've got to move tonight." They packed quickly and left the Coral Court.

At the Town House, Hall inspected Apartment 324 closely. He walked around, looked at everything and then said he was satisfied: "It looks like a good place. I think I'm going to like it here."

He suggested they send down for a couple of Cokes, but Ollie said: "No, you go ahead and have one. I'm going to pick up that girl for you. I'll see if she has a friend, and we'll have a real celebration." Johnson said Hall "brightened up considerably" at this. He asked how long it would take to get the girls, and Ollie said about a half hour. "Okay," said Hall, "when you get back, knock three times and say: 'Steve, this is Ollie.' "

The "girls" Ollie went to get were Lieutenant Lou Shoulders and Patrolman Elmer Dolan.

Shoulders had arranged to meet Johnson at the rear of Ritzer's Bar at 4910 Delmar Boulevard, not far from the Town House. Dolan, who was the lieutenant's chauffeur that evening, drove there between 7:30 and 8:00 P.M. Shoulders was in plain clothes, Dolan in uniform.

Oliver Johnson was waiting for them. After a brief conversation, they drove to the Town House. Ollie told them the password and warned them that "Steve" had a gun.

They went up to the third floor, and Shoulders whispered to Ollie to stand back in the corridor where "Steve" couldn't see him. Then Shoulders and Dolan drew their revolvers, and Dolan knocked on the door. "Steve," he said, "this is Ollie."

Hall opened the door and saw two men pointing guns at him. They came into the apartment fast and hard. Hall took a step or two back into the room, staring at the guns. And seeing, at last, the demons and furies.

"Get your hands up," Shoulders said. "You're under arrest."

"What the hell for?" Hall asked.

"Never mind the questions," said Shoulders. He gave Hall a quick frisk, to see whether he had a weapon, and then told him to sit down in an armchair.

"Keep him covered," he told Dolan. "If he makes a grab for you, shoot him." Dolan stood in front of Hall, with his gun trained on the seated man.

Shoulders reached into the breast pocket of Hall's coat and took out the keys to the suitcase and footlocker, which were in a closet. Hall could not see the closet from where he was sitting, but he heard Shoulders go into it and he thought he heard him open one of the bags.

"I think the jig is up," said Carl Hall. Then, apparently trying to cover his slip, he asked Dolan: "What's this all about?"

"I don't know," said Dolan. "Somebody probably made a complaint against you. Are you in trouble with someone?"

At this point, Shoulders came back into the room. If he had opened the suitcase or footlocker and seen the money, he didn't mention it. But he had heard Hall's remark. "What do you mean, the jig is up?" he asked.

"I don't know what I meant," Hall said.

Then Shoulders saw Hall's briefcase, picked it up and opened it. In it was the $20,000 that Hall had transferred from the larger bags. Also in the briefcase was his wallet, containing almost $2,500.

"Looks like you've got quite a bit of money here," Shoulders said. "Where did you get it?"

"I'm a liquor dealer," Hall said, lying glibly. "I've got a liquor business in Illinois with my brother, but I live in Kirkwood [a St. Louis suburb]. I sold a liquor company—another guy and I sold it. That's where the money came from."

Hall gave his name as John D. Byrne. He had a Social Security card, a photostat of an Army discharge, an Army hospital record and two driver's licenses, all in that name. These identification papers, he said later, had been given to him by Ollie Johnson. But also in his wallet was an insurance agent's card in the name of Carl Austin Hall.

Shoulders finished looking through the briefcase, closed it and told Hall: "I want you to notice I'm putting it back exactly where it was." He looked at the money and identification papers in Hall's wallet for a few moments and then said: "Notice that I'm putting the money back in the wallet, too."

"What's this all about?" Hall asked again. "What am I being arrested for?"

"Be quiet," Shoulders said. "When I get ready to tell you, I'll tell you." But then he added: "Some woman called us about you. She . . . uh . . . she said we should investigate you." The big policeman, Hall said later, sounded "very vague" about this.

"Do you have a gun?" one of the cops asked.

115

"No," said Hall. The gun was in a desk drawer, and Ollie Johnson had told Shoulders and Dolan about it, but they appeared to accept Hall's word and made no search for the gun.

A few moments later, Shoulders told Hall to put his coat on; they were leaving. The whole thing had taken about ten minutes.

As they came out of the Town House, Hall looked for the rented Plymouth in which Ollie Johnson had gone to get the "girls," but he didn't see it.

However, he did see another car. This one was parked at the side entrance to the Town House, with its interior light on. In the car was a woman with short blond hair. Hall said later that she was looking around as if interested in something. There had been a mystery man the day before, when Hall bought the used car, and now there was a mystery woman. Again, the newspapers rose to the challenge. Hall got only a glimpse of the woman before Shoulders and Dolan put him in the police car.

In the shadow of the St. Louis Cathedral, and not far from May Traynor's whorehouse, was the Newstead Avenue police station. Thus was the city defined.

The cathedral is still there, at Lindell Boulevard and Newstead, not soaring but solid, so faith can have faith. At 14 North Newstead, a block and a half from the cathedral, was the police station. On Forest Park Avenue, a short distance from the station, was May Traynor's brothel, which was to figure in the search for the missing Greenlease money.

At the Newstead Avenue station, Corporal Raymond Bergmeier, the acting desk sergeant, booked Hall on a holding charge, for "investigation." Police records showed that the exact time of booking was 8:57 P.M. The time was later to be very important.

Shoulders put Hall into a holding cell and told the turnkey, Lyle Mudd, not to allow him to make any telephone calls and to keep him separated from the other prisoners.

Then Shoulders and Dolan left the police station. Shoulders said later that he had an errand to run: He had promised his woman friend that she could use his car that night, so he drove it to her house. The lieutenant was separated from his wife and was living with this other woman, whose name was June Marie George. Dolan followed him in the police car and brought him back to the station. They were gone about an hour, or perhaps more.

There may have been some mild surprise when Shoulders left the station, but no one really thought twice about it, because as far as the other cops

116

knew, "John D. Byrne" was just another drunk. Someone had complained about him, he would be held for a few hours, like so many others, and then he would take his hangover and go home.

Alone in his cell, Hall was silent for a while. But then he called to the turnkey. When Mudd came to the cell, Hall told him he wanted to make a phone call, but Mudd said no. Then Hall spoke urgently:

"Listen, I'll give you $2,000 to get hold of that cop who arrested me."

"Who do I have to kill?" Mudd joked.

"Where is that big guy who brought me in?" Hall asked. "I want to see him. I want to talk to him. I can tell him where the rest of the money is."

But the money in the suitcase and footlocker had not been counted yet. What did Hall mean by "the rest of the money" unless he knew that when it *was* counted, $300,000 would be missing? And how would he know that unless he himself had hidden it somewhere?

On the other hand, Hall was in terrible shape—close to a complete collapse. He was coming off months of saturation drinking that had culminated in the mammoth two-day binge in St. Louis. He couldn't remember where he had been or what he had done. When he wasn't crying, he was incoherent. The reference to "the rest of the money" could have been drunken maundering.

Later, on his way to Kansas City to stand trial, Hall talked to a deputy United States marshal, Leslie S. Davison. He was sober now and more calm, but when he poked around in his sodden memory he found only half-images and blurred recollections. *Had he hidden the money?* On balance, it seemed he hadn't, but there remained a tantalizing and frustrating possibility that he had:

"I wish to God I could remember what I did with that money, but I can't. I remember trying to bury some money. It was on a bottom road near a river [the Meramec]. I remember there were automobiles passing nearby, and I guess I decided it wasn't isolated enough, so I gave that up. But I still had the idea of burying the money when they got me."

In an elevator at the Federal Courthouse in Kansas City, handcuffed and surrounded by guards, Hall began mumbling. His head down, a man at the end of greed's road, he muttered one word over and over:

"Money, money, money."

And again: "Money, money, money."

117

Chapter **14**

*I*n the beginning, however, the focus was not on the missing money but on the abduction of Bobby Greenlease. The kidnapping was receiving nationwide publicity, but it was not known that the boy was dead, and no one knew the kidnappers had fled to St. Louis; they might have gone anywhere. When they were caught, it was their crime that was the center of attention, not the disappearance of half the ransom.

It is not clear when—or how—Lieutenant Shoulders learned that Hall was not an embezzler but a kidnapper. He said later that he *did* open Hall's luggage at the Town House, and when he saw the money he began to think "John Byrne" might be Bobby's kidnapper. But if he suspected Hall was involved in a crime that big, a crime that had horrified the nation, why did he leave the police station to run a minor errand?

Dolan said he and Shoulders left the station at about 9:20 P.M., took Shoulders' car to his girl friend, and got back between 10:15 and 10:30. Shoulders went back to the holdover to talk to Hall while Dolan kept an eye on the suitcase and footlocker, which were in Shoulders' office.

At 10:40, according to the police log, Shoulders put out a radio call for detectives attached to the Newstead Avenue station. When they arrived, he told them to go to the Arsenal Street apartment, taking Hall along to help them find it, and arrest Bonnie Heady. Assuming all these times were correct (at least one of them was disputed), it was sometime between 10:15 and 10:40 when Hall admitted to Shoulders that he and Bonnie had kidnapped Bobby Greenlease.

Later, Shoulders told the St. Louis police board that he believed the insurance card with the name "Carl Austin Hall" on it was the main reason Hall confessed. He said he showed Hall the card and questioned him about it. Who was he—John D. Byrne or Carl Hall? "When I called him 'Carl,' he almost swallowed his necktie," Shoulders said.

When he got back to the station, he had Hall transferred to an end cell for greater privacy; he explained that he didn't want a bunch of "nosy cops" to hear. Then Shoulders stood close to the bars and told Hall: "Talk low." They began a murmured conversation. A big, hard cop and a drunken, cornered murderer, standing close together, confidingly, their heads almost touching. Priest and penitent, whispering between the bars.

According to Shoulders, it began with Hall offering him one of the suitcases full of money if he would let him go:

Hall: "For Christ's sake, officer, you got that money, and I'm in here under the name of John Byrne. For Christ's sake, take me out and release me and take one [of the suitcases] and give me one and get me out."

Shoulders: "Listen, fellow, that's out. Let's not talk about anything like that. You are in back of these bars and it is gonna be a long time before you get out."

Then, according to Shoulders, he told Hall: "Listen, Carl, you are the kidnapper. I've got the ransom money . . . and I've got you. We've got those serial numbers [on the money], and we've got your full name, Carl A. Hall."

Hall: "I knew when you opened that door, when you put those guns in my belly, that I was done. All my planning is for nothing."

At this point, Shoulders said, Hall retreated into the cell, sat down on his bunk and put his head in his hands.

Shoulders: "Come up here. I know a red-headed woman went in [the school] and got the boy. Who is the woman?"

Hall: "For Christ's sake, it's not a red-head; she has as black a head as you are."

Shoulders: "Who is she?"

Hall: "Why do you have to bring her in? You got the money. You got the case broke. You got all the money."

Finally, Shoulders said, Hall gave him Bonnie's name and told him she was in an apartment on Arsenal Street. But:

Hall: "Listen, she's an alcoholic. She doesn't know what she's doing."

119

Shoulders: "The hell she didn't." Then: "Where's that boy? Is he alive?"

Hall: "Sure he's alive.". . .

Shoulders: "Where is he [the third kidnapper] and did he get his cut? Did you split [the money] with him?"

Hall: "No, I am fucking him, and her too. Why should I split?"

Shoulders: "You mean you are screwing your accomplices out of this?" Then: "How much is in these suitcases?"

Hall: "I never counted it. There ought to be $600,000 in there."

When he turned away from the cell, Shoulders said, "I had the admission that he was the kidnapper [and] the name of the woman that went in and got the Greenlease boy. I was pleased. . . ." He said he went back to his office and told Dolan: "Christ Almighty, we got the kidnapper, and I know where the woman is."

Later, Shoulders told reporters he pushed Hall hard about his identity— wasn't he really Carl Hall, not John Byrne?—and suddenly Hall broke. Shoulders quoted him as saying: "It's all up. You got me. I know the thing is up. I'm the kidnapper of the Greenlease boy."

But Hall, in his confession to the FBI, didn't mention the identity question as a factor. He said he broke when Shoulders pressed him about the money in his luggage and then informed him that he had been "implicated" in the kidnapping.

Implicated? Implicated by whom? Did someone tell Shoulders that Hall was a kidnapper? If so, who? Or was Shoulders bluffing when he told his prisoner: "Listen, Carl, you are the kidnapper"?

When Hall was interviewed on Death Row by St. Louis Police Chief Jeremiah O'Connell and Prosecuting Attorney Edward L. Dowd, there was this exchange:

O'Connell: "What conversation did he [Shoulders] have with you?"

Hall: "Well, he said: 'There's a lot of money out there [in the suitcase and footlocker], isn't there?' I said: 'Yes.' He said: 'You are wanted in the kidnapping, aren't you?' I said: 'That's right.' There wasn't any use to deny it."

So it probably came down to this:

1. Hall was ready to confess. Deeply drunk, sleepless, weary, frightened, pursued beyond further endurance by the demons and furies, he was simply ready to give up. He had come to the edge, and Shoulders pushed him over. *"There wasn't any use to deny it."*

2. Someone may have told Shoulders that Hall was a kidnapper, but there

was never any indication that anyone did. More likely, a suspicion and then a realization simply came to him, prompted by instinct and experience, after which he tried a bluff that worked.

But a spark of self-preservation lingered in a burnt-out life: Hall was not ready to admit that he was a murderer as well as a kidnapper.

The FBI disputed Shoulders and Dolan on a point of time. FBI agents said their investigation showed that the lieutenant and his driver didn't get back to the Newstead Avenue station until a few minutes before 11:00 P.M. That would mean the errand took them an hour and forty minutes, whereas Dolan said they were gone about an hour—from 9:20 until 10:15 or 10:30. The time conflict later became an important issue, but the police log seemed to support Dolan. It showed that Shoulders put out a radio call for "special officers"—policemen temporarily assigned to detective work—and it noted that the call went out at 10:40 P.M.

In response, four "specials" assigned to the Newstead station hurried back to duty, arriving about 11:30 P.M. Their names were Edward Bradley, Norman M. Naher, William Carson and Lawrence King. Shoulders told them to take Hall with them, find the apartment on Arsenal Street, and pick up Bonnie Heady.

It wasn't easy. They went to the wrong apartment first, and scared the bejesus out of a couple of innocent citizens. It is tiresome to keep saying it, but Hall was drunk. He had only a vague memory of the apartment building where he had left Bonnie; all he could tell the detectives was that it was in the 4500 block of Arsenal.

Hall rode with Carson and King. King was a rookie, less than two years on the force; he later rose to the rank of lieutenant. Carson was an older cop, a member of the force since 1929, a family man.

King remembered only fragments of the conversation as they drove through the dark streets. He recalled asking Hall where he had picked up the ransom money. "A bridge someplace in Kansas City," Hall mumbled. Then:

"I had six hundred thousand dollars. For a while, I had six hundred thousand dollars."

They got to the 4500 block of Arsenal and parked while Hall tried to recall the address. "I just can't remember which house it is," he said, but he might be able to find it if they first found a tavern where he had had a drink. So they started driving around, looking for the tavern. Bradley and Naher followed them in a second car.

They found a bar that Hall said might be the one, and he tried to give them

121

directions from there. No luck. Carson began to think maybe it wasn't the 4500 block of Arsenal after all, so they spent about ten minutes driving up and down other streets, but none of them looked right to Hall. They ended up on Arsenal again, and this time they decided to try it on foot.

"Now, we're gonna walk you up there," Carson said. "You know the house, and you're gonna have to pick it out and pick it out right now. I think you're stalling us."

"I am not," Hall replied. "I think I can pick it out." They walked up the street and he indicated a building near the corner.

"Who's in there with her?" Carson asked.

"She's all by herself," Hall said.

"Are you sure?" Carson was an experienced cop; he wanted to know what they might be up against.

"Oh yes, I know she's by herself," Hall repeated.

Carson told King to go around to the back of the building, in case anyone tried to escape from the rear. Then, taking Hall with them, Carson, Bradley and Naher went in the front. Inside, Hall pointed to a first-floor apartment.

Carson rang the bell—and a man opened the door. All by herself, huh?

"Grab him!" Carson shouted.

"Honey, the jig is up, the jig is up!" Hall cried.

The cops rushed into the apartment, and for a few moments it was the Burning of Rome. There was turmoil and noise and disorder. A door slammed; someone apparently had left the room in a hurry. One of the cops grabbed the astounded man and held on tight. The man was protesting, in the outraged tones of innocence the world over. What's this all about? No answer, because no one knew. What's going on here? No answer, because no one ever knows. Another cop had Hall in his grasp; it would not do to let the prisoner get away in the confusion. Hall was still calling out to Bonnie, wherever she was: "Honey, the jig is up!"

Carson had heard the door slam. It sounded as if someone had run into the next room and might be escaping. Or might be waiting in there—perhaps with a gun. Bradley and Naher were guarding Hall and the other man. King was watching the back of the building. That left Carson. He went to the door of the other room. The family man, alone. He opened the door.

There was a woman in the room. Carson said later that "she seemed to be excited." Very understated cops in St. Louis.

"Somebody just grabbed my husband!" she screamed.

"Who is that man?" Carson asked.

"He's my husband! Who are you?"

122

"We're the police."

"My God, what happened?" the woman cried.

After the bombs have gone off, the soldiers have been killed, the leaders indicted or the financiers arrested, explanations are offered. Carson described the situation, but it took a while to quiet the woman down. She and her husband had been sitting peacefully in their apartment when the doorbell rang and a group of large men burst in. They grabbed her husband, and God alone knew what they were going to do to him. She dashed into the next room and slammed the door.

When she had calmed down a little, the woman told the cops that she and her husband occupied the front apartment and there was another apartment in the rear. She said a man and woman had recently moved into the rear unit. Detective Bradley went into the back apartment. Bonnie Heady was there, in bed. He arrested her.

As soon as Bonnie had been brought in, giving him both suspects in custody, Shoulders called Chief O'Connell and told him the kidnappers of Bobby Greenlease had been caught. The chief, who was at home, called I. A. Long, a St. Louis banker who was president of the Board of Police Commissioners (a group, usually of leading citizens, appointed by the governor, usually not a leading citizen, to exercise civilian control over the police department). O'Connell also called Joseph E. Thornton, the agent in charge of the FBI office in St. Louis.

O'Connell, Long, Shoulders, Thornton and another FBI agent, Joseph R. Connors, gathered in the office of Captain Thomas Dirrane, the commander of the Newstead Avenue station. Hall was brought in and the questioning began, with O'Connell and Thornton doing most of it.

At first, it was impossible to get anything coherent out of the suspect. As related in Chapter 1, his responses were "mumbled and inarticulate." He was crying and vomiting and lolling slackly, helplessly, in his chair. At 2:40 A.M., he "blacked out completely" and had to be taken to the hospital.

Meanwhile, Bonnie Heady was admitting nothing. Throughout the investigation—and at the moment of their execution—she was tougher than Hall. FBI agent Phil King told the author that Bonnie was "very antagonistic toward Hall" in the first hours after their arrest. She spoke scornfully of him as a weakling. King believes this was the reason she held out against confessing longer than Hall.

When Hall was brought back from the hospital, he was "still in a miserable physical condition," but after a while he revived a little, and some information began to emerge, in bits and pieces. But at first it was what governments call disinformation. Hall said Bobby Greenlease was alive and well and should have been released Monday in Pittsburg, Kansas, in front of the Hotel Besse. But Robert Ledterman and Norbert O'Neill, the elder Greenlease's friends, had been at the Hotel Besse since Monday and were still there—and had heard nothing.

The boy hadn't been released? There was no sign of him? Hall said he couldn't understand it. It was a mystery to him. This pathetic blather did not impress the grim men in the captain's office. They had had years of experience in dealing with liars.

The questioning continued, and now Hall began to mumble something about Bobby being in Parsons, Kansas, not Pittsburg, in the care of another man. He said this other man had taken part in the kidnapping. By prearrangement, the man had met Carl and Bonnie in the Katz Drugstore parking lot after the kidnapping, and they had turned Bobby over to him. The other man was supposed to take Bobby somewhere and guard him. So said Hall.

He named the other man. He was a derelict, a skid-row bum whom Hall may have encountered somewhere in his boozy wanderings. In his desperation, Hall apparently just dredged up a name from the drunken past, threw it into the case and hoped it would send vengeance chasing off after an *ignis fatuus,* a will-o'-the-wisp. But it soon became clear that this other man had nothing whatever to do with the kidnapping. For this reason, his real name is not being used in this book. He will be known here as John Martin.

The FBI conducted a nationwide search for John Martin. But with all its resources and expertise, it was never able to find him. Much later, the author tried to locate him, but after more than thirty years it was impossible to trace an obscure piece of human driftwood on the vast American sea.

The problem was that Martin's real name began with an "M." This was the initial Hall had used in his telephone calls to the Greenlease home. Many persons—Robert Ledterman among them—believed Hall's use of "M" was an effort to make people think it was Martin who had made the phone calls, whether he was part of the plot or not. The FBI agents and the St. Louis police never believed Martin was involved at all, but until Hall's second confession there was a *chance* that he was. There was a possibility that when Hall called himself "M," it was a conscious or subconscious reference to an accomplice. So an effort had to be made to find Martin.

*   *   *

In the early hours of Wednesday, Hall made a formal confession. In this statement and in subsequent interrogations over the next three days, he told some of the truth. He said he had known about the Greenlease family for many years, having attended military school with their adopted son, Paul Greenlease. He said he knew the Greenleases were wealthy, knew they had a younger son, and had thought about kidnapping the boy for "about two years." Then he began disinforming again.

He told a long, detailed and mostly untrue story about encountering John Martin at a bar in Kansas City. It was, as related by Hall, a meeting of true minds; each quickly realized the other was an ex-convict. In their second or third conversation, Hall said, he asked Martin if he would be interested in a "real good caper." Martin, ever a practical man, asked, "How much?" At least $100,000, Hall boasted. "I'll go in on anything that big," Martin replied.

According to Hall, he and Martin began planning the kidnapping. Hall gave the locations of their meetings, described Martin's car, named the hotel where he was living and furnished many other details. As Hall told it, they virtually lived in each other's back pocket for weeks—but then he claimed he could not remember what Martin looked like. He said he couldn't give any physical description of his accomplice, none at all.

Continuing Hall's mendacious account: Because of Bonnie Heady's "drunken condition," he said, he could not entrust Bobby Greenlease to her while he was in Kansas City arranging the payment of the ransom. So it was agreed that Martin would take the boy to Bonnie's house and keep him there while Hall was in Kansas City. After the ransom was paid, Martin would take Bobby to the Hotel Besse in Pittsburg and release him there. Hall said he and Martin agreed to split the ransom fifty-fifty. And he said he gave his gun to Martin because the accomplice said he might need it if he ran into the police while he had Bobby. That shifted the murder weapon to Martin.

Now the kidnapping itself. Hall told of coaching Bonnie Heady in her role and sobering her up long enough to take Bobby from the Notre Dame de Sion school. When Bonnie brought the boy to the drugstore parking lot, Hall said, he took Bobby from her and told her to go shopping—he would meet her in an hour. Then he drove to an agreed rendezvous on Westport Road, met Martin and turned Bobby over to him. That, he said, was the last he saw of John Martin.

Then he picked up Bonnie and they went back to her house. Hall said he left Bonnie in the station wagon and went into the house. In the basement, he found the body of Bobby Greenlease. Hall's gun was lying

125

on the floor beside the body. So here was the first version: John Martin had murdered Bobby and had left the body in Bonnie's basement.

Question: "Was he [Bobby] dead when you got there?"
Hall: "Yes."
Question: "Where was the other man?"
Hall: "I don't know."

It had taken hours to get Hall to this point, but finally he had admitted the boy was dead. A photograph did it.

During the night, Kansas City's chief of police, Bernard C. Brannon, was notified that two suspects in the kidnapping were being held in St. Louis. Brannon and his chief of detectives, Major Eugene M. Pond, made a fast trip across the state, arriving at the Newstead Avenue station about 8:00 A.M. They apparently brought a large photograph of Bobby with them, or perhaps the FBI had obtained it elsewhere. At any rate, Brannon said later that as Hall was being questioned, the photo was placed on a table, facing him.

And so Hall saw Bobby Greenlease for the last time. The demons and furies danced and capered inside his skull, screaming at him. Look, they cried, look, look. He could not help himself; in the grip of a terrible fascination, his eyes went to the picture of the little boy.

"Hall would look at it for a moment and then turn his eyes away quickly," Brannon said. "He kept coming back to the photograph with his eyes again and again."

Brannon said he told Hall: "Carl, we just can't buy your story. It's full of holes. I know and you know you killed him. For the sake of the parents, let's get it over with and get the boy's body back."

Hall looked at the photograph once more, Brannon said, and suddenly it was over. The hotel in Pittsburg, Kansas, the child to be returned alive and unharmed, the first edifice of lies, all swept away.

"He's in the flower bed," said Hall.

But he claimed he had not wanted Bonnie to know the boy was dead. He said he went out to the station wagon and told her to go downtown and pick up his laundry and while she was at it, do some more shopping. As soon as she had gone, he said, he got a shovel and dug a grave in the yard.

When he had finished, he carried the boy up from the basement, through the kitchen and out to the yard. But then he decided the grave was not "suitable," apparently meaning it was not deep enough, so he thought of a better plan.

He would wait until Bonnie got back, put the body in the station wagon, take it to the Missouri River and dispose of it there. Having decided on the

126

river, he carried the body back down to the basement to await Bonnie's return.

But then he changed his mind again. By this time, Hall said, he was "extremely nervous and panicky." He was in a fever of indecision: the river or the grave? It would be the grave after all. He carried the body upstairs a second time.

Then, incredibly, he carried it back down again. By now, he no longer knew what he was doing. He was given over entirely to fear; there was nothing in his cosmos but terror. With the pathetic bundle in his arms, he stared around the basement. He is in a place, a well-known place, but how can he be here? There are familiar things—the furnace, the washing machine, the gardening tools—but they are not real; he can look through them, as through phantoms. He is in a world of indistinct apparitions and horrid noises, the shrieks and gibberings of the damned. And no way out.

When Bonnie returned, Hall said, she was drunk and went to sleep, either in the bedroom or on a couch in the living room. After she passed out, he brought the body up for the third and last time.

Reverting for a moment to the river plan, he said he put the bundle in the station wagon. This was his way of accounting for the blood in Bonnie's car, because he was claiming that he and Bonnie had not committed the murder and therefore had not transported the body. But then, Hall continued, he again decided not to dispose of the body in the river. So he buried Bobby after all, and then did what he could to clean up the basement. He said Bonnie was asleep all this time; he insisted—falsely—that she did not know the boy was dead.

The grim men did not believe him. They told him his confession was full of lies and contradictions. They were convinced that he and Bonnie and no one else, no John Martin, had murdered Bobby. Hall sweated and trembled and cried—a blubbering misery encircled by retribution—but he stuck to his central story: He and Bonnie had kidnapped the boy, but they hadn't murdered him.

"I didn't do it, I didn't do it, I didn't do it," he sobbed.

A few hours after the confession, reporters were brought into the captain's office to interview Carl and Bonnie. Whereupon, the murderers played a play.

Hall was sober now but very nervous. Bonnie, seated next to him, kept her eyes down much of the time, staring at the floor. But she looked up when a reporter mentioned the freshly planted chrysanthemums in her yard.

"You mean to say you put the flowers on the boy's grave?" the reporter asked.

Bonnie's eyes widened; she had heard that ladies widened their eyes when surprised. She looked at Chief O'Connell and exclaimed: "You mean they found him? He's dead?" The chief nodded.

Bonnie shuddered; ladies did that, too. She put her hands over her face and said in a low, horrified voice: "In my back yard."

Hall reached over and patted her hand comfortingly. "You didn't know," he said.

The reporters, too, were skeptical about John Martin, but Hall stayed with his story.

"I didn't expect it to pan out that way, that the boy would be hurt or killed, but then I thought, 'Oh, well, might as well go ahead with it.' " In other words, collect the ransom.

Another reporter asked: "Did you plan to kill Bobby or harm him in any way?"

"God, no!" Hall said. He began to cry again. "I didn't shoot the boy. John [Martin] did. I never would have done a thing like that."

Left, Bobby with his governess, Elsie Utlaut, on a vacation in Europe shortly before the kidnapping

Below left, Bobby's mother, Virginia Greenlease

Right, Bobby's father, Robert C. Greenlease

Above, Lieutenant Louis Shoulders (standing, left) and Officer Elmer Dolan with Bonnie Heady and Carl Hall. Dolan is showing the murder weapon to Heady and Hall. *Below*, Bonnie Heady shortly after her arrest. Her face shows marks of a recent beating by Hall. Carl Hall (right), with Deputy U.S. Marshal Lester Davison

Joe Costello

Below, Lieutenant Louis Shoulders (left) and Officer Elmer Dolan

May Traynor   John Vitale

Below, St. Louis Police Chief Jeremiah O'Connell (left) and I. A. Long, president of the Board of Police Commissioners

Chapter **15**

*I*n the death of a child is the infinite sadness of the world. . . .

During the long night in which Carl and Bonnie had yielded part of their secret, Bonnie had given the FBI permission to search her home in St. Joseph. At about 5:30 A.M. Wednesday, several agents arrived from Kansas City. They found the house empty, with some of its windows open. There was no car in the garage and no sign of any ransom money. The agents noticed an area in the back yard in which the earth had been freshly dug and chrysanthemums planted, but at first they had no idea of its significance.

Later in the morning, Agent Donald S. Hostetter called from Kansas City and told them the boy's body might be buried in the yard. Agent Norman L. Casey began digging under the chrysanthemums.

About fourteen inches down, "an odor was detected." At two and a half feet, Casey and another FBI agent saw a white substance that was later determined to be lime. At three and a half feet, they encountered "something blue." Casey dug deeper and saw that it was some blue plastic material—the plastic sheeting in which Hall had wrapped the body. Part of the plastic was loose, and under it Casey could see human flesh. It was Bobby's right knee.

133

The yard quickly filled with law enforcement officers and the neighborhood with voyeurs. A local radio station had broadcast a report that digging was under way for Bobby's body, and crowds of people immediately surrounded the house. Police lines were set up to keep them back, but some managed to infiltrate anyway. There was a fence around the back yard and inside the fence was a dense hedge of honeysuckle, but several sightseers got over the fence and pushed aside the honeysuckle to watch the digging. The streets around the house were clogged with traffic; hours after the body had been taken away, cars were still going by, bumper to bumper, cretin to cretin.

Slowly and carefully, the body was exhumed. When most of it had been exposed, Prosecuting Attorney John E. Downs of Buchanan County knelt in the grave and brushed the dirt and lime away from Bobby's face, but the features were too decomposed to permit an identification.

Shortly after noon, the body was taken to the Meierhoffer-Fleeman Funeral Home in St. Joe. There the Greenlease family dentist, Dr. Hubert Eversull of Kansas City, identified it from dental records. Bobby had six fillings, all of them in deciduous ("baby") teeth. All of the fillings shown in the records exactly matched the fillings in the body's teeth, as did the dental X rays that Eversull had brought with him. The dentist said his identification of the body as that of Bobby Greenlease was "definite and positive." In his examination, Eversull also found that Bobby's two upper front teeth and one lower tooth were missing; Hall had knocked them out in the struggle with the boy.

An autopsy was performed by Dr. Homer F. Mundy, coroner of Buchanan County, and Dr. Clement C. Dumont of St. Joe. They found a bullet hole approximately one and a half inches behind the right ear; this was the entry wound. There was another bullet hole two inches above the left ear—the exit wound. The physicians said death was caused by the gunshot wound, "loss of brain substance" and "fatal hemorrhaging." From the condition of the body, the doctors estimated that the child had been dead more than a week. (Bobby was kidnapped and murdered on September 28, and his body was found on the morning of October 7—nine days later.)

Hall had beaten Bobby in the face with his gun or fists before shooting him. The doctors found that Bobby's lips were cut in two places and "distorted," his gums were torn and jagged, and the flesh around his nose and left eye was damaged. These injuries, the autopsy report said, could have been caused by "severe" blows. The doctors did not find any bullets in the body. The FBI discovered two spent bullets later, in Bonnie's station wagon. One had struck Bobby; the other had missed.

When the autopsy was finished, the body was taken to Kansas City. Two days later, on October 9, at St. Agnes Church in Mission Hills, the suburb where he lived, a high mass of the angels was said for Bobby.

Twenty sheriff's deputies were needed to handle the traffic at the mass, as the community came to grieve, and to try to understand, and to fail. More than seven hundred mourners filled the church, and hundreds of others stood outside, in weak autumn sunshine. Some who were there remembered how quiet it was, almost tranquil.

The Greenlease family arrived in two limousines: Bobby's mother and father; his older brother, Paul; his sister, Virginia Sue, and Mrs. Greenlease's mother, Mrs. Irene Pollock. Bobby's mother was dressed in black but wore no veil; her face was very pale.

At 9:30 A.M., the small coffin, bronze with silver fittings, was brought into the church. On top of the casket was a single bouquet of lilies of the valley. The pallbearers were business associates of Bobby's father, among them Robert Ledterman and Norbert O'Neill—the intermediaries who had tried to save the child.

The high mass of the angels, which is for children, was sung by the pastor of St. Agnes, the Reverend Herman J. Koch. Archbishop Edward Hunkeler of Kansas City, Kansas, then addressed the congregation, several times speaking directly to the Greenlease family.

The dead child, the archbishop said, "was Christlike—and Christ suffered. If Christ suffered, ye also must. The just are in the hands of God and torment cannot touch them. . . . Your sorrow is not in that the cheery person has gone, but in the agonizing fear that he was in the hands of evil persons. God said: 'Suffer the little children to come unto Me, for of such is the Kingdom of Heaven.' Do you think that in God's omniscient presence He can be less than helpful to you? God created him [Bobby] through the cooperation of his parents. He took him into His fold at baptism. In such short time, His purpose was fulfilled."

Thus comforted, the family came out of the church. Mrs. Greenlease appeared close to collapse. Her husband helped her into the car for the trip to the cemetery.

At Forest Hills Cemetery in Kansas City, a burial service was held. Father Koch and another priest, assisted by two acolytes, stood under the rotunda of Forest Hills Abbey, a large mausoleum. The rotunda was filled with flowers, among them a large cross of white carnations from Bobby's classmates in the first grade at the Notre Dame de Sion school. Father Koch

135

read the burial service, part in Latin, part in English, and then the coffin was placed in the family crypt.

St. Agnes Church, where the high mass was sung for Bobby Greenlease, was named for a martyr who perished in the Diocletian persecution of the third century. St. Agnes was tied to a stake to be burned, but the fire went out, so her head was cut off instead. She was twelve years old.

The investigation now had four parts:

1. Because the FBI—or at least *most* of the FBI—believed Hall was lying when he said a man named John Martin had committed the actual murder, agents continued to question Carl and Bonnie intensively, in the hope of breaking down their story.

2. At the same time, however, the FBI conducted a nationwide manhunt for John Martin. Donald Hostetter, who directed the early part of the Greenlease investigation, did not believe Martin was implicated at all, and his colleagues agreed with him. But the FBI's renowned director, J. Edgar Hoover, eight hundred miles away in Washington, knew better than the men in the field; what else is renown for? Hostetter reported that "no confirming evidence has been obtained . . . to indicate the existence of this alleged third kidnapper" and recommended against issuing a formal charge against Martin. But Hoover wrote on the report: "I don't agree at all." So the manhunt went on.

3. In addition, investigators began searching for physical evidence in the case, concentrating first on Bonnie's house in St. Joe and then fanning out to the many other places that Hall had mentioned in his confession.

4. Now, too, began the fourth and longest phase of the investigation. The FBI started looking for the missing half of the ransom money. Carl and Bonnie were executed only eighty-one days after the kidnapping—a swiftness of justice inconceivable today—but the hunt for the missing $300,000 went on for years.

With four major investigations under way simultaneously, the first several days were filled with confusion. It was not surprising that some mistakes were made—and one of them involved Bonnie Heady's identity. It turned out there were two of her. One "Bonnie Brown Heady" was in the FBI's files in Washington. The other "Bonnie Emily Brown Heady" was in jail in St. Louis. For a few hours, the FBI thought they were the same person. The population of the United States in 1953 was more than 150 million people; that was a lot of people, but even so, was it possible there were two Bonnie Brown Headys? The FBI assumed it wasn't. Alas, it was.

Based on information from the FBI, the nation's newspapers of Wednesday, October 7, identified the female kidnapper being held in St. Louis as Bonnie Brown Heady, "widow of a gunman." Her deceased husband was said to be Dan Heady, an old-time bank robber, presumably to be played by Paul Newman. In December 1935, Dan Heady and five other men were in jail in Muskogee, Oklahoma, suspected of robbing a bank. His wife visited him and kissed him tenderly as he stood close to the bars of his cell. Somehow Dan obtained a pistol; his wife was accused of slipping it to him as they kissed, but the charge was later dismissed. At any rate, Dan and the others broke out of jail in the old-fashioned way: They shot people. Muskogee's chief of detectives, Ben Bolton, was killed in the gunfight. A few days later, a posse surrounded a farmhouse in which Dan Heady was hiding. There was another gunfight, and Dan was killed. When told of his death, his wife was reported to have smiled. "That's too bad," she said.

A tough cookie. Played by Meryl or Jane or Faye. But she was not Bonnie Heady of St. Joseph, Missouri, divorced wife of V. Ellis Heady and mistress of Carl Austin Hall. The FBI retracted its identification the next day, and the wire services sent out urgent bulletins informing newspapers that Bonnie Heady, the kidnapper, was not Dan Heady's widow.

After questioning Hall in the early hours of October 7 and getting his first, incomplete confession, Chief of Police O'Connell, Police Board President Long, Lieutenant Shoulders and FBI Agent Thornton questioned Bonnie—but she was even more incomplete.

"I'm trying to help you as much as I can," Bonnie told them. "[But] I'm just so hazy on some things that I can't remember. If you had been drunk as long as I had, it does something to your brain. I just travel around in a haze most of the time."

She said she remembered picking up Bobby at school and taking him in a cab to the Katz Drugstore parking lot, where Hall was waiting in the station wagon. This much was true. Then, Bonnie said, Hall drove them to "the Plaza" [presumably the Country Club Plaza shopping mall, where Hall had seen Bobby's sister and had considered kidnapping her]. At the Plaza, Bonnie said, Hall let her out and drove away, taking Bobby with him. She said Hall was gone about two hours, and when he came back, "the boy wasn't with him." None of this was true.

Then Bonnie's central lie: "I asked where the boy was, and he said he took him back to the school." Bonnie was pretending that she still believed Hall's story that he was Bobby's father and only wanted to take the child from school for a little while so he could see him.

Next morning, Bonnie said, she read a newspaper story about the kidnapping, "and I was dumbfounded." She said she asked Hall "what he did with the boy and where he was and everything, and that is when he got mad and wouldn't say anything and told me to mind my own business."

Question: "Did he hit you then?"

Bonnie (indicating the bruises on her face): "Yes . . . I been running around looking like this ever since."

Bonnie said she remembered very little about the trip to St. Louis and had only a vague memory of the apartment on Arsenal Street: "I was just blind [drunk]. I was just staggering; he [Hall] had to lead me in."

But she was not too drunk to see the ransom money. After they got into the apartment, she opened Hall's luggage and "saw a lot of money."

Question: "You knew the boy had disappeared? Why didn't you call the police?"

Bonnie: "I should have, I know that, but I thought if I called the police they'd come and take him [Hall] away, and I love him very much and want to keep him. We had been very happy together, and I wanted to keep him."

So it was Dryden: All for Love. A woman blinded by passion, helpless in its grasp. That was one side of Bonnie—the side she turned to the men in the police station. A group of *men*. You do understand, don't you? A helpless woman.

There was, however, another side. On October 13, the *St. Louis Post-Dispatch* published a story based on interviews with two women who were prisoners in the city jail, where Bonnie was being held. Two *women*.

They said Bonnie had talked to them several times about the murder of Bobby Greenlease—and had not shown a trace of sorrow or remorse. One of the prisoners said Bonnie was so detached and emotionless when she spoke of her part in the murder that it was as if "she was talking about someone else."

"When she came back from giving the signed confession, she was actually laughing and acted as if she had had some very good news," the other prisoner said. "In fact, she seemed so elated that I remarked that everything must be going all right. She answered: 'Yes, I feel fine.' "

The women said Bonnie told them about the murder in considerable detail: how she and Carl had taken Bobby to a lonely field, how the child became "very frightened" and began to struggle, how Carl "beat him with his fists," knocking out his front teeth, and then shot him, and how they took the body back to Bonnie's house and buried it in the yard. Bonnie spoke of all this, her cellmates said, in "calm, matter-of-fact" tones, with one exception:

"I was awfully nervous during the actual killing," she said.

And what of her love for Carl Hall—the man with whom she had been so happy that she could not bear to turn him in? He was a bungler, Bonnie told the two women, a nothing, a wimp. Her only disappointment, she said, was that the kidnapping had not succeeded—and she blamed Hall. She spoke of him with scorn.

"Before the kidnapping," she said, "I thought Carl was a big tough guy with a lot of nerve. But when the chips were down, I found out he was nothing but a weakling. He certainly had me fooled."

It was the scorn of a woman scorned. And hurt? Was that possible with someone like Bonnie Heady? She was forty-one years old, starting to go matronly in breast and buttock, and Hall had left her alone in the apartment on Arsenal Street and had gone off to spend the night with a younger woman. "If he had stayed with me," Bonnie told her cellmates, "everything would have been all right." Crushed petals in a cesspool?

The law moved swiftly. In Kansas City, warrants were issued charging Carl and Bonnie with extortion, and in St. Joe, Prosecutor Downs charged them with first-degree murder—John Martin or no John Martin. Downs said he believed Buchanan County had jurisdiction in the case because of the bloodstains in Bonnie's house. "There is every indication the murder was committed there," he said.

But it was not yet known exactly where Bobby Greenlease had been murdered, so there was some initial confusion over jurisdiction. The St. Louis prosecutor, Edward L. Dowd, protested the decision of his own police department to turn Carl and Bonnie over to the FBI. Dowd said it was a state case. In Washington, Attorney General Herbert Brownell, Jr., at first agreed with Dowd. He announced that the federal government would give the prisoners back to the state of Missouri for prosecution. Brownell's decision was based on the assumption that the victim had not been taken across a state line and therefore the federal kidnapping statute—the Lindbergh Law—did not apply. This caused consternation within the FBI, which feared the investigation might be taken out of its hands.

So it appeared for a while that Carl and Bonnie would be tried under state law, which meant in some Missouri county. But which one? The Jackson County (Kansas City) prosecutor, Richard K. Phelps, wanted the trial held in Kansas City if it turned out that Bobby had been murdered there. However, Buchanan County's Downs sent an assistant to St. Louis to bring Carl and Bonnie back to St. Joe—in which effort he was unsuccessful. It was kept dignified, but both Kansas City and St. Joe wanted that trial.

139

It turned out that Brownell's decision was premature. A short time later, it was discovered that Bobby *had* been taken across a state line, into Kansas. The federal government then took jurisdiction for good: Carl and Bonnie were tried in a federal court in Kansas City.

John Martin. Who was he, and where was he? Information about him was in the FBI's files, which in our society made him a real person. Also in the files was a photograph of Martin, a mug shot taken at the Missouri penitentiary.

But there was a problem. Carl Hall refused to identify the mug shot as the John Martin he was talking about. He said the man he claimed had murdered Bobby Greenlease was not the man in the photo. To make the whole thing more dubious, Bonnie Heady said she had never seen the man in the photo and had never heard Hall mention anyone named John Martin.

So there were three possibilities:

1. In refusing to identify the photo, Hall was trying to protect Martin— trying to make it more difficult to find him.

2. Or Hall's John Martin was not the John Martin in the FBI files but another John Martin altogether. Like the two Bonnie Headys, were there two John Martins? In that case, the FBI would be looking for the wrong man.

3. Or Hall had made up the whole story. He had known a drifter named John Martin, somewhere, sometime, and had just tossed in his name as the killer.

Prosecutor Downs, in St. Joe, had issued a murder warrant against Martin at the same time that he had charged Carl and Bonnie. But the United States attorney in Kansas City, Edward L. Scheufler, held off. Scheufler and FBI agent Hostetter reasoned that if a federal warrant was issued against Martin, charging him with extortion in the Greenlease case, the public would always suspect that a third kidnapper had been involved. Even if the investigation later disproved this, the damage would have been done.

However, the murder warrant in St. Joe made it necessary for Scheufler to charge Martin with unlawful flight to avoid prosecution, which he did. As a result, Martin was officially a fugitive, and the pressure was on the FBI to find him, whether or not it thought he had anything to do with the case. There were two days of telephone calls and messages between Kansas City and Washington, in which Hostetter argued that there was no evidence that a third kidnapper had been involved. Predictably, he did not prevail against Hoover. On the night of Thursday, October 8, the FBI ordered a nationwide manhunt for a skid-row bum.

In announcing the manhunt, the FBI said Martin had a long record of arrests and convictions for robbery, larceny, drunkenness, child molesting and "sex deviation." It said he had been jailed thirty-three times in Springfield, Missouri, for being drunk. Residents of a small Missouri town where Martin had lived for a while described him as a "wino" and "the village bum." The FBI said he had served fifteen months in the Missouri penitentiary for sexually abusing a child. He was released in October 1951. Carl Hall had done time in the same prison, but his sentence had begun in January 1952, so he apparently had met Martin somewhere in his wanderings, not in prison.

Martin was born in 1916, in a small town near Chicago. His childhood was aimless. His early years were spent in another small Illinois town, where he was a chronic school truant and a constant problem for the authorities. The town's former police chief was quoted as saying the boy lived a "dog-eat-dog" existence on the streets and had the reputation of "an all-round no-good kid."

Was that it? Just no good? In February 1929, the Cook County juvenile court committed him to a state school for the feebleminded. He was then twelve years old, but the school superintendent said he had a mental age of six years, nine months. His I.Q. was 52. He was described later as "extremely illiterate." Martin made a "good adjustment" to the school, the superintendent said, but in November 1932, when he was sixteen, he just walked away.

After completing his education, he became a derelict. He wandered around Depression-era Missouri and Illinois, working occasionally as a "low-class laborer" but mostly drinking and getting into trouble—an anonymous bum until Carl Hall, in desperation, dredged up his name and offered him as the murderer of Bobby Greenlease.

The FBI described Martin as a white male, thirty-seven years old, five feet six inches tall and weighing 190 pounds, which gave him a "stocky" build. His hair was brown, his eyes blue and his complexion ruddy. And he was extensively decorated. He had tattoos on many parts of his body, some of them with sentimental inscriptions and others fierce and piratical; all he needed was a motorcycle. Lastly, he had two physical deformities. They were relatively minor but nevertheless noticeable. These disfigurements were widely publicized at the time as part of Martin's description. However, they are being withheld from this book to avoid identifying him if he is still alive, since he had nothing to do with the kidnapping.

As soon as the description was circulated, the American people began seeing him. Reports flooded into FBI headquarters. Men resembling Martin were seen in Dallas, Denver, Philadelphia, St. Louis, San Diego and

141

Washington, D.C. He was in York, Pennsylvania. No, he was in Montgomery, Alabama. Now he was in Mount Vernon, New York, and then he was in Ogden, Utah. Another bulletin just in: He has been seen in Maine.

The FBI investigated dozens of these UFOs, but none of them led anywhere:

- A passenger on a TWA flight from St. Louis to Washington was observed to have a physical disfigurement similar to one of Martin's. The plane circled over Pittsburgh until FBI agents could get to the airport—at last, an explanation for the frequent delays—and then landed. The passenger was questioned, but he was sixty-seven years old and had no tattoos.

- A man answering Martin's description was seen in a tavern in Ankeny, Iowa. The tavern owner, a woman, said the man claimed to have been the Greenlease family's chauffeur. She said he "kept talking about the kidnapping." An FBI agent drove to Ankeny, made inquiries, and found no reason for further investigation. Bar talk.

- A man in New Orleans said he met another man in a bar on St. Charles Street. The first man said the second man was "identical with John Martin." He said the man had $500 and boasted he "could get $60,000." The first man said he left the bar when the other man invited him to his hotel room. A nonconsenting adult; no further investigation.

- Two men registered at a motel in Cottage Grove, Oregon. The motel owner said one of them looked like Martin and had tattoos on his arms. One said, "I love you, Dorothy," and the other said, "I love you very much, Margie." Neither of these tattoos resembled Martin's tattoos, but the motel owner said the men should be investigated anyway, because they had acted suspiciously. Dorothy and Margie were also suspicious.

- A woman got on a bus in Chula Vista, California. A few minutes later, a man got on. The woman noticed he had a disfigurement similar to one of Martin's. The man took out a crucifix and began crossing himself and saying, "God bless you," again and again. When some children boarded the bus, the man said: "God bless little children." The woman called the police, who notified the FBI. An agent interviewed the woman. Nothing more on this one.

- A man advised that he was in a club in Omaha, Nebraska, and met three prostitutes. The whores were accompanied by a man whom the informant "positively identified" as Martin. The informant couldn't give much information about the man, but he remembered the whores very

142

well. He gave their names and described them in alluring detail. He said he phoned a hotel in Chicago, made a reservation, and told all three hookers to meet him there. No further investigation; they skip the good parts.

- An Atchison, Topeka and Santa Fe train stopped in Manzanola, Colorado. A man threw some things out of the train, including a newspaper, a train schedule and a book entitled *Sixty-three Funny Stories*. Written on these items were several messages. One said: "Important information for FBI. I am not dead. John Martin." Another said: "I am John Martin, if you will look at paper on car middle entrance 570 Thirty-first Street you will find car diagram for lost money. You will never get me."

They never got him.

Chapter **16**

7he money was counted twice. Elmer Dolan and the four detectives—
Carson, King, Bradley, and Naher—opened the suitcase and footlocker,
took out stack after stack of $10 and $20 bills, and made a careful tally.
Money seemed to fill the room, awakening it. The dark corners twinkled
with money. It was not a miser's hoard of gold suddenly come to light, or
a glittering heap of rubies and emeralds, but it fascinated nevertheless,
drawing the eye irresistibly, exciting the imagination. Even though it was
only half the ransom, it . . . was . . . so . . . much . . . money.

A little later, it was counted again, by a team of two FBI agents and two
St. Louis policemen. Agent John H. Poelker, who was an accountant and
who later became mayor of St. Louis, was in charge of this count. Both
times, the total was the same:

In the black suitcase: $151,000.

In the green footlocker: $137,510.

That made a total of $288,510 in Hall's luggage. Smaller amounts were
recovered later from various persons: from Bonnie Heady, the $2,000 that
Hall had put in her purse; from Oliver Johnson, $1,180 of the money Hall
had given him; from Bernard Patton, the $500 that had arrived in the mail,

and from Sandra June O'Day, after her arrest in Kansas City, $110 of the $1,200 Hall had given her. In Hall's wallet, the FBI found $2,490, and in his pockets he had $740. Lastly, some small amounts were recovered from various stores at which Hall had made purchases. Added to the money in his luggage, this made a new total of $295,790.

In the months and years that followed, the FBI retrieved an additional $2,250, some of it from banks and some from persons who had received $10 or $20 bills in ordinary ways and had taken the trouble to check them against the lists of serial numbers published in newspapers and circulated to banks and business firms. Thus, a grand total of $298,040 was eventually recovered. It was later returned to Bobby's father, Robert Greenlease.

The last ransom bill was recovered in January 1956. After that—nothing. Greenlease had paid a ransom of $600,000, but $301,960 had disappeared. Year by year, the trail grew fainter, and finally it seemed to fade away altogether.

At Bonnie's house in St. Joe, FBI agents found bloodstains on the basement floor, on the steps leading from the basement to the kitchen, in the kitchen itself, and on a fiber mat on the back porch. Hall had tried to scrub out the stains, but many easily identifiable traces remained. More bloodstains were found on a cushion and a bedspread, on one of Carl's suits—the suit he had taken to the cleaner—and on one of Bonnie's suits and a blouse, all of which were hanging in bedroom closets. The agents also found the shovel that Carl and Bonnie had used to dig the grave, and the empty lime sack.

In a small pile of incinerator ashes in the yard, they found a cartridge case from a .38-caliber revolver. Sifting through more ashes in a trash barrel, they found two more .38-caliber casings. One of the casings was from the bullet that had killed Bobby, another was from the bullet that had missed, and the third was from a shot that Hall had fired one night when drunk.

A short time later, the agents examined Bonnie's station wagon. The bullet that had killed Bobby was embedded in the floor mat on the driver's side. The bullet that had missed was in the left front door panel. There were bloodstains in the station wagon—and on the floor under the passenger seat were fragments of human bone.

Hall's first confession was riddled with inconsistencies, and one of the most glaring was the station wagon. If he had turned the child over to John Martin and had then driven the station wagon back to the shopping mall to pick up Bonnie Heady—as he insisted he had—then why were the bullets and bone fragments found *in the station wagon*? If Martin had murdered Bobby, he must have done it in his own car (which Hall had described in deceitful detail) or in Bonnie's house or somewhere else—but not in the station wagon. However, there was clear evidence of murder in the station wagon. Hostetter and the other investigators reasoned that this went a long way toward ruling out the derelict, John Martin.

It was not hard to find Sandra June O'Day. Ollie Johnson had given her name to the police and FBI, as well as the name of her aunt, Molly Paine. The investigators had Sandy's telegrams to Molly, and the other cab driver, Herman Dreste, told them he had driven Sandy to Kansas City. Dreste said he had reserved a room for Sandy at the Muehlbach Hotel, but Sandy met another sister of the cross of shame, got drunk with her, and ended up at a different hotel. There, on Wednesday, October 7, she was arrested.

The FBI found no ransom money in her suitcase and overnight bag. This eliminated two pieces of luggage in a luggage-ridden investigation, but the agents could not ignore the possibility that Sandy had hidden the money somewhere before she was arrested. They booked her into the Jackson County jail as a material witness—at least, everyone *thought* she had been booked as a material witness—and began questioning her.

Sandy was held in jail for twenty-three days. She was finally freed by an acute and resourceful Kansas City attorney named James L. McMullin. It happened this way:

McMullin was representing a woman who was accused of killing her boyfriend. The woman said he had swindled her out of some money and, to make things worse, had boasted that he had a new girl friend. So she shot him. McMullin defended the woman, and she was acquitted. Later, the same woman got into a fight with another boyfriend and stabbed him in the heart, of which he died. McMullin got her off on that one also. Altogether, McMullin told the author, this woman killed seven men between 1953 and about 1975; she had a hasty temper. McMullin defended her every time and won six acquittals. In the seventh case, the woman poured gasoline on a boyfriend while he was sleeping, lit it, and burned him up. She pleaded guilty to that one, sparing other boyfriends.

While on trial for the first killing, the woman was being held in the Jackson County jail. She shared a cell with Sandra O'Day, and after her acquittal she told Sandy about the marvelous lawyer who had defended her. When the woman was released, she smuggled out a note from Sandy to McMullin. In it, Sandy told him of her plight and said: "They won't let me have a lawyer."

McMullin filed a writ of habeas corpus demanding Sandy's release. At this point, the United States attorney in Kansas City suffered an embarrassment. Everyone in his office thought someone else had filed the necessary papers to hold Sandy as a material witness. The age of communication had begun: Apparently no one had filed them. No papers could be found. McMullin agreed not to reveal this lapse, and in return the government agreed not to oppose habeas corpus. Sandy walked.

"But I wondered—as did the government—whether she got some of the money," McMullin said.

Everything was happening at once, pell-mell. The kidnappers had been caught, Hall had made a partial confession, Bobby Greenlease's body had been found, and it had been discovered that half the ransom money had disappeared—all in a few hours. The newspapers reported the fast-moving developments in big front-page headlines:

KIDNAPPED BOY MURDERED, BODY FOUND; TWO HELD HERE WITH $293,992; THEY ADMIT ABDUCTION.

NATIONWIDE MANHUNT ON FOR ACCUSED KILLER OF BOY; THREE MURDER WARRANTS ISSUED.

KIDNAPPERS WAIVE HEARING; SEARCH FOR MARTIN, LOST RANSOM GROWS.

This crime struck more deeply than most: the brutal, terrifying murder of a child. The St. Louis prosecutor, Edward Dowd, summed up the prevailing opinion. The death penalty, he said, was "too good for the murderers of Bobby." It was an old answer, but who was to give it? "Dearly beloved," wrote the Apostle Paul, "avenge not yourselves . . . for it is written, Vengeance is mine; I will repay, saith the Lord." No, no, that would not do.

The search for the missing $300,000 began immediately, and at first it focused on the most likely culprit, Hall. On Thursday, FBI agents took him on a five-hour tour of the St. Louis neighborhoods that he and Bonnie had frequented. The master criminal's recollections were hazy, but he guided the agents to as many of the bars, motels and alleys as he could remember.

It was an erratic and incomplete journey, and all the evidence it produced was negative. The first find was the duffel bag that had originally contained the ransom money. After much driving around, Hall located the alley in which he and Bonnie had transferred the money to the suitcase and footlocker. In a garbage can, the FBI men found the duffel bag, but it was like the rest of the first day's search: empty.

In the succeeding days, with information from Hall and from the various cab drivers who had taken the kidnappers around St. Louis, the FBI pains-takingly reconstructed the bleary itinerary of Carl and Bonnie from their arrival in the city early Monday morning until they were arrested Tuesday night. Agents questioned dozens of tavern owners, bartenders, drinkers, whores, sales clerks, used-car salesmen, motel employees, apartment-house managers and others who had had contact with Carl or Bonnie.

The investigators were trying to find anyone who had seen or heard Carl or Bonnie say or do anything that might provide a clue to the missing money. They showed photographs of the kidnappers and asked the same questions again and again:

Have you ever seen this man? Or this woman? When did you see him (or her or them)? What time did he come in and how long was he here? What did he do in your bar (or restaurant or store or whatever)? Was anyone with him? Do you know the other person or can you describe him? Did you hear anything they said to each other? Did the suspect display any money? How much? Did he have any luggage with him? Did he open it? If so, did you see what was in it? Did he take the luggage with him when he left? Did he talk to you? What did he say? Did he seem nervous? Did he say or do anything suspicious? Did he talk to anyone else in the bar? Do you know the person he talked to or can you describe him? Did you hear what they said? Did he make any phone calls or receive any? Did you hear what was said or get the number he called? Did he write any notes or letters? Do you have any idea what they said or who they were to? Did he go to the bathroom or anywhere else? Could he have hidden anything? Did he buy anything? Did he say what he wanted it for? Do you have any of the money he paid you? When he left, did he leave anything behind? Did he say where he was going? Did he leave in a cab or a car or on foot? Did you see the cab number or license number? Did you see the direction he went? When he left, did anyone go with him? Do you know that person or can you describe him?

And on and on and on. And none of it produced any clues to the missing money.

During the Thursday tour, Hall led the FBI to the hardware store where he had purchased a shovel and the plastic bags and garbage cans in which he had planned to bury the money. Then he took the agents to the area along the Meramec. At the riverside cottage named for "Thelma," they found the garbage cans and plastic bags, and in some nearby underbrush, the shovel. However, the cans and bags were empty, and Hall said he had not buried the missing half of the ransom money. But could he be believed? With Hall, that was always the crucial question.

There was some confirmation. Three of the cab drivers who had taken

Hall here and there in St. Louis—Irwin Rosa, Howard Lewis and Oliver Johnson—had had to lift his suitcase and footlocker at various times, and they told the FBI that the luggage was very heavy—Rosa said it was so heavy he could hardly lift it. They estimated the combined weight of the suitcase and footlocker at seventy-five to eighty pounds. The full $600,000 in ransom money, when it was assembled in Kansas City, weighed just under eighty-five pounds. So the recollections of the cab drivers were circumstantial evidence that all of the money was in Hall's possession on Monday and at least part of Tuesday.

Hall himself told the FBI that the golden luggage weighed essentially the same when he was arrested Tuesday night as it had on Monday morning, when he had filled it with $600,000. During the entire time, he insisted, the footlocker weighed between forty and fifty pounds and the suitcase thirty to thirty-five pounds. If true, this meant that the ransom was virtually intact when the kidnappers were caught.

Hall said he never counted the entire ransom; he didn't have time. But while he was alone in the Town House apartment, waiting for Ollie to return with women, he apparently took heed of his finances. On an envelope, he jotted down a rough accounting of the money he had spent or planned to spend the next day, in order to determine how much he would have left. The figures he wrote down were "2,4,1,4, 20." Hall said the "20" referred to $20,000 he had transferred to his briefcase, and the other numbers represented his cash flow. It added up to $11,000 in three days. That was spending in the modern style, but the numbers on the envelope nevertheless indicated that Hall still had most of the ransom money when he was arrested. Unless, of course, he had hidden half of it after all.

And that is where matters stood on Thursday, October 8—twenty-four hours after the arrest of Carl Hall and Bonnie Heady. One of the most brutal crimes in the nation's history had been solved, the kidnappers were behind bars, a chimerical third kidnapper was being sought, $300,000 in ransom money had vanished, and the FBI had three prime suspects in its disappearance—Hall himself and Oliver Johnson and Sandra June O'Day. The kidnappers had been quickly caught—largely because they were among the most inept in the annals of crime—but the search for the missing money was to prove more difficult—much more.

It was a job for Superman, but the FBI had jurisdiction. In the year 1953, the Federal Bureau of Investigation was without question the premier law enforcement agency in the United States and one of the most renowned in the world: a disciplined, efficient and highly trained corps of professional investigators backed up by impressive scientific resources and led by a legendary government official named John Edgar Hoover. If anyone could find the missing money, it was the FBI.

Many Americans did indeed think of the FBI as a group of supersleuths. This image was assiduously promoted by Hoover, who at the time of the Greenlease case was nearing thirty years as the bureau's director and whose tenure was to last an astounding forty-eight years, until his death in 1972. A veteran FBI agent once described Hoover as one of the two indisputable public relations geniuses of the twentieth century—the other being Douglas MacArthur—and Hoover's blue smoke and mirrors played an important role in the FBI's rise to eminence and power. So did his files. But Hoover's FBI also solved a great many crimes and caught a great many criminals. Moreover, it was the major stimulus to police professionalism in the United States, an incomplete process.

There were some people who feared the FBI under Hoover as a Komitet Gosudarstvennoi Bezopasnosti (the Russians have even greater need of initials than we), but in the 1950's this was a minority view. The director was a hero to millions of Americans. They remembered and admired his battles against the gangsters of the 1930's—although they admired the gangsters, too—and now they applauded his unrelenting vigilance in the face of the Communist peril. They read the adulatory books and articles about Hoover and listened to a popular radio program that recounted the FBI's exploits; the program's musical theme was taken from an opera by Sergei Prokofiev, a Communist.

Hoover's reputation raised expectations; surely the FBI would find the missing Greenlease money. But it was the agents in the field who would have to fulfill the expectations. And this exposed, once again, the central fraud of public relations: No matter how much you magnify them, humans can only behave as humans. That is all they are, *all*. Each generation learns this about its children, its parents, its leaders and its investment bankers. The FBI agents assigned to find the Greenlease money were good investigators but they were human. They were not supermen. They left that to Hoover.

And got on with the job.

The federal government's nerve center in St. Louis was the United States Court and Custom House on Twelfth Street. On the fourth floor was the St. Louis office of the FBI, with a complement of sixty to seventy agents headed by Joseph E. Thornton, the Special Agent in Charge, or SAC. (In the FBI's terminology, all agents are called Special Agents. There are no plain, ordinary agents. It mystifies the laity.)

Thornton, however, did not direct the Greenlease investigation. The St. Louis office's regular work had to go on, and the Greenlease case was so big that it clearly had to be handled separately. To do this, a special team was set up, headed by a veteran FBI agent who had been involved in the case from the beginning. His name was Donald S. Hostetter. He was forty-five or forty-six years old and had been with the FBI since 1934.

Mary Kay Eifert, who was in charge of the Greenlease files in the St. Louis office, remembers Hostetter as a big man—about six feet three inches tall—and a no-nonsense type; he had once been a football coach. Mrs. Eifert describes him as "a big, rough man—rather rough-spoken—but a good man to work for." He was born in Warren, Arkansas, in 1907 or 1908—the FBI's records are not clear which—and he had a law degree from Washington and Lee University in Virginia. He retired from the FBI in 1962 and died ten years later.

When the Greenlease case broke, Hostetter was in Newark, New Jersey, in charge of the FBI office there. He was sent immediately to Kansas City, where he took command of the kidnapping investigation—operating under limits set by Bobby's father. Then, when the scene shifted to St. Louis, Hostetter went there to head the separate squad, which was known as the Greenlease Special. An acronym was used to identify the case: Grenap.

The first requirement was manpower, lots of it. Many of the agents regularly assigned to St. Louis worked on the case in the early stages and some of them stayed with it for a long time. In addition, twenty-five or thirty agents were sent in from FBI offices in Kansas City, Little Rock, Louisville, Denver and other cities. Mrs. June Michael, who was working in the St. Louis office then, estimates that at the height of the investigation almost one hundred agents were assigned to it. After a while, however, the Greenlease team shook down to a group of thirty to thirty-five men. Once the evidence against Hall and Heady had been assembled, it was these agents, primarily, who spent the ensuing months and years trying to find the missing $300,000.

They worked in anonymity. The names of the Grenap agents were not in the newspapers, their faces were not on television, and they were not given to writing their memoirs. The Greenlease file at FBI headquarters in Washington—File Number 7-6920—consists of more than ten thousand

151

pages. Part of the file is available to the public under the Freedom of Information Act, but in this mountain of reports, memoranda and documents, the agents who did the work are denied to posterity. With only rare exceptions, their names have been blacked out.

Who were they?

The Grenap roster included Phillip M. King, Earl C. Porter, Howard Kennedy, John S. Bush, A. S. Reeder, William G. Simon, E. J. Stoltz, Otto G. Heinecke, G. Wayne Mack, W. Clark Fuller, James Cadigan, Robert Bender, Jack C. Pollock, Charles W. Nail, Jr., Max E. Richardson, Walt M. Sirene, Don W. Walters, Frank F. Staab, Jack S. Fisher and Joe M. Pearson.

Other agents who worked on the case at various times in St. Louis, Kansas City or St. Joe were Edward M. Moreland, John H. Poelker, Hugh Small, Joseph R. Connors, Jerome J. Hoefferle, Finis Y. Sims, J. R. Meigs, Fred J. Maloney, Fred G. McGeary, Richard E. Martin, John J. Buckley, Charles G. Cleveland, Norman L. Casey, Paul R. Casey and Harry J. Maynor.

These lists are not complete. After more than thirty years, memories are imperfect; some names undoubtedly have been omitted. And those agents who *have* been included will not be rescued from anonymity by being mentioned in a *book*.

For approximately three months, the Greenlease investigation was a "bureau special," meaning that it had been set up by FBI headquarters in Washington as a national operation. Early in 1954, however, Washington changed its mind. The national investigation was costing a lot of man-hours and money, with no sign of the elusive $300,000. Hostetter was instructed to turn over the case to the St. Louis office. It then became an "office special" under the direction of J. Earl Milnes, who had succeeded Thornton as St. Louis SAC. Milnes' assistant SAC, Herbert K. Moss, supervised the Grenap squad on a day-to-day basis and played a leading role in the investigation from then on.

The Grenap team had begun as thirty to thirty-five agents, but as the years went by without a breakthrough the squad was gradually reduced in size. Former agent Edward Moreland, who worked on the case, recalls that as the squad grew smaller its nucleus became agents Phillip King, Earl Porter and Howard Kennedy—and of those three, the key figure was Phil King.

Of all the investigators involved in the Greenlease case, none worked on it longer than Phil King. This agent spent years trying to track down the missing ransom money. He pursued innumerable leads, questioned and requestioned scores of informants, traveled from coast to coast. Although he worked on many other investigations over the years, the Greenlease case never really left his mind. He was not obsessed with it, being a practical man who did not go in for fixations, but he was a very persistent detective. The Greenlease case nagged him; he plugged away at it for years.

King was born in Savannah, Georgia, on August 7, 1922. His father and mother were government employees (''it's a family tradition''). In high school, he was a three-sport student—football, baseball and basketball—and he won a football scholarship to George Washington University in Washington, D.C. In 1942, he joined the Army Air Force, ''but I ended up in the tank corps and spent seventeen months in Europe.'' After the war, he went back to GWU, graduating in 1950 with a B.A. in government. While in college, he played baseball in the Yankee farm system, first as a pitcher and then a first baseman; football had been his favorite, but a knee operation ended that. After graduation, he took Civil Service exams for the Secret Service and the FBI. He was accepted by both and chose the FBI. In 1953, he was assigned to the St. Louis office. He retired from the FBI in 1975 and now lives in New Orleans, where he operates a private security firm, King Investigations.

All these men—Donald Hostetter, Herbert Moss, Phillip King, Earl Porter and the rest—came under severe pressure to get full confessions from Carl Hall and Bonnie Heady and to find the missing $300,000; in other words, to clear up the Greenlease investigation in a hurry. And in the Hoover era, pressure was *pressure*. A St. Louisan who knew several of the FBI agents working on the case—and knew some of the suspects too—told the author: ''Hoover wanted this case solved in the worst way. There was an assistant directorship waiting for the man who broke it.''

Chapter **17**

*O*n Thursday, FBI agents began questioning Carl and Bonnie again, and the interrogation continued until Sunday night. Hour after hour, the agents strained and pushed for a breakthrough—an admission of murder—but they could not get one. Often the captors were as tired as their captives; they were locked together in a dance of exhaustion.

Again and again, the agents took Hall back to the glaring contradictions and discrepancies in his story, battering at the weak spots. But he clung stubbornly to his central lie. He admitted the kidnapping, but he insisted he and Bonnie had not killed the child.

At times, he edged close to the abyss: "I know I am more responsible than anyone else because I planned the kidnapping and it resulted in the death of Bobby Greenlease." But then he would draw back: ". . . he continued to steadfastly claim that there was such a person as John Martin, and emphatically and emotionally denied that he [Hall] was the actual murderer. . . ."

Hall did not have a lawyer with him during the questioning. He didn't ask for one, and ultimately an attorney had to be assigned to represent him at his trial. William Rosenthal, a St. Joe attorney, had arrived to represent

Bonnie Heady, but Rosenthal told reporters: "Hall has no lawyer. He didn't seem to want to talk to me. He just sits there and grunts." However, Rosenthal said he had given Hall some advice about his legal rights.

In Chicago, Mrs. Troy Baker learned that her niece was in custody, accused of a terrible crime. It was devastating news for the woman who had raised Bonnie after her mother died. Nellie Baker was seventy years old and appeared to be in poor health. Her face was deeply graven by age and grief, and there were immense dark circles around her eyes. Nevertheless, she came to St. Louis.

The aunt and niece talked for a half hour at the city jail. Afterward Mrs. Baker told reporters: "I don't think she would be involved in this if she hadn't got mixed up with the wrong crowd.

"I just wanted to come down and tell her I was behind her," she said. "Bonnie was an only child. She hasn't anyone in the world but me." Then the elderly woman, loyal and loving, left the jail.

On Sunday night, Hall broke. He made a second confession in which he admitted he had murdered Bobby Greenlease. He said Bonnie had been with him when he killed the child, and he acknowledged that John Martin had not been involved in any way. After days of lying, dodging and twisting, he finally told the whole truth.

Bonnie may have confessed first. If she did, it was surprising, because agent Phil King believes she was the stronger of the two, and because she had held out longer than Hall before admitting the kidnapping. Nevertheless, FBI reports gave this chronology of the developments Sunday night:

Hall was being questioned in the jail's chapel by Hostetter and another FBI man. At 9:35 P.M., a third agent—probably Arthur S. Reeder—came into the chapel. He told Carl that Bonnie had just said she had lost her hat in the field where the child was murdered—and that "she had seen Hall kill the victim."

Hall burst into tears. "It's true, it's true," he said.

And that was it: "She had seen Hall kill the victim." Carl began to talk. He talked and talked, admitting everything.

Why did he confess? For four days, the FBI agents had been calling him a murderer in every language except Swahili, and he had held out. Then one of them came in and told him Bonnie had said he did it. Wouldn't he assume the agent was bluffing—that it was a trick? But he didn't. He assumed it was true. Perhaps he was just worn out. Or perhaps he figured the hat would be found and that would be the end for both of them. The hat must have been a stunning blow. It would place Bonnie at the scene of the crime, and where she was, he was; he wouldn't be able to wiggle out of that one. Or perhaps it was simply the words "Bonnie says" that cracked him open. He was a weak man, Carl Hall, vicious in his deeds and stubborn when cornered, but weak nevertheless, and although he would put her down and say nasty things about her, he was very dependent on Bonnie. They broke him with a few words from her—and her brown velvet hat.

In the confession, Hall told of driving south on Highway 69 to a large farm "with a fence around it and a big lake. . . . We turned west and drove to a big hedgerow, a distance of two miles or so, and turned [into a field] and stopped. There was a large barn there and an airplane behind the barn." This was specific enough for the FBI to locate the field where Bobby Greenlease had been murdered.

A team of agents arrived at the field off Lenexa East Road not long after midnight. Using flashlights, the agents began to search through the wheat stubble. It was difficult work in the dark, but at 2:20 A.M. Monday they found a woman's brown velvet hat, later identified as Bonnie's, and a few minutes later they discovered a plastic pencil with the name of the Greenlease-O'Neill Oldsmobile dealership on it. Bobby had taken the pencil with him when he left the Notre Dame de Sion school with the woman who said she was his aunt.

So the truth was known at last.

But truth creates so many problems it is no wonder people don't use it much. Carl and Bonnie were telling the truth about the kidnapping and murder; there was no question about that. Their confessions were completely convincing, and the FBI was rapidly uncovering a massive amount of physical evidence that ultimately proved their guilt beyond dispute. The new situation rang with truth—and that was the problem. If Hall was telling the truth about the crime itself, was it possible he was also telling the truth about the ransom money? It was a question that nagged at Hostetter and the other agents, tentatively at first, and then, as the days passed, more insistently.

But what was Hall saying about the money? His early statements were a farrago of vague recollections, uncertainties and confusion.

First there was the remark to Ollie Johnson: "I feel relieved. I just shipped out a bundle." Hall insisted this merely referred to the $500 he had sent to Barney Patton for someone. But he had sent the $500 in a letter, not a bundle. Why did he say "bundle" to Ollie? He might have been thinking of $500 as a bundle of money—people do talk that way—but there were other things. There was the man who had mailed a package from the East St. Louis Post Office. There was the strange interlude at the Greyhound bus station, when Bonnie might have been planning to take some of the money to an accomplice in the Dakotas, or ship it there. And there was the mystery man in the Studebaker at Columbo's Tavern.

Then there was the period in which Hall indistinctly remembered looking for a place to bury the ransom. He didn't *think* he ever found a suitable place; he didn't *think* he buried it—but he wasn't sure. He just couldn't remember.

The FBI continued to treat Hall as the chief suspect in the disappearance of the money. He was, after all, the person who had had it in his possession. He was, after all, not sure whether or not he had buried it. Nevertheless, some doubts began to creep in.

Lieutenant Lou Shoulders, who had arrested Hall at the Town House, had a theory about the $300,000. He told the *St. Louis Post-Dispatch* he believed gangsters had stolen it from Carl at the Coral Court motel. Here was a brand-new possibility.

Shoulders and Officer Elmer Dolan had become celebrities, instantly. The newspapers were interviewing them every hour on the hour, they were appearing on television, and their superiors in the police department were issuing statements praising them. When Shoulders talked, people listened. The lieutenant said he felt "certain" Carl and Bonnie had the entire $600,000 with them when they got to St. Louis, and he added: "From my experience and from statements made by the two kidnappers, I feel equally certain that Hall kept the ransom with him until he got to the Coral Court with the O'Day woman. . . .

"All the evidence points to the fact [that] there was quite a party at the cabin that night—more than has been disclosed so far. It appears almost certain that other persons besides Hall, the O'Day girl and the taxicab driver were present.

"Hall was drinking, and he had taken dope," Shoulders continued. "If he had visitors—it wouldn't take long for the hoodlum element to locate a fellow throwing money around like that—they could easily remove half of the $600,000 without his knowing it."

Shoulders' theory carried the implication that Sandy or Ollie might have tipped off the gangsters. The lieutenant speculated that the heist had taken place at the Coral Court, but there was also the possibility that Hall had been the "angel" in Ollie's cab in the middle of the night and that after they left the Chestnut Street bar, Ollie had delivered Carl and the money into the hands of gangsters. Or Hall himself might have hidden half of the money at that time, with Ollie's help. Or . . . or . . . or . . .

After all that, it is a pleasure to clear up one loose end. As a result of Hall's confession, the FBI called off its search for the derelict, John Martin. The agents on the scene had never believed Martin was involved, and now Hall told them "there never was such a person as John Martin." When he was arrested, he said, "he immediately concocted the idea of blaming the actual murder of Bobby Greenlease on some 'fall guy.' "

At ten o'clock Monday night, Carl and Bonnie were spirited out of the St. Louis jail and taken to Kansas City. It was done very quietly, because feelings were running high against them in Bobby Greenlease's hometown, and the authorities were worried that something might happen if people knew they were coming.

Hall, in handcuffs and leg irons, was in a car driven by Deputy U.S. Marshal Leslie S. Davison, with Deputy Marshal Roy L. Kirgan and St. Louis Police Sergeant Tom Fuller as guards. Bonnie was in a second car driven by Marshal Omar Schnatmeier, with his wife and Mrs. Davison guarding her. Bonnie was handcuffed and the cuffs were chained to a metal belt around her waist.

As she saw Carl being put into a separate car, Bonnie exclaimed, "Oh, can't we be together? We have so little time left." She was told regulations did not permit this.

They arrived at the Jackson County courthouse at 3:40 in the morning. "Did you get any rest, dear?" Bonnie asked. "A little," Hall muttered.

They were put in cells on the eleventh floor. Security was tight; although there were about 250 prisoners in the jail, Carl and Bonnie were the only ones on that floor, and five guards were assigned to watch them. Carl's cell was at one end of a corridor and Bonnie's at the other, with six empty cells between them. The furnishings consisted only of a steel cot, a mattress and gray sheets and blankets. A bleak outcome for the master criminal.

Here they would remain until their trial. On the floor above them was a reluctant and unhappy prisoner, Sandra June O'Day.

No one ever successfully accused Louis Shoulders of being the smartest policeman in St. Louis, Missouri. If he had been smart, he never would have mentioned gangsters.

However, Shoulders' theory about the missing money was not the reason

158

a nagging question arose in the minds of the FBI agents—a suspicion that perhaps, just perhaps, Carl Hall was telling the truth about the $300,000. But it was a long time before anyone other than the FBI knew what Hall had *actually* said about the money. The news media, the public and the St. Louis police department were not aware that the FBI had withheld some things Hall had said in his confession. These things, and the FBI's subsequent investigation, raised the nagging question.

However, the two Teds were on the job, which meant the government secrecy was not complete. Theodore C. Link of the *Post-Dispatch* and Theodore Schafers of the *St. Louis Globe-Democrat,* both nicknamed Ted, were tough, persistent investigators, and both were trying hard to crack the remaining puzzle in the Greenlease case. The missing $300,000 put the newsrooms of both papers on a war footing.

The first result was a story on October 17. Not surprisingly, it concerned another mystery man. The story said "authorities" were investigating reports that an unknown man had appeared at the Town House at about the time that Hall and Oliver Johnson got there. Mrs. Jean Fletcher, manager of the apartment building, said she saw the man and was positive he wasn't Hall or Ollie. She described him as a well-dressed businessman type who had black hair and spoke "excellent English." That was all the newspapers could find out about the man at this point, but it was an opening wedge. It turned out that the mystery man at Columbo's Tavern and the mystery woman in a car outside the Town House had nothing to do with the missing money, but the third time is a charm. There was a *real* mystery man *inside* the Town House, and he became a very significant figure indeed.

This was a tantalizing disclosure, but there was a much bigger bang the next day. An abrupt and dramatic development was reported in the search for the missing $300,000. The revelations were sensational, and their implications were dismaying.

The newspaper stories of October 18 were a major turning point in the case. The FBI's secrecy had been penetrated, providing a glimpse of a startling new line of investigation. It was only a glimmer, but it produced a radical change in public perceptions, which is to say, people were shocked. Because the newspapers were suggesting that something might have gone wrong—very wrong—in the St. Louis police department.

DISCREPANCIES REPORTED FOUND BY FBI IN POLICE AC-COUNT OF KIDNAP MONEY said the *Post-Dispatch*'s three-column headline. "Currency said to have been brought in an hour after abductor" was the subhead.

The story began: "Agents of the Federal Bureau of Investigation, who are searching for the missing half of the $600,000 ransom paid to the kidnappers of Bobby Greenlease, have found a number of discrepancies in the police account of the arrest of Carl Austin Hall and the recovery of part of the ransom money. . . ."

The next paragraph noted that the police report on Hall's arrest had stated that the suitcase and footlocker containing the ransom money were brought into the Newstead Avenue station *at the same time* that Hall was brought in.

Then an astonishing third paragraph: "But the FBI has determined that when Hall was taken into the police station, *no suitcases were brought [in] with him,* an informant reported [emphasis added]."

And finally: ". . . More than an hour elapsed . . . before the money-laden suitcases were brought in. . . . [This] is one of the major discrepancies being investigated by the FBI."

That was the heart of it. The police report, written by Shoulders, had said Hall was booked at the Newstead station at 8:57 P.M. and that his luggage was brought into the station *at the same time.* Now the newspapers, quoting an anonymous informant, were disputing Shoulders' version. They were saying the FBI had discovered that the suitcase and footlocker were brought in *more than an hour later.*

If this was correct, where was the golden luggage during that time? Had it been left in Hall's apartment when Shoulders and Dolan took him to the station? Or had it been taken somewhere else? Either way, it could mean the $300,000 was removed *after* Hall was arrested. In that event, he had not hidden the money. Someone had stolen it.

Of course, it didn't *have* to mean that. Hall could have secreted the money somewhere *before* he was arrested, or it could have been stolen from him *before* his capture. If that's what happened, then the delay in bringing in the luggage had two possible explanations: Either Shoulders and Dolan simply forgot to bring it with them, in their excitement and haste, or they decided for some reason to leave the bags in the apartment and go back for them later.

So the Greenlease case, as usual, was full of "ifs" and "could haves" and "might haves." The conditional tense never had a finer hour. However, FBI agents and journalists and citizens could ask themselves some commonsense questions:

Would Shoulders have walked out of that apartment and left behind a suitcase and footlocker full (or half full, depending on the scenario) of money? Could he have forgotten all about the luggage? He was an experienced cop with hundreds of arrests to his credit. And if he didn't actually forget the luggage, could he have made a conscious decision to leave it in the apartment, unguarded, with only a locked door between it and cupidity?

And sure enough, Shoulders insisted he had *not* left the luggage behind. He might be accused of various things, but by God they weren't going to get him for sloppiness. Just before he left the apartment, the lieutenant said, he ducked out into the corridor and handed the suitcase to Ollie Johnson, telling him to take it downstairs and put it in the police car. Then, he said, he went back into the apartment, got the footlocker and carried it down himself. Dolan carried Hall's briefcase, Shoulders said. That took care of all the bags that had money in them (Hall said he had put about $20,000 in the briefcase). The suitcase that Ollie had bought for Hall, to put new clothes in, *was* left behind, Shoulders said. He explained that he had opened this one also and found it empty.

There it was, and Shoulders stuck to it. Nothing could shake him. The bags, he insisted, were brought into the station with Hall, at 8:57 P.M.

And Dolan and Johnson backed him up. They told it just as Shoulders told it. Dolan said the lieutenant "passed [the suitcase] out the door to Johnson" and carried out the footlocker himself, while Dolan carried the briefcase. They then drove directly to the Newstead station, with Hall and the luggage, and took the prisoner and the bags in at the same time, Dolan said. Johnson's version was just as corroborative. He said Shoulders came out of the apartment, handed him the suitcase, and said: "Take it down and put it in the back seat of the police car," and he said that was what he did.

There was no wiggle room in their story. They swore the luggage had not been left in the apartment, which ruled out any chance that someone had stolen the $300,000 after Hall was taken to the police station. So only two possibilities remained:

1. If Shoulders and his companions were telling the truth, the bags were only half full when Hall was arrested. This meant he had hidden the $300,000 himself or someone had stolen it from him earlier.

2. If Shoulders and the others were lying, the bags contained the entire $600,000 when Hall was arrested. The luggage then turned up at the Newstead station more than an hour later, and when it did, $300,000 was missing.

For eleven days, from October 7 to October 18, the public had believed the first possibility was the *only* possibility. When the ransom was counted and it was discovered that half of it was missing, it was immediately and universally assumed that the money had been hidden or stolen *before* the kidnappers were caught. There seemed to be no other explanation. Then came the newspaper stories of October 18. They were Copernicus on the celestial order, Darwin on the origin of man, and television evangelists on morality. They cast a new light on things.

161

Chapter **18**

hy did the FBI challenge Lieutenant Shoulders? What did it have that caused it to doubt the hero of the hour, the intrepid officer who had solved a lurid crime and apprehended two despicable criminals? The agents had two things: the confession and the police station.

1. The confession. It is important to realize that *only* the FBI had Hall's second statement—his admission of murder. The St. Louis police department had no knowledge of what was in it. Nor did the newspapers or the public. They had to rely on what the FBI told them. It was an accurate account—but it was not a *complete* account.

When Carl and Bonnie confessed the *kidnapping,* senior St. Louis police officers were present, but no one from the police department was present when they admitted the *murder.* It was the same with the newspapers. After the first confession, reporters were allowed to question the kidnappers and get their story directly, but there were no interviews or press conferences after the second confession. The FBI simply announced that Hall and his mistress had admitted killing Bobby Greenlease and described the basic details of the murder—but certain things Hall had said were withheld.

The murder confession was announced on October 12, but the information that had been suppressed did not come to light until November 17, when the confession was read in its entirety at the trial of Hall and Heady. For almost five weeks, therefore, only the FBI knew what Hall had said about the ransom money, the luggage and the unknown man at the Town House. If true, it was sensational.

"I am certain that at the time of my arrest, I had about $570,000 in the two suitcases and about $22,000 in my briefcase," Hall told the FBI.

If he was at last telling the truth about the money, it could be very troublesome for Lou Shoulders and Elmer Dolan, of the police, because it would mean he had about $592,000 in his possession when they arrested him. That would be all but about $8,000 of the ransom, which was approximately the amount he had spent in St. Louis.

It was the most specific statement Hall ever made about the money, but the FBI's Grenap squad had to look at it two ways:

On the one hand, there was Carl Hall, the Master Liar. If he had hidden the $300,000 or had shipped it off to an accomplice, he would of course lie and say he had almost all the ransom when he was caught. He would be trying to divert attention away from himself by casting suspicion on Shoulders and Dolan.

On the other hand, he had finally told the truth about the murder, and it was straight stuff. Virtually every fact, every detail checked out as accurate. So, because he had come clean about the murder, the FBI had to consider the chance that he was also speaking the truth *about the money*. That was the possibility that began to nag at Hostetter and the other agents.

· And there was more. The newspapers had got a small whiff of the unknown man at the Town House, but Hall said a good deal more about him, in another portion of his confession that was withheld by the FBI.

As they started to leave the apartment, Hall said, "the large officer [Shoulders] stayed at the door, and the uniformed officer [Dolan] and I walked the entire length of the building looking for the rear steps leading [down] from the third floor.

"We were unable to locate any steps there, and as we turned to go back, looking up the hallway I noticed a man standing at the end of the hallway facing my room. I am not positive, but this man appeared to be talking to someone in the direction of my room, but I was not able to hear any of the conversation.

"This individual was wearing a light tan snap-brim hat, a pair of rust-colored slacks with matching jacket, which was a short jacket gathered at the belt line. This man was about medium height and decidedly slender. I can give no further description of him as I observed only his profile.

163

"I am positive this man was not Oliver Johnson and that I have never seen this individual before. When the uniformed officer and I arrived at the end of the hall . . . this man had disappeared."

Then the luggage. "Neither the money nor the suitcases were brought to the police station with me," Hall said. "I am positive neither of the officers carried any suitcases or [the] briefcase when we left the apartment. . . ."

2. The police station. The conflicting versions collided head-on at the Newstead Avenue station. This was the place they could be checked. The Grenap squad found seven persons—four policemen, a police clerk and two civilians—who had been in the front room of the station when Hall was brought in. The agents questioned these persons. All of them had seen Hall being booked at the front desk. None of them saw any luggage.

The seven were:

Corporal Raymond Bergmeier, who was in charge of the booking desk on the night of October 6. Bergmeier was fifty-one years old and a veteran cop. He signed Hall in and wrote down the preliminary information about the arrest.

Corporal Alexander Magee, who was assigned to a patrol car that night and came into the Newstead station at about 8:30 P.M. to use the bathroom. Magee was sixty-five years old and had been a cop since 1914.

Officer Thomas Crowe, twenty-six years old, a member of the force for three years, who was in the patrol car with Magee and came into the station with him.

Officer Karl Schottler, who was walking a beat that night and also came into the station at about 8:30, to check some information. Schottler was thirty-nine and had been a cop for nine years.

Police clerk Walter H. McDowell, twenty-one years old.

Esther Wells, a twenty-seven-year-old woman who came to the station that night to try to see two friends who had been arrested. She was denied permission to talk to them but was still in the station when Hall was brought in.

Barbara Cupp, seventeen, who came to the station with Esther Wells, on the same unsuccessful mission.

On October 19, the St. Louis police board announced that it would investigate the situation—without knowing very much about it. The newspaper stories of the previous day had cast a sudden dark cloud over the police department, but the stories were short on details. However, they were all the board had to go on; it was unaware of the damning things Hall had said or what the seven witnesses had told the Grenap squad. The cops were compelled to play catch-up ball with the FBI, in ignorance of the inning and the score.

Despite these unsatisfactory conditions, they covered much of the ground. They questioned the people who had been in the Newstead Avenue station and discovered what they had told the FBI:

Chief Jeremiah O'Connell: "When Lieutenant Shoulders came into the station with the prisoner, did he [Shoulders] have anything in his possession?"

Corporal Bergmeier: "No, sir."

O'Connell: "Did he have any grips or suitcases?"

Bergmeier: "No, sir."

O'Connell: "Did you see Dolan with a briefcase?"

Bergmeier: "No sir, I did not see any briefcase of any kind."

It was the same with Corporal Magee:

O'Connell: "Did you see Lieutenant Shoulders and Officer Dolan bring in any luggage?"

Magee: "No, I did not."

O'Connell: "At no time while you were there and they were booking the prisoner or after they placed him in the holdover, you did not see Lieutenant Shoulders and Officer Dolan bring in any luggage?"

Magee: "No, I did not."

Assistant Chief Joseph E. Casey: "Did you see Officer Dolan carrying anything at that time?"

Magee: "No, sir."

Casey: "A briefcase or a suitcase or anything?"

Magee: "No."

A tragic sense began to settle on the police department. . . .

Next was Officer Thomas Crowe, the young cop who was working with Magee that night and came into the station with him.

O'Connell: "Did you see Lieutenant Shoulders or Officer Dolan bring any luggage into the station at any time?"

Crowe: "No, sir."

Patrolman Karl Schottler said he was on the phone checking some information. As he was doing so, he saw Shoulders and Dolan booking a man whom he later identified as Hall. Schottler said he was curious, because "Lieutenant Shoulders bringing in a prisoner was sort of unusual," so he watched what was going on as he talked.

Casey: "You were in a very good position to see the prisoner [and] Lieutenant Shoulders and Patrolman Dolan, and at no time did you see them carrying in any luggage?"

Schottler: "No, sir, I didn't."

Esther Wells and Barbara Cupp were at the station trying to see two friends who were being held on charges of obtaining money under false pretenses. The women spoke first to the turnkey, Lyle Mudd, and then to Bergmeier and Magee, all of whom said they would have to get permission from the captain.

"Where is the captain?" Esther asked.

"He's not in now," said Bergmeier.

So they sat down to wait, although they knew they had little chance. Miss Cupp said she saw Shoulders, Hall and another man come into the station and go to the booking counter. She identified Shoulders and Hall from photos and accurately described the lieutenant's suit and his horn-rimmed glasses. She could not positively identify Dolan's photo, however.

Captain Ola McCallister: "Did you observe whether or not any of the three men were carrying anything?"

Miss Cupp: "I don't recall them carrying anything. I think I would have saw it if they were carrying anything."

Esther Wells said she first noticed the three men when they were standing at the booking desk. She identified Shoulders and Hall but not Dolan.

McCallister: "Did you see any luggage or anything else at the feet of Lieutenant Shoulders or Hall?"

Mrs. Wells: "No."

The women remembered something else. Both of them said Shoulders received a phone call while he was booking his prisoner. They said he talked "for a very short time" and then hung up. He then went to a phone booth a few feet away, and as he did so the phone in the booth rang. Shoulders answered it and again talked for a few moments, the women said. They said they didn't hear any of the conversation.

Shoulders said later that the call was from his girl friend, June Marie George. He said he had told her to call him about their date that night. When she did, Shoulders said, he told her something had come up at the office, he couldn't keep the date, he would drop the car at her house, he would see her later, etcetera, etcetera, the course of true love. The FBI didn't believe any of this.

Thus far, four policemen and two civilians had testified that they didn't see any luggage. That left the young police clerk, Walter McDowell. He was the only uncertain witness.

When he was questioned the first time, on October 21, McDowell said the booking counter was too tall for him to see whether or not Shoulders and Dolan had any luggage with them when they brought Hall in. He explained that his desk was situated in such a way that he did not have a full view of the booking area.

Casey: "In other words, you . . . could [not] tell whether they were carrying luggage at that time?"

McDowell: "No, sir."

At another point, however, he was more definite:

O'Connell: "At any time while you were on duty . . . did you see Lieutenant Shoulders or Officer Dolan bring any . . . trunks or luggage into the station?"

McDowell: "No, sir, I don't remember them bringing any trunks in. The only time I recall seeing any trunks or cases was the next day. . . ."

Then on December 7—six weeks later—McDowell made another statement. "About an hour and 20 minutes" after Hall had been booked, he said, he saw Dolan come in the main entrance of the station carrying "a light green-painted metal valise or suitcase."

McDowell said it was about three feet long and a little over a foot wide. He said, too, that it seemed to be heavy—Dolan had trouble getting it through the door.

Inspector George Parker asked McDowell why he hadn't mentioned this when he was questioned the first time. The clerk said he simply hadn't remembered it until later, and when he did he came forward to amend his statement.

The situation had now become acutely uncomfortable for Shoulders and Dolan. The police board was anxious to question them—but Shoulders called in sick. His physician told Chief O'Connell that the lieutenant was in "a nervous condition" and needed rest. His health might be adversely affected if he had to undergo an interrogation, the doctor said.

But Dolan was available. Twenty-five-year-old Elmer Stephen Dolan, who had been Shoulders' driver on the night of October 6, and had been at his side the entire time. Chief O'Connell summoned Dolan to police headquarters on October 19 for questioning.

The interrogation lasted three hours. O'Connell and other senior officers took Dolan over the details of the arrest again and again, trying to trace the handling of the luggage and find out how $300,000 happened to be missing from it. The questions were skeptical—and later were to be even more so—but Dolan stuck to his story.

He said Shoulders carried the footlocker out of the apartment, and he (Dolan) carried the briefcase. With Dolan holding on to Hall and Shoulders behind them, they went down the rear stairs, came out the rear entrance of the building and walked around to the front, where the police car was parked.

Dolan said Shoulders put the footlocker in the back seat of the car and he tossed the briefcase in with it. He said he didn't actually see what happened to the suitcase, but Shoulders told him he had handed it out the apartment door to Ollie Johnson, who took it downstairs and put it in the police car. At any rate, Dolan said, he happened to look in the back seat of the car when they got to the police station and saw the suitcase was there, as well as the footlocker and briefcase. In other words, they had all three bags with them when they left the Town House and when they got to the station.

(And to cover the few minutes in between, both Shoulders and Dolan insisted they made no stops on the way to the station, that the luggage was never out of their possession during the brief ride, and that no one took anything out of it.)

Dolan's account continued: When they got to the station, Shoulders went in first, holding Hall by the arm. The lieutenant was not carrying any luggage at this point. Dolan was a few steps behind them, carrying the suitcase and briefcase. When they got inside, Shoulders told him to take these bags to Shoulders' office and Dolan did so. He then returned to the front room, where Shoulders was standing with Hall.

As soon as Dolan rejoined them, Shoulders went out to the police car and brought in the remaining piece of luggage—the footlocker—while Dolan guarded the prisoner. Hall was then booked and put in a cell, after which Shoulders took the footlocker to his office and put all three bags in a locker. Then Shoulders and Dolan left the station, to take the lieutenant's car to his girl friend—the gallant gesture that the FBI doubted; by this time it was doubting much about Lou Shoulders.

Captain McCallister: "Relative to this article in the Sunday *Post* [*Dispatch*] . . . wherein it says, 'Currency said to have been brought in [an] hour after abductor.' How long after Hall was brought in were the suitcases brought in?"

Dolan: "Right away."

Chief O'Connell: "Within a few minutes?"

Dolan: "Yes."

On October 26, Dolan was recalled for more questioning. By this time, the police department brass had talked to the four cops who were in the Newstead station that night. The questions, in consequence, were even more skeptical.

O'Connell: "Can you tell me how it would be impossible for Corporals Magee and Bergmeier and Patrolman Crowe and Patrolman Schottler not to see you bringing in this suitcase if they were standing right in [the room]?''

Dolan: ''No, sir.''

Casey: ''You still say definitely that you carried one of those grips into the station?''

Dolan: ''Yes, sir.''

Dolan hadn't wanted to drive for Shoulders that night. And he had been thinking of quitting the police department anyway.

After roll call on the afternoon of October 6, Shoulders stopped Patrolman Karl Schottler. ''Say, Karl . . .'' he began, but before he could finish, he saw Dolan. ''Never mind,'' he told Schottler, and then he beckoned to Dolan: ''Oh, Elmer, come here.'' He told him not to leave the station; he wanted him to be his driver on that shift.

Dolan was not happy about this, because he had planned to duck out after roll call and borrow an hour or two from the police department. He was going to apply for another job—with the American Automobile Association.

He had had it with being a cop, which was a little surprising because he came from a police family. Sure and hadn't his father, Frank Dolan—Cozy Dolan, he was called—been a cop, and his brother, too, and wasn't his mother, Helen, a police matron? Elmer himself had started with the department in 1944 as a telephone operator, when he was not yet seventeen years old, and had become a probationary patrolman in 1949, at the age of twenty-two. His future had looked pretty good; there was his family background for one thing, and he had set a record for rookies by scoring fifty bull's-eyes out of fifty shots on the police firing range.

But after almost four years on the force, he was making only $320 a month—$3,840 a year before withholding tax—and his wife, Mary Frances, was expecting their first child. It was time to get a better job. But he never made it to the American Automobile Association.

Dolan was born on December 20, 1927. He attended elementary school and had one year of high school; his only other education was a two-month accounting course. In later years, he had various jobs, among them regional sales manager for a beer and liquor importing company. He could never escape his past, of course, but he did his best to fashion an ordinary existence: Elmer Dolan, husband, father, provider, a slightly-built, ordinary man, just getting along, nothing unusual or exceptional about him. *Fallentis semita vitae;* the pathway of an unnoticed life—except for the Greenlease case. Dolan died on May 26, 1973, after a heart attack at the age of forty-five. He was survived by his wife, eight sons and a daughter.

169

*O*n Wednesday, October 21, Shoulders unexpectedly appeared at police headquarters. Apparently his nerves were better; at any rate, he announced that he was ready to face the police board. Because he was a bigger fish than Dolan and because the situation was rapidly becoming more serious, it was deemed advisable to bring a lawyer into the picture, which is how it is determined that situations are becoming more serious. Therefore, Herman Willer, the only attorney on the board, did most of the questioning. It lasted six and a half hours.

The police board's investigation, like the FBI's, was secret. No reporters were present, and no information was given out about Shoulders' testimony or that of any other witness. The citizenry knew only that Shoulders had appeared and had been questioned—supplemented by whatever bits and pieces the newspapers could obtain from the public benefactors known as anonymous sources. On January 17, 1954, Theodore Link of the *Post-Dispatch* managed to get a copy of the Shoulders transcript, but this was almost three months after he had testified; many things had happened in between, and the public presumably had made up its mind about Lou Shoulders. After Link's story appeared, the transcript was forgotten for years, until it and more than one thousand pages of other material from the police board's investigation were made available to the author, through the courtesy of I. A. Long, who was president of the board at the time of the Greenlease case.

The crucial question of Hall's luggage can be dealt with quickly: Shoulders' story was the same as Dolan's. He said he gave the suitcase to Ollie Johnson to put in the police car, and carried out the footlocker himself. Dolan carried the briefcase and they went down the rear stairs, with Dolan holding on to the prisoner and Shoulders right behind them. All three bags were in the back seat of the car, the three men sat in the front, and they drove directly to the Newstead Avenue station, not passing Go and not collecting $200. All this was exactly as Dolan had said.

"I know they [the bags] were brought in" with the prisoner, not an hour and twenty minutes later, Shoulders said. He was unequivocal: "Those grips came in with Hall, definitely so."

Thus the lines were drawn: Two cops say they brought some luggage into a police station at 8:57 P.M. or a few minutes before or after, and seven witnesses say they didn't see any luggage brought in. And when the pie was opened, the birds began to sing. And when the bags were opened, three hundred thousand dollars were missing.

But the luggage didn't come first. The interrogation of Shoulders had hardly begun before it took a surprising turn.

Willer: "Have you ever or do you now have [any] financial interest in the Ace Cab Company?"

Shoulders: "I should say not. I have been accused of it."

Willer: "Who has accused you of it?"

Shoulders: "I wouldn't say accused. Let me change that. It has been rumored."

Willer: "You absolutely deny you have any financial connection with Ace or any other cab company?"

Shoulders: "Absolutely not, and if it is checked it can be proved."
Then:

Willer: "Do you know Joe Costello?"

Shoulders: "I have known Joe Costello since 1922. I knew him well while he was driving a cab."

Willer: "Have you been intimate with him in recent years?"

Shoulders: "Not intimate. I have never associated with him since I was a policeman. No one has ever saw him out with me. . . ."

Joseph Costello operated Ace Cab—the company that employed Ollie Johnson. The St. Louis cops considered Costello one of the city's foremost criminals. He was an ex-convict—having been in prison in the 1930's for the burglary of a jewelry store—and in the years since then he had been arrested many times on suspicion of many crimes. In 1958, Captain John Dougherty, a tough cop who headed the hoodlum squad, told a Senate committee that Costello was "known as a top fence for diamonds and so forth . . . diamonds or anything, he will fence anything."

Robert F. Kennedy, chief counsel of the committee, asked Dougherty if Costello was "close to Vitale and [his] mob." John J. Vitale and Anthony G. Giordano were the reputed leaders of the Mafia in St. Louis.

"Yes, sir," Dougherty replied.

Why did Willer suddenly inject the name of Joe Costello into the Greenlease case? Unless there had been an interagency leak, the police did not know Hall had told the FBI he had seen an unknown man in the corridor at the Town House. But it was well known in certain circles that Shoulders and Costello had been friends for years—the circles being police and criminal circles. Presumably Willer had been briefed to ask Shoulders about Costello. And, incredibly, Shoulders himself talked about Costello a few moments later.

Willer: "Did you get a call on October 6 from Mr. [Ollie] Johnson?"

Shoulders: "I got a call at 3:30 [P.M.]. He did not, I am sure he did not tell me who he was."

Willer: "Will you tell me what the conversation was. . . ?"

Shoulders: "He told me he had something real hot, real good. [He said], 'If you meet me around 7:30 around Union and Pershing this evening, I will explain it.' I said, 'Who is this?' He said, 'I will know you and you will know me.'"

Then Shoulders volunteered the information that he had received *another* phone call, and that this one was from someone he *did* know:

Shoulders: "I got another phone call that I recognized his voice. He didn't tell me his name; he didn't have to. . . . I know there will be suppositions drawn from people at this table who have a strong idea of who it is, but I don't want to go on record to say that. Maybe later I can explain.

"I was told by this caller I was going to get a real good pinch, really good. . . . It was to be an insurance embezzler, something big, an insurance embezzlement. . . . He said, 'I will either see you or you will hear from me later on this evening.' He even said, 'Didn't you get a previous call?' and I said yes. I promised him in strictest confidence of not involving him, and I am not going to involve him at this time by name, this person."

172

Not involve him? Who did Shoulders think the police board would assume it was, Benito Mussolini? It has already been explained that the lieutenant's intelligence was not an adornment of mankind, but this was exceptional, even for him. Willer had merely asked him if he knew Joe Costello. Well, yes, he did. He could admit that much without doing any great mischief. The matter might have rested there—if he had simply stonewalled from then on. Let them prove Costello was involved, if they could. Without any help from Shoulders.

Instead, Shoulders *volunteered* that he had received a second phone call from someone whom he knew, and then he refused, protectively, to identify this person but said "suppositions" could be drawn as to who he was. They sure could. And if Costello had been the second tipster, it meant he had known about Hall—and about the money. Given his reputation, the police board would assume he had had covetous intentions. With a single imprudent remark, Shoulders had thrust Costello squarely into the missing-money investigation.

The FBI made the same assumptions, and it had a little more to go on. As soon as Hall told of seeing a man in the corridor, the Grenap squad showed him photographs of various St. Louis gangsters, including Costello. The newspapers reported that Hall had been unable to identify Costello or any of the others as the man he saw, and this was partly true, but What is truth? said jesting Pilate. Years later, former agent Phil King told the author that Hall *had* made an identification after all—but it was extremely tentative. He had more or less picked out Costello as the man he had glimpsed. However, King emphasized that "it was only a half-assed identification. It was never definite." No way was it proof, but it was enough for the FBI to consider Costello a prime suspect from then on.

But that did not end the matter; the Greenlease case was as infinite as ignorance. In addition to Costello, there was *another* unknown man in the corridor that night. Hall did not see him, but someone else did. . . .

Willer and his colleagues tried hard to get the name of the second informant. They did not succeed, but they got some other information along the way:

Willer: "He told you . . . you were to get something hot on an embezzlement?"

Shoulders: "Yes."

Willer: "Did he tell you how?"

Shoulders: "Yes. He said, *'I will have him later this evening.'* I said,

'Where—in the police station?' [He said], *'No, no, in St. Louis'* [emphasis added]."

It was about 3:45 in the afternoon when Costello called Shoulders. At that time, Hall was still at the Coral Court, which was in the suburbs, out of Shoulders' jurisdiction. However, Costello said he would have Hall in St. Louis that evening. How could he have known this unless Ollie Johnson had told him? Ollie had rented an apartment for Hall at the Town House, which was in the city, and he knew Hall intended to go there. Something was being worked out.

Willer [referring to Ollie's call to Shoulders at 3:30—the first tip-off]: "You think he [Costello] was responsible for Johnson getting in touch with you?"

Shoulders: "Yes."

Willer: "Do you think Johnson told him about [Hall] first?"

Shoulders: "I know positively he talked to him."

At six o'clock that evening, while Shoulders and Dolan were eating dinner at the apartment Shoulders shared with June Marie George, there was another call from Costello. Shoulders told the police board this conversation was brief; the informant (Shoulders was still refusing to identify him) merely told him to stand by for further instructions.

At 7:20 or 7:25, Costello called again. This time, he told Shoulders to "get right over to Union and Pershing and . . . meet Ollie Johnson. He will be on the corner. . . . Dolan and I grabbed our coats and went out." Hall was now at the Town House; the trap was set.

Willer then questioned Shoulders for several hours about the arrest at the Town House and the handling of the luggage, and about Hall's confession. At the end, however, Willer came back to Costello, still unidentified but a household name by now. He asked Shoulders if he suspected that Costello had stolen the $300,000.

Shoulders: "I suspected that he knew who stole it. I always suspected."

Then Shoulders began to soar. After it was discovered that half the ransom had vanished, he said, he vowed to do "everything in my power" to find it. And he said his informant did the same. Together, "using the same sources," these two stalwarts tried to track down the missing money.

Still soaring, Shoulders said it wasn't only that he had given his word not to identify the informant; he was also trying to protect him from unnamed menaces at the Coral Court motel. And in his fervor, he let Costello's name slip out at last, together with a reference to his own ephemeral fame:

"What if I get him killed?" Shoulders declaimed. "I had to kill in this

174

department, and it isn't pleasant, and if I want to be responsible and the big shots out at Coral Court, and if Joe Costello gets killed because one time he done me a favor which made me a great guy and the next time a thief . . ."

The Coral Court was central to Shoulders' theory about the money: ". . . I don't think they would ever let him [Hall] get away from there without clipping him, and that prostitute gave him a mickey. See, Johnson was out there twice, and he stated to me that when he took him out there he was drinking with them and he was showing off [the money], and what if she sent him to notify her pimp, or for a mickey? He says she sent him to her house for her clothes. Now Johnson had been laying [a woman] and I believe she used to run a joint over in East St. Louis [and presumably would know some crooks]. . . . I think this steal was made Monday night in [the] Coral Court. . . . I am . . . inclined to believe that this Sandra might have mickied him and then let somebody in there. . . . I do know this, that the FBI found some fellow that was having a party close by and looked out and saw some guy going over a fence."

So that was how it had happened, according to Shoulders. There was a drunken evening at the Coral Court (which was true enough), during which Sandy O'Day slipped chloral hydrate or some other potion into Hall's whiskey, after which she and Ollie Johnson rolled him for $300,000. Or she sent Ollie to her apartment not for clothes but to fetch her pimp (ignoring the fact that Ollie himself was her pimp). Or to tell a woman to get word to some criminals in East St. Louis. Someone then hurried out to the Coral Court, committed the robbery, and got away, via a fence.

Or *was* that the way it happened? Shoulders kept coming back to Joe Costello. Maybe Hall *hadn't* been rolled by Sandra O'Day and Oliver Johnson, in league with some pimp or East Side gangster. Maybe Costello had taken the $300,000 after all.

"Knowing him and the type of thieves he runs with, I can't figure why they took only half," Shoulders said. "[If they] didn't think it was a government case [a kidnapping] but an embezzlement case, why didn't they take it all? The type of people he bums with would kill you for less."

The next day, the *St. Louis Post-Dispatch* disturbed the public again. A front-page headline said: JOSEPH COSTELLO CALLED BEFORE RANSOM PROBE IN SURPRISE MOVE. The newspaper said the police board had questioned Costello for three hours "about his knowledge of the activities of Carl Austin Hall prior to the kidnapper's arrest.

175

"It was reported that Costello, shortly before Hall was taken into custody, made several telephone calls indicating he knew of Hall's presence in the city," the story said. It added that Costello was aware that Hall was spending money freely.

This was big news, startling news, the kind that made people think. And when they thought of Joe Costello, they thought of dark nights and dirty work.

Nonsense, said Costello. It was all nonsense about him being a criminal. He was just an ordinary, hardworking businessman who ran a company that sold gasoline and other supplies to Ace Cab drivers. Then why did people think he was a crook? Costello had an explanation for that—a familiar explanation, a vintage explanation favored by many persons: It was all the news media's fault.

"The newspapers have made me a big boogey-boo," he said. "I don't know why. I know I don't deserve it . . . why do the newspapers always [write] 'notorious St. Louis hoodlum' every time I spit on the sidewalk? . . . every time I am arrested I am a notorious St. Louis hoodlum or a racketeer . . . I have been accused of everything but the Crucifixion. . . .

"I am up at 6 in the morning and I am working around that place [the cab company] as late as 10 or 11 or 12 o'clock at night, and I go out on accidents all hours of the day and night, and work my ass off . . . and still I am a hoodlum."

Criminal or businessman, Costello was called in. The police board wanted to question him. It awaited answers. And awaited and awaited:

Willer: "Now, starting with October 1st of this year . . . have you had any occasion to talk to Lieutenant Shoulders on the phone?"

Costello: "Yes."

Willer: "Can you tell me when you spoke to him on the phone?"

Costello: "I'd rather not answer that."

Willer: "Can you tell me how many times you have spoken to him on the phone?"

Costello: "I would rather not answer that, sir."

Willer: "Can you tell me—you say that you want to co-operate with the police?"

Costello: "Yes, sir, I do."

Willer: "And yet you are refusing to answer these questions."

Costello [cryptically]: "Maybe I *am* co-operating with the police."

Willer: "Are you co-operating by refusing to tell what happened?"

Costello: "I told you I don't want to get myself hurt, and of course I don't want to make you mad, but that's all I am going to tell you."

176

Inspector George Parker: "How do you figure you are going to get hurt by these men on this panel? They are in the police department."

Costello: "I don't trust anybody." . . .

Willer: "Did you talk to Lieutenant Shoulders on the phone—"

Costello (interrupting): "Colonel Willer, I am not going to answer."

This was going to be a difficult case.

Costello said he was refusing to talk because if he did, someone might harm him or his family: "I am afraid if anything gets out of here, they hear I am trying to help you people, me or some of my family will get hurt. . . . I wouldn't be helping my family to get myself put out in Calvary [cemetery]."

The rest of Costello's testimony—if that's the correct word for it—was a mixture of denials and refusals. He denied that Ollie Johnson had told him about a man who was spending a lot of money and might be an embezzler. He denied that he had told Ollie to call Lou Shoulders and tip him off about the "embezzler." And he denied that he had been at the Coral Court:

Inspector Parker: "When is the last time you used the Coral Court?"

Costello: "Me? I am too old for that [he was 47]."

Parker: "Have you visited anyone out there lately?"

Costello: "I am too old for that, Colonel. I am satisfied."

Willer: "Have you . . . been there within the last year?"

Costello: "No, sir. I am satisfied."

It was a quaint tribute to wedded bliss—as the lady said, the peace and quiet of the double bed after the hurly-burly of the chaise longue—but no one really thought Costello had been summoned by Sandra O'Day and had gone pelting out to the Coral Court to roll Hall. No, it was the Town House, not the motel, that was important.

And on that crucial question—whether he had been at the Town House on the night of October 6, whether he was the man in the corridor—Costello was implacably silent. He was willing to say he hadn't been at the Coral Court, but when it came to the Town House he wouldn't say anything at all:

Willer: "When were you last there?"

Costello: "I am going to refuse to answer that."

Willer: "Were you there at any time since October 1st of this year to date?"

Costello: "I am going to refuse to answer that, sir."

On one point, however, he was very talkative, positively voluble. He insisted he had nothing to do with the disappearance of the $300,000. He said it again and again, in a variety of ways:

177

- "I didn't know anything about the case until I heard about it over the radio, and that's all I can tell you. Are you people trying to frame me?"

- "It just so happened that my driver (Ollie Johnson) co-operated with the police and [they] arrested a stinky, dirty son-of-a-bitch that should be killed. I don't know nothing about the case and I don't want to know anything about the money, and if I seen it laying out in the street I wouldn't even touch it. . . ."

- "They [the FBI] checked me from A to Z, they checked my ex-wives, my ex-wives' mothers, they checked where my wife bought the automobile, they checked where I had it financed. They wanted to know what kind of childhood I had. They can check me to doomsday and they [will] find I don't know nothing about it. I don't care if they even checked my grandmother."

- "I don't know anything to tell you, but I will tell you one thing: I don't have to be ashamed to look at my kids, because I don't know a thing about it."

- "Regardless of what anybody says about me, I wouldn't touch a penny of that money. I wouldn't give a shit if my family was starving. If the stinking son-of-a-bitch had to kill that little boy . . . there ain't nothing anybody could do to that son-of-a bitch that would be too good for him. . . ."

Chief of Detectives James Chapman: "And I guess your associates are the finest?"

Costello: "Who are my associates?"

Chapman: "Well, I will tell you about one of your associates: Vitale."

Costello: "Vitale? Where have you seen me associate with him? . . . I am not crazy enough to be seen with Vitale. . . ."

Chief O'Connell: "How long have you known Vitale?"

Costello: "All my life."

O'Connell: "All your life?"

Costello: "Practically. I was born and raised downtown here, and so was he."

178

Chapter **20**

"**W**ho knows what evil lurks in the hearts of men?
"The Shadow knows!"

A sepulchral voice on radio, years ago. Still good for a laugh, due to age. Rock music will be similarly remembered someday, but everything is too late.

As a young cop, walking a beat, Lou Shoulders made it a practice to prowl through back yards and alleys, looking for thieves, numbers runners and other evil. He did this so often and so successfully that the other cops began calling him "the Shadow." As time went on and he was promoted to sergeant and then lieutenant—and started putting on weight—the stealthy forays grew less frequent, but the nickname stayed with him.

A legend of sorts gathered around the Shadow. He was the kind of cop who was talked about—sometimes admiringly and sometimes not. He was tough and courageous—and also dangerous, with at least two killings on his record. He had shoved and slugged his way through the mean streets for a long time; men feared him.

But there was another side to the legend: Shoulders reputedly had been on the take for years. He had been the subject of several departmental investigations—suspected of accepting bribes from pimps, prostitutes and gamblers in return for allowing them to operate freely in his district. Nothing was ever proved, but it was widely believed in the police department and underworld that Shoulders was a crooked cop. Former FBI agent Phil King says flatly: "He was a thief in uniform."

Legends have many sides. When he was seventeen years old, Shoulders married, and when he was eighteen he had a son. There was a divorce, and Shoulders was left with the child. He had little money and less education, but he cared for and raised his infant son. Between father and son there was deep and lasting affection. "He was my old man," says Bruce Shoulders, "and I loved him."

They were farmers originally, first in Tennessee and then in Kentucky. Lou Shoulders' grandfather was named Ensley P. Shoulders, and he had two sons—W. C. Shoulders and Ira Pleman (or Pleam) Shoulders. Ira and his wife—he had married Kate Cox, known in the family as Katie—had their first child on August 26, 1898. They named him Louis Ira Shoulders.

Shoulders' formal schooling was brief. At the police board hearing, he said sorrowfully: "You [Willer] are a lawyer, and I guess that was why you were selected to question me. I have only an eighth-grade education." On another occasion, this time in tears, he said his schooling had ended in the "fifth grade, second quarter." He remembered it down to the quarter.

Sometime after 1900, Ira and Katie moved to St. Louis, where Ira got a job as a streetcar motorman. Streetcars ran on rails and were powered by electricity from overhead wires. They have mostly vanished, since they were unable to pollute. Young Lou went to work as a machinist in a can company.

He was in his teens when he went into the factory and in his teens when he married. His wife's name was Agnes. On March 21, 1917, Agnes gave birth to a son; they named him Bruce Sterling Shoulders. The marriage foundered, and in October 1919 they were divorced.

Bruce Shoulders was sixty-eight years old when he was interviewed for this book, and time had done for him what it does for the fortunate; it had made his memories endurable. "You know," he said, "when I was younger I wouldn't have talked to you or anyone else about that business. But when you get to be my age, it doesn't make any difference what people say. He was my old man, and I loved him."

So he went into memory's albums and attics. He recalled that his mother and father separated when he was about fifteen months old. Agnes left the baby with Lou, and the young father raised his son. Bruce didn't hear another word from his mother until he was eighteen years old. "She called me up one day," he says. "She told me she had remarried."

In 1922, Lou decided to give up the can factory and try hacking instead. For the next three and a half years, he drove a cab. During this time, he met another cabbie named Joe Costello. They became friends.

This Side of Paradise had been published in 1920. The Roaring Twenties had begun—the Era of Wonderful Nonsense, the Jazz Age. But the world of F. Scott and Zelda and Hemingway was not the world of Lou Shoulders and Joe Costello. They had never heard of the Left Bank or stately, plump Buck Mulligan or some goddamn pigeons on the grass, alas. What they knew was a grimy, gritty, hardworking city, a beer-and-sausage city of frame and brick, corner grocery stores and cars with running boards. Men wore straw hats in the scorching summertime and went out to Sportsman's Park to try to cool off by watching the Cardinals or Browns, and people slept on upstairs porches, with electric fans on all night, but jesus, it didn't do any good, and nothing helped in the winter. What else did they know? They knew the Irish and Italians and rednecks labored, sweated, drank, fucked and fought, and the Germans and the big shots downtown had all the money, so screw them. The machine ran the town, people were voted from their last resting place, the cops were paid off, and life was a tough proposition generally; an honest man couldn't get anywhere.

However, the two worlds of the 1920's intersected at some points. Lou and Joe knew about speakeasies, flappers, floozies and hooch—and also the hoochie-koochie (a native dance). And bootleggers, rumrunners, revenue agents, blind pigs, alky, home stills and near-beer, good-time Charlies, big butter-and-egg men, rubes, hayseeds, suckers, con artists, bunco games, craps, five-card stud, ribbon clerks (the guys who dropped out when you raised), bookies, horse parlors, hotel rooms, bellboys, whorehouses, pimps, pussy, clap, syph and blueballs, dance halls, set-up joints (later Joe ran one of those), gin mills, girlie shows and gangsters. Especially gangsters.

Lou and Joe reacted to this rich store of knowledge in ways that were different and yet the same; paradox is God's joke.

In December 1922, Lou married a woman named Melissa. This second marriage was a short one; Melissa sued for divorce after a few months, and

181

the decree was granted in October 1923. They had no children. In September 1927, Shoulders got married again, this time to a woman named Florence. This union, which was the longest, produced three children. When he married Florence, he was no longer a cab driver. In October 1926, he had joined the police department.

In 1937, two young men—Alvin Mott, eighteen years old, and Ray Rusch, nineteen—escaped from a prison in Michigan. It was learned that they had come to St. Louis and were staying at a hotel on Olive Street. Shoulders and other cops went there to arrest them. The kids had guns, the cops had guns, and there was a fusillade of shots. Detective Sergeant Thomas Sullivan was killed, and so was Ray Rusch. His pal, Mott, ran out of the hotel and jumped into a car. Shoulders went after him in another car.

"I shouted to him to pull over to the curb. He ducked his head and made a move toward his belt. We found later he had two revolvers in his belt. I fired one shot from our car. The bullet went through the glass of the [car] Mott was driving, and hit him in the head." Mott died.

Three years later, Shoulders killed a man named Erther Johnson. He said he surprised Johnson in his home, burglarizing it. "I asked him what he was doing there," Shoulders said, "and he started to run for the door. I shouted to him to halt. When he continued running, I shot him in the left leg. He drew a pistol. I fired again, hitting him in the body." Johnson died.

(Elsewhere in the records there are vague references indicating Shoulders may have killed another man at some point, but this could not be verified.)

In the late 1930's or early 1940's, rumors began to circulate about Shoulders. They came into the open in 1943, when the police board and a grand jury investigated the slot-machine racket in St. Louis. The inquiry centered on the Lucas Avenue police district, just north of the downtown area. Eight of the district's nine sergeants were demoted, and some of the higher ranks, including Shoulders, were censured.

The life and death of Buck Newell figured prominently in Shoulders' difficulties. Joseph Newell, known as Buck, was a labor boss who, to increase profits, also ran gambling houses. Shoulders admitted that he had been a frequent guest at Newell's home in Jefferson County, and had often entertained Buck in return. However, he said he broke off the friendship when he learned Buck was a labor racketeer and gambler. Shoulders also admitted Newell had offered him a bribe if he would help one of his relatives out of a jam. Shoulders said he had rejected the bribe, but there was much skepticism about this.

Ingratitude in Jefferson County: The relative then shot and killed Newell.

After his death, an FBI report said, Buck's assets "more or less disappeared." The circumstances "indicated Lieutenant Shoulders might have secured these assets," which included $40,000 in bonds.

As soon as the Grenap squad began investigating Shoulders—sculpting feet of clay for the hero of the Greenlease case—it found a host, a horde, an infestation of informers, tattletales, underworld gossips, stool pigeons and snitches. All of them said the lieutenant was, like themselves, corrupt.

An informant told the FBI he had paid Shoulders "many twenty-dollar bills" over the years in return for doing business without police interference. The business was dice games.

A prostitute said she had paid five dollars a month to each of six cops in the Newstead Avenue district, and she "understood" from other prostitutes that the cops split the money with their commanding officer, Shoulders.

Numerous other whores told of payoffs that they believed were shared with Shoulders. Although they hadn't given him money directly, they said it was understood in the sisterhood that they could not operate unless Shoulders got his cut.

A "PCI" (private confidential informant) told the Grenap squad he knew "positively" that Shoulders had operated two whorehouses on Chestnut Street when he was a sergeant. He said Shoulders was well known for "illegal activities around the city."

An anonymous letter said May Traynor had paid Shoulders $200 a week to allow her to operate her brothel on Forest Park Avenue. The letter writer described Shoulders as "the whoremaster's keeper in St. Louis." (In 1958, May herself testified before a Senate committee and said it was nothing like $200 a week. She said she gave Shoulders "a present" of $25 "every three or four months.")

Other informants told the FBI that Shoulders associated with various gangsters in St. Louis, New York, Cleveland and elsewhere. Joe Costello headed everyone's list, of course, but one source brought in a bigger name. He said Shoulders had "done business" (the nature of which was not specified) with a prominent New York hood who had the unlikely name of Joe Adonis. The handsome lad adored by Venus and Proserpina? No, probably another Adonis.

One of the FBI's most specific informants was a man who had operated a whorehouse in St. Louis in the 1940's. This man had been a driver for the Yellow Cab Company back in the twenties, when Costello was also hacking for Yellow and Shoulders was driving a Black and White cab. The informer had known Joe and Lou in those early days and had kept in touch with them over the years—in the line of business, so to speak. His statements about them were not evidence, but Phil King says the FBI considered his information reliable.

It was certainly reliable as far as the Eleventh Police District was concerned. This midtown area, familiarly known as the Newstead Avenue district, had been "notorious" for years as "a hangout and playground for pimps, prostitutes, gamblers and hoodlums," according to the informant. A superb choice of words; it was an adult playground. During World War II, the recreational facilities became very crowded after dark—and by then Shoulders was the night commander at the Newstead Avenue station.

"[The informant] stated that he never had any specific working arrangement with Shoulders, but that on numerous occasions between 1941 and 1948 he handed out money to Shoulders in various amounts ranging from $50 to $200 at a time. He stated that Shoulders never asked him for money, but it was generally understood that if a person operated in the Eleventh District it was necessary to pay off Shoulders or serve [sic] the consequences by being molested by the police."

The source named several other persons who he said had paid off Shoulders. Among them was a man who operated a hotel on Olive Street a few blocks west of Grand Avenue. The informant "stated that he knows of his own knowledge that [the owner of the hotel] was receiving protection from Shoulders and that [he] was making regular payments to Shoulders."

The memory of this hotel, which had the same name as a famous Civil War general, has been erased by many middle-aged St. Louisans of the utmost respectability. In their youth, they wore smooth the steps leading up to its second floor, in search of life's meaning. Dost thou think, because thou art virtuous, there shall be no acknowledgment? No thin girls who lay fleetingly and awkwardly with thee? No Yvonne or Jill or Penny, with protruding pelvic bones and poor complexions, no "Penny's roommate," the only name she ever had, her existence's sole summation? Nothing for them? No recollection?

Then there was the question of Shoulders' wealth. The St. Louis underworld and many cops, too, were convinced he had accumulated fabulous sums from graft. It was said he had buried Buck Newell's money, it was said he had real estate investments, it was said he played the stock market. It was said, it was said, it was said . . .

The problem was that the FBI couldn't find any of these riches. No bank accounts, no real estate except his home, no safe-deposit boxes, no brokerage accounts. Either Shoulders had concealed his assets very cleverly, which was always possible but didn't seem to be in character, or he didn't have any hidden wealth. The FBI was good at this sort of thing—many of the agents were trained accountants—and it tried hard to determine whether Shoulders was a closet millionaire, but it found nothing.

The investigation began, as is traditional, with the wife. In September 1952—a year before the Greenlease kidnapping—Shoulders and his third wife had separated, after twenty-five years of marriage. Florence Shoulders was preparing to sue for divorce; her petition cited the customary "general indignities," but the specific grounds were desertion—Shoulders had left her and had gone to live with another woman.

"Mrs. Florence Shoulders . . . was interviewed by [two FBI agents], at which time she advised that as far as she could ascertain, Shoulders was always 'poor as a church mouse.' She stated that there were times during their married life that she barely had enough money to buy necessities for herself and her children.

"With regard to her present income from Shoulders, [she] related that [he] had been furnishing her with small amounts of money monthly, and that the payments [were] $75 to $100 to $200 per month. . . . She stated that Shoulders has never paid her by check, and as far as she knows, he maintains no checking or bank account. She stated they do not have a safety deposit box and have not had [one] for a number of years. She advised that she knows of no additional property owned by Louis Shoulders other than his interest in the house [on] Theodosia. . . ."

It was a sad interview.

Shoulders and his wife had lived in a house on Theodosia Avenue for many years. It was in a north St. Louis neighborhood, and its size and magnificence were indicated by its tax assessment. The house, lot and garage were valued at a total of $5,700.

A modest life-style. But perhaps he owned other property. Perhaps he had secretly become a real estate mogul, without notifying Florence. But when the Grenap squad checked deed records in St. Louis and the suburbs, the search "failed to reveal any additional real estate owned by Louis Shoulders. . . ." Either he had purchased it under assumed names or had, like the Japanese, bought up other cities. Or he just didn't own any.

Well, if he hadn't socked his ill-gotten gains into real estate, maybe he had gone into the stock market. The Grenap squad made inquiries at Goldman Sachs, Newhard Cook and ten other firms. The theory was that if Shoulders had been active in the stock market, someone would remember it. How many cops, on their salaries, could afford to buy into the American

185

fantasy? Presumably it would have attracted attention. But no one had heard a thing.

The Grenap squad summed up the results: "Investigation re [Shoulders'] financial status failed to locate assets other than interest in one house [in] St Louis, and money received from pension and retirement funds and loan on car."

But if he had been on the take for years, where had the money gone? In a similar situation involving the unhappy stockholders of the New York Central Railroad, Diamond Jim Brady replied poetically that it had gone where the woodbine twineth. It is possible that Shoulders had a twining bower of greenbacks somewhere, as a refuge in his old age, and that the Grenap squad hadn't been able to find it. But his character argued against this: He was not notably clever and not especially provident. In his later years, there were no indications that he was drawing on hidden reserves to maintain himself in comfort. No Sun City, no condo, no golf eternal. He earned his living by managing some rooming houses—pretty much a janitor actually. FBI agents, checking on him occasionally, would see him wrestling trash cans out to the curb, his big body shrunken, worried about his heart, often breaking into tears if he was reminded of the past. When he had been, briefly, a hero.

So two other possibilities were more likely. The first was that the FBI's underworld informants had exaggerated the bribes and payoffs. Most of them had no affection for Shoulders, and when he got into trouble they were ready to make things worse for him if they could. When the FBI agents came round, they may have remembered the graft as larger and more frequent than it actually was.

The second possibility—since there unquestionably had been *some* graft—was that Shoulders simply spent the money as it came in. It was never really *big* money. It was just tens and twenties and an occasional hundred. It was just bits of money that dribbled in and then dribbled out again, and he used it to pay for the things that a cop's salary never quite covered:

The gas company, the electric company, the telephone company, the insurance company, the mortgage company, the finance company, the doctor company, the dentist company . . .

Finally, the easy life. The extra money enabled Shoulders to hold his own with the easy guys—the guys who always had money in their pockets for a good cigar, a good drink of whiskey, a good game, a good bet, a good suit, a good lay. The guys who didn't have to live from paycheck to paycheck, with nothing left over. The guys who never had a pinched look around their mouths, or worried eyes.

186

He could never be that kind of guy on his salary. And that was the key to Shoulders, the explanation: his salary. As a police lieutenant in St. Louis in 1953, with more than a quarter-century on the job, he was paid $5,000 a year. After withholding taxes and other deductions, he took home $169.10 every other week. The taxpayers got what they paid for.

Chapter 21

*A*t one o'clock in the morning on October 24, a car drove up to a house on Romaine Place in St. Louis. Two men got out, making as little noise as possible, and went up to the front door. At the same time, another car eased into the alley behind the house and parked. The men in the second car did not get out. They sat silently, waiting.

The house was Ollie Johnson's. There had been trouble between Ollie and his wife, ending in a separation, and Ollie had been staying at a cheap hotel. But when he had suddenly found himself thrust into the tumult of the Greenlease case, he had sought the security of his wife and family. A temporary truce had been arranged, and Ollie had come home. He was there now, sleeping.

At the front door, the two men checked their watches. Satisfied that the other car had had time to get into position behind the house, they knocked loudly, disturbing the stillness. Ollie's wife came to the door. She saw two roughly dressed men, one wearing a corduroy jacket, the other in a red shirt.

They told her they were FBI agents. But they didn't look like J. Edgar Hoover's button-down, coat-and-tie boys, not at all. It was the middle of the night, and Ollie's wife was frightened. However, the men showed her their credentials, so she let them in. They went to Ollie's bedroom and woke him up. They talked fast and loud. They were rushing him, trying to give him no time to think.

"Come on, get up," said one of them. "We want you to come down to the office."

Ollie sat up in bed. "Who the hell are you? What are you doing in here?"

"FBI. Come on, get your clothes on. We want you downtown."

"I don't believe you," Ollie said. "Let me see some identification."

The men flashed their credentials at him, but Ollie stayed where he was. In bed, at a disadvantage, but unmoved. Surprisingly in a timid age, he declined to be bullied by loud, confident authority. Or perhaps, having been questioned several times already by the police and FBI, he was just fed up with law enforcement.

"The hell with it," he said. "I'm not going anywhere just because you say so. You want me to go downtown, you'll have to arrest me."

The agents apparently had expected paralyzing fear and a rapid capitulation—the usual result of the dread knock on the door in the dark of night, the menacing secret police, the cowering citizen. Instead, here was defiance, here was the turning of worms—and the possibility of a suit for false arrest. They wanted Ollie to come with them, but they didn't want to arrest him. They hesitated.

"Okay," one of them said finally, "if you want to consider it that way, come on." Ollie's brief resistance faded. He got out of bed and put on his clothes.

Downtown, they got tough again. "We're going to find the money, and you're going to tell us about it," they said.

"I've told you everything I know," Ollie said. "If I had it, I'd give it to you."

The agents didn't believe him. "You know where that money is," they said "and you're going to tell us. This will only take a few more hours. We'll have it all cleaned up by then. *You're going to tell us.*"

"I've told you everything I know," Ollie repeated.

They went at him for eight hours. The night ran down wearily, and daylight came. Ollie could hear the city's morning sounds outside, but still the questioning went on. It was insistently repetitious; Ollie recalled later that the FBI men said over and over that they were going to find the missing $300,000 and "you're going to tell us."

But he did not tell them. If he knew where the money was—or had a pretty good idea—he wasn't talking.

When he got home, his wife told him about the second car that had parked behind the house; he hadn't known about it till then. He may have wondered why the FBI had gone to so much trouble. Did they think John Dillinger was going to burst out of Romaine Place, spitting bullets from every orifice?

It was pretty much like that. Ollie Johnson was only part of a major FBI operation that night. Earlier in the evening, a large force of agents and St. Louis cops had surrounded a hotel on North Broadway and had sealed it off.

This was an old hotel, full of old pensioners and old bums; only the whores were middle-aged. They watched in rheumy-eyed surprise as cops and FBI men swarmed into the lobby and stationed themselves in strategic places, evidently expecting the outbreak of World War III. Some of the raiders rushed into the elevators and then waited impatiently as the ancient machinery bore them slowly up to the eleventh floor.

Emerging at last, they dashed down the corridor and found the room they were looking for. They broke down the door and burst into the room, where they arrested one prostitute, two suitcases and an overnight bag.

The prostitute was called Betty Bradley (her professional name). The FBI had been informed that a man had occupied her room, which was likely enough, and that this man had the missing $300,000. He was said to have stayed in the room for several days, never venturing out.

If there was any truth to this rumor, the man was long gone by the time the agents got there. But Betty *was* there, a blond woman with an arrest record as long as her dreams. Large, rough men surrounded her and began pounding her with urgent questions. Who was the man? Where was he? Where was the money?

She said she didn't know any man who had $300,000; she didn't move in those circles. She knew a lot of men—of course she did, it was natural, a girl had to eat—but no one like that. No, definitely not.

When this failed to satisfy her inquisitors, she grew frantic. She cast around in her mind for someone to finger. She desperately needed a Christian for the lions. So she said she knew a woman who had part of the ransom money and was trying to sell it at a discount. She named the woman and said she had seen the money in her possession.

They took Betty to the city jail, booked her under her real name and left her to languish. The suitcases and overnight bag found in her room were taken into custody because in the Greenlease investigation all luggage was suspect. They contained, generally speaking, Betty's life. That is, nothing.

Meanwhile, the armies of the night went in search of the woman who allegedly had some of the ransom money. She, too, was a whore, and apparently she frequented a hotel on Olive Street. It was the hotel with the famous Civil War name whose owner reputedly had paid off Lou Shoulders; this is called the short arm of coincidence. A group of cops raided this hotel, found five women, and arrested all of them. None of them was Betty's friend. She was never found, but it didn't matter, since Betty had made up the whole thing.

The night was filled with activity. Another group of agents went to a rooming house in midtown, and arrested a man. It is not entirely clear why this individual was picked up, but apparently there had been a tip that he might have the missing money. People were seeing suspicious persons and mysterious occurrences all over town, and the FBI was hurrying from place to place, *va et vient,* trying to track them down.

Other agents went to Slay's Bar, which thought it had seen all it was going to see of the Greenlease case. As related in Chapter 7, Carl and Bonnie had come into this bar on the morning of October 5, shortly after arriving in St. Louis. Now the FBI, pursuing another rumor, swooped down on Slay's and arrested one of its employees. The man, who was an ex-convict, was questioned and then released.

Altogether not the FBI's finest hour. In a fast-moving series of raids, two hotels, a rooming house, a bar and a private residence (Ollie's) had been entered, nine people had been arrested and others had been badly frightened, for which they could thank J. Edgar Hoover, although their gratitude was restrained. And it was all for naught; the raids produced no trace of the missing money.

Betty Bradley was charged with giving false information to the FBI. Her bail was set at $1,000, which she did not have. She stayed in jail for five days, until a professional bondsman with the memorable name of Sam Silk put up the money. Betty was released and disappeared from the narrative.

On October 25, Lou Shoulders resigned from the police department. "After 27 years as a police officer," he said, "to be castigated and have my character assassinated, on the heels of performing my duty with the highest sense of responsibility, is more than I can endure with any degree of self-respect and pride."

Then he talked to the newspapers, bitterly. He said the police board had no business investigating him: "I don't think this hearing should ever have taken place. There are always discrepancies in a case like this [the vexatious question of Hall's luggage]. They are honest discrepancies, not . . . an effort to hide anything. Police reports are made by policemen, not lawyers.''

The law was moving rapidly to punish the murderers of Bobby Greenlease. On October 27—three weeks after the capture of Carl and Bonnie—a federal grand jury convened in Kansas City to consider indictments against them. U.S. Attorney Edward L. Scheufler, who presented the evidence, said the jury would ''go into all phases'' of the crime. It quickly became clear that this meant not only the kidnapping and murder but also the missing ransom money.

The jury summoned Shoulders, Dolan, Oliver Johnson, Sandra O'Day and Joe Costello. For the first time, the leading characters were assembled in one place and questioned about the missing $300,000. Shoulders was interrogated for three hours, Ollie Johnson for three and a half, Sandy for two hours, Costello for more than an hour (and a week later he was recalled for more questioning).

Shoulders refused to tell the waiting reporters anything about his grand jury testimony. ''Not one word about the case,'' he said. ''I'll talk about the weather if you want to.'' The media tried a different tack; they asked how things were going for him in St. Louis. ''Things aren't so good for me in St. Louis any more,'' the big cop said sorrowfully.

Costello had nothing to say to the press; he said he had been sworn to secrecy, and anyway he was in uxorious haste to get back to St. Louis: ''My wife is expecting a baby.'' Ollie Johnson said he had agreed not to discuss his testimony, but he indicated that the jury had taken him step by step through the twenty-eight hours he had spent with Carl Hall.

When it was Sandy's turn, the reporters and photographers displayed remarkable devotion to duty; the people's right to know was paramount. Except for Bonnie Heady, who was close to the mysterious age at which the media lose interest, Sandy was the only woman in the case. The press jostled and pushed and tumbled all over itself to shout questions and take pictures as U.S. marshals rushed her into the grand jury chamber. The public, too, was fascinated; some three hundred persons gathered at the Federal Building to see the beautiful blond witness—they are always beautiful and blond—and others leaned from windows to catch a glimpse.

And Sandy *did* look good that day. It was her first time out of jail in three weeks, and she had taken pains with her appearance. She was wearing a powder-blue suit, a light-blue off-the-face hat, and handcuffs. Her hair was freshly washed and neatly combed. At first she was annoyed by the photographers—she was unaccustomed to media events—and said some unladylike things about them, but later she relented and agreed to an interview. In response to the most important question, however, she said she had been unable to tell the grand jury the whereabouts of the missing $300,000.

"They asked me about it time and time again," she said. "I have to tell you [the reporters] the same thing I told them. I simply don't know anything about it."

On that same day—October 30, 1953—the grand jury indicted Carl Hall and Bonnie Heady for the kidnapping of Bobby Greenlease. The indictment consisted of one paragraph.

The grand jury charged that "the defendants on or about September 28, 1953, did unlawfully, knowingly, wilfully and feloniously transport in interstate commerce from Kansas City, Missouri, into the state of Kansas one Robert Cosgrove Greenlease, Jr., who had theretofore been unlawfully seized, confined, inveigled, decoyed, kidnapped, abducted and carried away for ransom, reward or otherwise, and that the said Robert Cosgrove Greenlease, Jr., a minor, was not liberated unharmed by the defendants."

Not liberated unharmed? How delicate. Why not say the child had been murdered? The reason was that murder was not a federal crime—and still isn't except for a few categories. It is a state crime. The federal law on kidnapping is based on the federal government's constitutional jurisdiction over interstate commerce—the transporting of goods or persons across state lines. (The Mann Act, relating to interstate transportation of persons for immoral purposes, is another example.)

The indictment of Carl and Bonnie was brought under the so-called Lindbergh Law, which had been enacted after the kidnapping and murder of the infant son of aviator Charles A. Lindbergh in 1932. It made kidnapping a federal offense if the victim was taken across a state line, and it provided for the death penalty if the jury recommended it.

Four days after the indictment, Carl and Bonnie were brought into a federal courtroom in Kansas City to be arraigned and enter their pleas. They were heavily manacled, their handcuffs fastened by chains to thick belts around their waists. However, they had been spruced up for the occasion. Hall was wearing a suit and tie, and his hair was freshly trimmed and slicked back; with a white handkerchief tucked neatly in his upper pocket he looked almost natty. Bonnie wore a brown gabardine suit and platform shoes. Neither she nor Carl seemed nervous, but Bonnie occasionally turned in her chair to look at the spectators in the crowded courtroom; reporters had noticed before that she seemed to enjoy being the center of attention.

U.S. District Judge Albert L. Reeves gaveled the hearing to order at

1:30 P.M., and two attorneys representing the defendants came forward. One was Marshall K. Hoag of Pleasanton, Kansas—Hall's hometown. Hoag had known Carl for years and had helped him settle his mother's $200,000 estate. Bonnie's attorney was Harold M. Hull of Maryville, Missouri, who had represented her in her divorce and had been administrator of her father's estate. Neither lawyer had a criminal practice; they said they didn't know whether they would represent Carl and Bonnie at the actual trial. But they were here today, and Judge Reeves asked them whether the defendants were ready to plead.

"Mr. Hall wishes to plead guilty," Hoag said.

"Mrs. Heady wishes to plead guilty," Hull said.

Until this moment, it had not been known for certain how Carl and Bonnie would plead, although "guilty" had been widely expected. Now it was official, and the courtroom fell into sudden heavy silence, death having entered.

The silence was broken by U.S. Attorney Scheufler. He briefly reviewed the circumstances of Bobby's kidnapping and murder, which he described as "premeditated, brutal and cold-blooded." Then he explained that there would be a trial, but because of the guilty pleas its only purpose would be to determine the punishment. However, even though the jury would not decide guilt or innocence, the prosecution and defense would present evidence and testimony, to aid the jurors in fixing the penalty.

Under the Lindbergh Law, Scheufler said, the jury could recommend the death penalty, life imprisonment or imprisonment for a lesser number of years. The judge could not sentence Carl and Bonnie to die unless the jury recommended it. If it did not, the maximum sentence he could impose would be life in prison.

"I would be derelict in my duty if I did not recite this [the jury's options]," Scheufler said. But he added that the evidence clearly demanded the death penalty.

Judge Reeves set November 16 as the trial date. That was less than two weeks away. Reeves would preside.

The judge was eighty years old. He had been on the federal bench for thirty-one years, and this would be his last major trial; he retired the following February. Before the Greenlease case thrust him into prominence at the end of his career, he had been known chiefly for his role in the downfall of the Pendergast political machine in Kansas City, and as the judge who presided at the espionage trial of Judith Coplon.

194

His face was long and narrow, his white hair was combed uncompromisingly flat across his head, his lips were thin and usually clamped severely together, and he wore rimless glasses. But he was not a caricature of puritanical righteousness; he was the real thing. He was an upright, old-fashioned man from a small Missouri town (appropriately called Steelville), a God-fearing soul who had once taught the largest men's Bible class in the nation, and a lifelong Republican from an era in which Republicans were the "good folk," the solid, virtuous, respectable folk, and only the town drunk voted Democratic. There were no moral struggles within Albert Reeves; a thing was either right or wrong, good or evil, with nothing much in between.

That would do admirably for Carl and Bonnie, but morality is hard on lesser sinners, unless they preach it on TV.

Chapter 22

*O*ctober 25:

"... tell you why I called. I heard you was short on dough—you know I'll always be glad to help. How about it, you short?"

"Nah, I don't want to ask nobody, you know that."

"C'mon, don't kid me, okay? That fucking pension, that's gonna set you up for life, huh?"

"Well, I sure could use some, and that's the God's truth. Things are tight as hell. I ain't got one nickel to my name right now. . . ."

"... listen, that stuff about me calling you—"

"Well, I didn't tell 'em—"

"—you know, they're blowing it out their ass that I tipped you off. I don't know where the hell they're getting that stuff. I can't help it if somebody used my name—you know, calling you up and saying it was me—"

"I know. I know you can't. Well, I sure as hell didn't take that money. For God's sake, June was down there [at the police station], and she saw it [the money]."

"I know you didn't have nothing to do with it. You're just a fall guy.

196

Now listen, you know I never talked to you about any of that stuff till that guy was arrested. . . . Now, look, if you're short I could give you a job, manager or something. . . .''

November 17:
". . . You know that business about Hall saying he didn't see no bags brought out? . . . Well, he's probably telling the truth all right, because I was very careful about that. He never did see Ollie bring the one bag down, and I stayed behind Elmer the whole time. I had him covered, see? He couldn't see a goddamned thing. He didn't see those bags brought out—he's telling the truth about that.''

"I think you handled it very shrewd.''

"I'll tell you something else. He says he didn't see me and Elmer bring them suitcases in the station. Well, how the hell could he see anything from where he was? He couldn't see anything from the station out to the front—he couldn't see shit. . . .''

November 24:
". . . I'll tell you what I think. I think somebody got that money out at the Coral Court.''

"So do I. I'm with you on that. They're barking up the wrong goddamned tree. They ought to be out there nosing around—knock hell out of some people.''

". . . They never have been checking anybody in East St. Louis, you know that?''

"They better start investigating some pimps.''

"Some big ones should be investigated, but they ain't doing it. Shit no, and you know why?''

"I know all right.''

"They're not gonna do it because they're so goddamned anxious to pin it on us. . . .''

In October, the FBI installed a listening device in Joe Costello's telephone at Ace Cab. However, Costello soon found out about it. The FBI then removed the bug, *while Costello watched them. And then the FBI immediately installed another bug in the same phone, and Costello watched them do that, too.*

197

When he learned his calls were being monitored, Costello called the telephone company and demanded that the bug be removed. Two men came to his office to investigate his complaint. One of them was a bona fide telephone man. They examined Costello's phone and then spoke blandly. Why, yes, there does seem to be something wrong. Well for heaven's sake, look at this: It's an electronic device.

Costello had recently purchased a larger desk. He said he wanted his phone purged of bugs and then installed on the new desk. The experts went to work, dazzling the customer with modern technology. Zip, zip, the bug was removed. Zip, zip, the phone was transferred to the new desk. Zip,zip, a new bug was installed.

The FBI agent then informed Costello solemnly that his phone was now clean. They train them to keep a straight face.

In November, Costello went into Faith Hospital in St. Louis for an operation. While he was there, the FBI tapped the hospital switchboard. This tap produced the startling information that Costello had an informant in the telephone company who had told him sometime previously about the bug on his office phone. Thus his complaint to the phone company.

Meanwhile, the second bug was humming along—and Costello remained deeply and properly suspicious. A source told the FBI that Costello was "certain that his telephone lines . . . are tapped." The source added that Costello had "called him from the cab company and [had] made statements as though he were broadcasting for the benefit of a third party. . . ." Shoulders, too, suspected his phone was tapped, and so did Elmer Dolan.

This exposed a central weakness: Wiretapping does little good if the victim believes he is being overheard, and takes evasive action. It requires only a modicum of acting ability, and Joe and Lou had a modicum. They were not professionals—they often sounded stilted and artificial as they delivered their lines—but the excerpts at the beginning of this chapter show that they were doing their best to divert the audience.

The hero is a courageous but unfortunate former policeman, played by Louis Shoulders. He is in need of money, not a nickel to his name, so how could he possibly have stolen the $300,000? Enter a faithful friend, Joseph Costello, who inquires solicitously about his financial condition. I will offer you a job, says the friend, to rescue you from your plight.

But the friend is involved in a subplot of his own. The audience understands, from a prologue, that two finks had told Shoulders about a suspicious man who had a lot of money. One of the finks was Oliver Johnson, but Costello wants everyone to know he was not the other one.

(Later, a new character named Buddy Lugar will be introduced as the second fink; he is dead.)

Returning to the main theme, Lou and Joe strongly imply that mysterious villains called pimps probably stole the $300,000. They attempt to convince the audience that the pimps should be sought in East St. Louis, a nearby village. But they agree, sorrowfully, that this opportunity will probably be lost. Instead, Lou and Joe will be unjustly accused.

There was no applause. The FBI didn't believe a word of it. Moreover, it knew that Joe and Lou knew they were speaking to a tape recorder. With everyone in the know, why bother? Well, there was always the possibility of a slip, an unguarded remark that might lead somewhere. The Grenap squad played a waiting game. The bug on Costello's phone was installed in October 1953. When agent Phil King left St. Louis in 1962, the bug was still there. Nothing had turned up.

Women. Were Bonnie Heady and Sandra O'Day going to be the only women in this case? There had to be some others; they are found everywhere. What about the blond woman in Chapter 13, the woman Hall had seen when Shoulders and Dolan brought him out of the Town House? She was sitting in a car, looking around as if interested in something. Shoulders told Hall that a woman had called the police to complain that a man at the apartment building had a gun. Was it possible Costello hadn't been the second fink after all? Could it have been the blond woman?

No, it couldn't. The FBI and St. Louis police located the woman. Her name was Viola B. Freeny, she was a waitress, and on the night of October 6 she was sitting in her car near the rear entrance of the Town House, waiting for a friend to get off work.

As she waited, Mrs. Freeny saw three men come out. She recognized one of them: Lou Shoulders. She explained that Shoulders had been a customer at a restaurant where she worked. Apparently she remembered him the way some other people did. "Who wouldn't know the big brute?" she said. The two men with him, she added, were a uniformed cop and a civilian, neither of whom she knew.

Then the crucial point: Mrs. Freeny said she saw all three men clearly—and none of them was carrying anything. No luggage, nothing. And the time was right, too. She remembered that it was between 8:45 and 9:00 P.M., because she was planning to listen to *Fibber Magee and Molly* on the car radio at 9:00. Shoulders and Dolan booked Hall at the Newstead Avenue station at 8:57 P.M.

199

Mrs. Freeny's statement was important. Seven persons had seen Shoulders, Dolan, and Hall come into the station, and none of them had seen any luggage. Now here was a witness who had seen them come out of the Town House and had not seen any luggage either. This supported Hall; he said the suitcase and footlocker were not brought with them when they left the apartment. Things seemed to be tightening up.

And then they seemed to come loose again. The St. Louis police were told that another woman had seen three persons loading some luggage into an automobile at the rear of the Newstead Avenue station early on the morning of October 7—the morning after Carl and Bonnie were arrested. This opened up a startling possibility: Had the missing $300,000 been stolen *at the police station*? Had it then been hidden somewhere in the station during the night of October 6–7 and smuggled out the next morning in some other luggage?

(Five pieces of luggage already had figured in the Greenlease investigation. The possibility that some more bags might be involved was almost more than flesh and blood could bear. Nevertheless, it would have been necessary to take the money out of the station in other bags because Hall's suitcase and footlocker were in the possession of the FBI from about 1:00 A.M. on.)

The woman's story actually created two possible scenarios:

1. The $300,000 could have been removed from Hall's luggage at the police station before the ransom was counted, then hidden in the station, transferred to other bags and taken away the next morning.

2. Or the $300,000 could have been stolen from Hall's bags *before* he was brought to the station—and then for some reason the money also was brought to the station, hidden there and then taken away in the morning. But this arrangement seemed tortuous beyond human comprehension. Why take the money to the station *after* it had been stolen, and then take it away again? Had some indecisive criminals been at work here? Perhaps an attack of conscience: We stole the money but we've decided to bring it back. Followed by a new resolve: No, we're going to keep it after all.

To say that the woman's story complicated the investigation is to win the Nobel Prize for understatement. If the money had been stolen at the Newstead Avenue station, then everyone who was in the station at any time that night—every cop, every civilian, even the FBI agents—would come under suspicion. Up to now, there had been only five major suspects—Shoulders, Dolan, Costello, Ollie Johnson and Sandra O'Day. But more than fifty cops, for example, had been in and out of the station at various times that night. The investigation could become a confused hue and cry involving scores of people.

The woman's name was Katherine Polke, and she was a refugee from Nazi Germany. Her experiences made her extremely reluctant to go to the police and tell what she had seen. Because of what she had undergone in the Third Reich, a police report said, "Mrs. Polke is afraid of all police officers and [is] highly nervous." An FBI report said she was afraid that if she got involved with the authorities, "she probably would be shot."

However, she confided in a friend. The friend, Eva Wilmont, worked for a prominent St. Louisan named Ethan Shepley. Although it is not certain, Shepley apparently persuaded Mrs. Polke to go to the police. Finally she agreed to. Because she spoke only a few words of English, Mrs. Wilmont served as interpreter.

About 8:00 A.M. on October 7, Mrs. Polke said, she was taking a shortcut through an alley alongside the Newstead Avenue station. She saw two cars parked in the alley, close to the station. A man and woman were trying to put a large brown suitcase or trunk into one of the cars. They "were very intent and appeared to be in a great hurry," Mrs. Polke said. A second man was on the other side of the car and seemed to be putting something—perhaps another suitcase—into the front seat.

Mrs. Polke said one of the men looked up, saw her watching them and "grimaced [at her] severely, which indicated to her that he was probably angry." She said she became "very frightened," so she turned around and walked rapidly out of the alley. As she did so, she heard both cars drive away.

The FBI lagged behind the St. Louis police on this one, but after a while it, too, found out about Mrs. Polke. Agents questioned her and showed her several photographs of suspects. She couldn't identify the woman at all, but she said photos of Shoulders and Costello "somewhat" resembled the men she had seen in the alley. However, she was extremely tentative. It was not a positive make at all, and she said she didn't think she would be able to identify the people in the alley if she saw them again.

There was no nourishment in this. It was sparrow soup, in which a pot of water is boiled, a window is opened, and a sparrow flies over the pot. The FBI probably would have dismissed Mrs. Polke's story as another of the many coincidences that bedeviled the Greenlease investigation—except for the window. There was a rumor about the window in Shoulders' office at the Newstead Avenue station.

According to the rumor, an unidentified cop was in the assembly room on the second floor of the station on the night of October 6—the night Hall was arrested. From this room, he could see the courtyard at the rear of the station. On the first floor, also overlooking the courtyard, was Shoulders' office.

The cop, it was said, saw a police car or a private car—the reports differed—parked in the courtyard. He saw someone take two suitcases out of the car and pass them through the first-floor window into Shoulders' office.

Like Mrs. Polke's story, this could change everything. The cop was supposed to have seen the suitcases come in the window at about 10:30 P.M., which was more than two hours before the ransom money was counted. During that time, someone could have got into Shoulders' office, removed the $300,000 and either spirited it away immediately or hidden it in the station overnight. And if some suitcases had come into the station through Shoulders' window, other suitcases could have been taken out the same way the next morning—and been seen by Mrs. Polke.

Of course, it was as improbable as social justice. Some person or persons had entered Shoulders' office, had scooped $300,000 out of Hall's suitcase and footlocker, and had made off with the loot—and no one had seen them do this? No one had seen a huge bundle of money being carried around the police station? (What's that you've got? Oh, this? It's my overtime.) Or if the money had been put into some replacement suitcases that had been speedily and providentially obtained, no one had seen a thief or thieves toting them around the station, looking for a place to hide them? No one had seen them being hidden? No one had seen them being passed out of Shoulders' window the next morning? In a busy police station full of cops, with people coming and going all the time, no one had seen *anything*?

Still, as implausible as it seemed, it had to be investigated. Every cop who had been in the station at any time that night was interviewed— fifty-two of them. Each was asked whether he had been in the assembly room and if so whether he had seen the suitcase-window incident. If not, did he know anyone who had seen it? Did he know anything at all about the rumor? Every answer was negative. The mystery cop was never found.

Many years later, it became clear that the suitcases-into-the-window rumor wasn't true and the alley episode reported by Mrs. Polke had nothing to do with the missing $300,000. In the meantime, however, both of these puzzles were put in the unsolved file, since there wasn't anything else to do with them. The investigation then shifted back to the shorter, tidier list of suspects. Whereupon, two new difficulties were encountered: the gro-cer's story and the old lady's story. Flesh and blood would have to endure suitcases a little longer.

The grocer had a small store across the street from the Town House. Shortly before 9:00 P.M. on October 6, he said, he saw three men come out the front door of the apartment building—and all three were carrying suitcases. He said he was positive one of the men was Shoulders, but he was equally positive that Elmer Dolan was not in the group. And he was fairly sure that Carl Hall and Oliver Johnson weren't, either.

The grocer had closed his store for the night and was walking to his nearby apartment when he saw the three men. "I was right in front of the [Town House], and I'm sure one of the men was Shoulders," he said. "He was in civilian clothes, had on a black tie and was wearing tortoise shell glasses. I was within two feet of him, and the lighting was good. He was carrying a shiny black suitcase.

"He crossed to the north side of Pershing to a car parked there. The other two men . . . walked . . . to the southwest corner of Union and Pershing. They were also in civilian clothes but were smaller than Shoulders. Neither was handcuffed. One man carried a two-suiter piece of luggage. The other had an ordinary-size suitcase and a briefcase."

The grocer put the time as shortly before 9:00 P.M. He said he was sure of this because he watched the beginning of the Veiled Prophet Ball on television when he got home, and the telecast began at 9:00. Like Mrs. Freeny's story, the time was right.

The grocer was sure Shoulders was one of the three men, but he was also sure Dolan wasn't; in that case, where was Dolan? Moreover, he said none of them was in uniform, whereas it was certain that Dolan was wearing his uniform that night.

Another problem: The grocer said the three men split up, with Shoulders going north and the other two southwest. But Shoulders, Dolan and Hall all said they rode to the police station together, in one car. Lastly, the grocer said they came out the front door of the Town House—but Shoulders, Dolan, Hall and Mrs. Freeny said it was the rear entrance.

Despite these discrepancies, the grocer's story appeared to be enormously helpful to Shoulders and Dolan on one key point: He said the men were carrying luggage. Hall and Mrs. Freeny said they weren't; Shoulders, Dolan and now the grocer said they were. That made it three to two for luggage. It was a narrow margin, but perjury raps have been beaten with less. Of course, there were seven witnesses who said no luggage came into the police station with Hall.

Now the elderly lady. She was seventy-one years old, and she lived at the Branscombe Hotel, a few doors from the Town House. She told the FBI she had been taking a walk in the neighborhood on the night of October 6, just before 9:00 P.M. She was about seventy-five yards from the Town House when she saw "two or three men" come out the front door, carrying luggage. It was now four to two for luggage.

She said she probably wouldn't have paid any attention to the men had it not been that they were in such a hurry, almost running. She said two of them went east, toward Union Boulevard, but she didn't see where the other went. Nor could she describe the men, although she didn't think any of them were in uniform.

The front door and the strange disappearance of Dolan's uniform were problems here, as they had been with the grocer. A larger problem, however, was that the old lady was dotty. Her brother told the FBI she had had "a complete collapse" five years before, and was inclined to hysteria. Her doctor said she had suffered two strokes, her mind was impaired and she had a tendency to delusions and fantasy.

For that reason, her name has been withheld from this narrative—and so has the grocer's. Because when the FBI took a closer look at him, according to Phil King, it turned out that he, too, was "peculiar." It was possible that both of them had seen some men near the Town House that night, carrying luggage. Then they heard about Hall's capture, and their imaginations, like China under Mao, took a Great Leap Forward. They would not be good defense witnesses after all.

*I*t was the oldest established seraglio in St. Louis, and so was its madam. It was conducted quietly and along classic lines: no fights, no spitting on the floor. No abductions, either. During its best years, there wasn't much walk-in trade; the customers would call ahead and specify what ecstasies gave them ecstasy. The madam had a little book, and when the client arrived, a suitable girl would be waiting for him. Many of the visitors were affluent; they could afford to stay two or three days and often did. When the New York Yankees were in town to defeat the St. Louis Browns, the mighty Babe Ruth would hit as many home runs as he felt like, and then he would go to May Traynor's whorehouse. His procedure there was as follows: He would screw every girl in the place, and then he would eat several pieces of cold corn on the cob. Ecstasy.

May's bordello was located at 4021 Forest Park Avenue, in midtown. The date of its founding is not certain—there was no ceremony—but at the time of May's murder in 1961, the St. Louis police said she had operated at that address for nearly forty years, so she must have started in the early 1920's. From time to time, some unbribed cops would raid the place, and then there would be fines to pay or perhaps May would be shut down for a while. But she always reopened. She never gave up, she kept the business going through good times and bad, she paid her bills and her taxes, met her payroll and payoffs and looked after her employees: an unyielding capitalist, a tribute to free enterprise.

Along the way, she had become a friend of Joe Costello, and this gave her the biggest trouble of her life; in fact, it may have killed her. In the underworld, it was said she was Costello's aunt, but May herself told a Senate committee that she was Costello's wife's aunt, by marriage. Actually, there may not have been any family relationship at all, but there was no doubt that May and Joe had been close friends for many years.

In the early phase of the investigation, when Carl Hall had been the chief suspect in the disappearance of the $300,000, the FBI's search had concentrated on places where Hall might have hidden the money. But when attention shifted to Shoulders and Costello as the more likely culprits, the Grenap squad was confronted with a different and vastly more difficult question: Where might Costello have hidden it? Unlike Hall, he had spent his entire life in St. Louis. The city had endless hiding places and willing accomplices for Joe Costello.

Of course, this was not the only possibility. Instead of hiding the money, he might have disposed of it by selling it, at a discount. The FBI was well aware that the missing $300,000 might have passed quickly into other hands and been taken elsewhere. It might not be in St. Louis at all but in some other city or even in a foreign country—laundered in Las Vegas, dry-cleaned in the Bahamas or stored anonymously with the Swiss. Nevertheless, Costello might have held on to the money and hidden it somewhere in St. Louis.

He boasted that the $300,000 would never be found in his house. He did this, of course, in the context of avowing his innocence; it wasn't there because he hadn't stolen it. He was heard to say, apparently in one of the wiretapped conversations: "I'll tell you and anybody else—they can take my house apart brick by brick, with my permission, and they won't find no kidnapping money around me."

But an informant told the FBI he had been in a tavern with Costello one night, and after a couple of drinks Joe had said some things about May Traynor. One of them, according to the informant, was that May had "a hiding place in [her] house that no one could find."

The informant said "there is no doubt in his mind that May Traynor knows the complete story as to the missing ransom money and that her place would be a logical place to hide [it]."

Logical, yes, but how to find out? There wasn't enough evidence to persuade a judge to issue a search warrant; it was all hearsay. And apparently the FBI didn't do a bag job—a surreptitious break-in. The conditions weren't favorable, since May's house was seldom empty. Or if they did, they found only the rumplings and stale smells of bliss.

Instead, the agents tried to locate prostitutes who had been working for May in October and might have overheard her say something about the money. They found a whore named Marie, but she said she had left before the Greenlease case broke. Well, who else was working there when you were? She named five women: Pat, Shirley, Nancy, Jerri and Juanita. However, she said the last three had worked for May only briefly.

So the agents concentrated on Pat and Shirley. They learned their real names, but even then it was hard to find them. The Grenap squad learned that Shirley had left May's place and then returned, but the files do not indicate whether she was interviewed. She was from Mount Vernon, Illinois, a small town in the southern part of the state, and she was described as "a very young, attractive girl," and that was her entire biography. As far as can be determined, the other prostitute, Pat, was never located.

So this led nowhere, but May continued to be a major target of investigation. The St. Louis police were putting the heat on; cops were stationed outside her house, asking people why they wanted to go in, which often caused them to decide they didn't. Even the laundryman, May said, was afraid to make deliveries, which created a professional difficulty. Costello, according to an informant, complained bitterly that May was being harassed. And May said unless it stopped, she was going to "go downtown and do some talking" about the payoffs she had made to an unnamed police captain.

On January 7, the cops raided the house and arrested three prostitutes; they may have been slow of foot to the hiding place. The Grenap squad was told that the raid threw Costello into "an extremely nervous state." The implication was that if the police kept this up, they might find the $300,000.

But the raid proved to be a blessing in disguise for May. One of the arrested prostitutes was questioned by the FBI. She said she had worked for Mrs. Traynor for almost a year and was in the house on October 6 and 7—the period during which the ransom money disappeared. Then the blessing: She said Costello had not been in the house at any time on either of those days.

"She stated that she is positive that Joseph Costello, either alone or accompanied by anyone else, could not have come into Traynor's place at any time [on] the sixth or seventh of October 1953, particularly if they were carrying any large suitcases, without this fact having come to her attention.

She [said] she usually went to the door when there were any callers, and . . . she believes it would have been absolutely impossible for any man or group of men to have been at Traynor's on practically any occasion without her knowing it.

"She stated that she had never been friendly with . . . Costello, although [she] knows him when she sees him, and said that she would have no hesitation whatsoever in advising the [FBI] if she had seen him in Traynor's place with any suitcases, or if she had any information [linking] him with the disappearance of the Greenlease ransom money. . . . [She] reiterated that she is positive that none of the ransom money . . . was ever brought into Traynor's place, nor was it ever at any time concealed [there]. She stated that she was there so much of the time that . . . it could not have been done without it coming to her attention."

A comprehensive witness. Downright voluble. She didn't take Costello off the hook—there were many other places he could have hidden the money—but she certainly helped May Traynor.

As the search for the missing money went on, spreading farther and farther, May's house gradually faded out of the investigation. In 1961, May's murder (which will be described in a subsequent chapter) finally closed the venerable establishment at 4021 Forest Park. Some years later, it was torn down to make room for a parking lot for the Allied Construction Equipment Company next door.

Forest Park Avenue is a broad street that sweeps west to the park for which it is named. In its prime, it was a proud boulevard lined with substantial residences, but it is silent now, with the quiet of old streets in old cities that have lost their people. To the east, however, the avenue provides a view of St. Louis's shining Gateway Arch. Perhaps the people will come back someday. Perhaps they will pass through the arch and find the city again, and wonder how it happened that they lost their way.

At Allied Construction Equipment, the author inquires about the house at 4021. The president of the company is John Gammon, a jovial man. "You mean May Traynor's place?" he asks, and then he explains that it was razed for the parking lot.

Gammon laughs hugely. "We tore it down just like it operated," he says. "Piece by piece."

On the morning of October 7, a large group of FBI agents descended on the Coral Court motel. John Henry Carr, the owner of the motel, said later there were twenty or thirty of them. They were looking for the money.

This was the morning after Carl and Bonnie had been caught. They had confessed the kidnapping but not the murder, and Hall had not yet told of seeing an unknown man at the Town House, so Sandra O'Day and Oliver Johnson were still prime suspects. They might have stolen the $300,000 themselves or they might have helped Hall hide it. Either way, the Coral Court obviously could have been the hiding place.

The agents searched Room 49-A thoroughly but found nothing. There aren't many hiding places in motel rooms, as adulterers have learned, and 49-A was barren. The agents dusted the bed, the furniture, the window air conditioner and other surfaces, looking for fingerprints. They found none the first time, so they dusted again and discovered several of Hall's prints on the air conditioner and one of Sandy's on the bed. But they didn't find the fingerprints of anyone else. There was no evidence that anyone had entered the room and stolen the money.

"Goddamn it, John," one agent complained, "you certainly have clean maids."

The agents fanned out. "They went from one end of the place to the other," Carr said. They searched the corridors, the furnace room, the grounds around the motel, poking into everything, even pulling off some of the molding—but they found nothing.

When the agents arrived, Carr had been doing some amateur landscaping—planting trees here and there. When the agents saw the saplings, their suspicions were aroused. They made him dig them up, but there was no money underneath. Then they searched the woods around the motel: no signs of buried money. They interrogated the maids and other employees: no knowledge of the money. Later they interviewed a number of persons who had stayed at the Coral Court on the night of October 5: no information about the money.

The whorehouse, the motel—and then the cab company. Thus far, the first two had been dead ends, although the FBI plugged away at them for months. But if Costello had stolen the money, then Ace Cab would have been another obvious hiding place.

A former Ace Cab driver told this story:

On the night the kidnappers were caught, he was in the company's garage, chatting with a supervisor and another man. At about 10:30 P.M., he saw Costello, Shoulders and Ollie Johnson drive up in Costello's Cadillac and go into the office. He said he was curious about this— apparently because he recognized Shoulders as a cop—so he slipped into an empty cab that was parked by the office window. He said the window was open and he could hear the conversation inside.

He said he heard Ollie Johnson tell Costello that he had discovered that a "friend" named Hall was the Greenlease kidnapper, and that Hall had $600,000 in ransom money. Ollie said he had wanted to steal the money by himself but was afraid his criminal record would make him an immediate suspect. So he called Shoulders, told him about Hall, and suggested that Shoulders arrest the kidnapper. He and Shoulders would then take half the money, Ollie said, and would be in the clear because they had caught Hall.

Shoulders told Costello, according to the informant, that they had come to him because they needed help in fencing the money and knew he had the necessary connections. Costello agreed to be the fence. The three men then counted the money and put half of it in Costello's safe. When they left the office, the informant said, they took one suitcase with them (it presumably contained the rest of the money, to be delivered to the police station) and left the other bag, empty, on the floor.

Beautiful. The big break. It was all over. The FBI would get a search warrant, open the safe and find the missing $300,000, and the informant's story would put Costello, Shoulders and Johnson behind bars.

Beautiful, but beauty too rich for use, for earth too dear. FBI agents interviewed the informant at the Federal Medical Center in Springfield, Missouri, where he was serving a three-year sentence for interstate transportation of a stolen vehicle. A prison official said the man had hinted that he hoped his story would win him a reduced sentence. He was in the medical center, instead of a regular prison, because he had been diagnosed as a schizophrenic, with "evidence of psychosis." Psychological tests showed he "exaggerated terribly." After further inquiry, the FBI concluded that his story was completely false.

Early in November, a man told the Grenap squad another story involving Ace Cab and the missing money. This tale seemed a little more solid; the agents who dealt with this informant said he appeared to be "sincere and honest in the information that he has furnished." They added cautiously that they didn't know yet whether the information was true, but they thought this man might "eventually be able to turn up some of the missing ransom money."

Many of the leads that reached the FBI at this time began the same way: A man met another man, and the other man told him something. This appears to be the way the world communicates; a better system is needed. And that's how it was this time: The informant said he met a

210

man, talked to him for a while and became friendly with him—and then the man said he had seen the missing money at Ace Cab on the night Hall was arrested.

According to the informant, the man told him the money was brought to the cab company on the night of October 6 and was put in a locker in the basement. Later it was moved to a safe in the office, and still later it was taken to some unknown place.

At this point, the new story became more specific and therefore more promising: The man said he himself took the money to the basement and put it in the locker. It was in a wrapped package or carton, he said, but before he stashed it away, he tore off some of the wrapping and saw bundles of money. In his conversations with the informant, he didn't say who gave him the package to take to the basement, but later he seemed to confirm that it was Ollie Johnson.

And there was more. The man told his new buddy, the informant, that Ollie had given him $10,000 in ransom money and had instructed him to take it to Detroit and "peddle" it there. He said he was getting ready to go to Detroit, but when the FBI "got hot on the case," he got scared and gave the money back to Ollie. However, the informant said he believed his friend could get it back and would be willing to sell it for thirty cents on the dollar.

They tried three times to set up a buy, with an agent ready to pose as a customer, but were unsuccessful. Once the locker man didn't show up, once the informant couldn't reach him, and once the informant himself got spooked and left town.

On December 8, however, the informant talked to the locker man on the phone while an FBI agent listened on an extension. On the major issue—whether he had some of the ransom money or could get hold of it—the conversation was disappointing:

"I don't know anything about that stuff . . . that money's gone . . . I don't know where it is," the locker man said. "I'm out . . . I'm out now. I don't know nothing."

But then the informant worked the conversation around to Ollie Johnson:

Informant: "Well, he's the guy who give you the money to carry downstairs, didn't he?"

Locker man: "Yeah, he is, Johnson, Johnson."

Informant: "That's what I'm saying. Well, then, Johnson gave you the money to carry downstairs, why, you know, Johnson . . . tipped Shoulders off and Shoulders is got the money. . . ."

Locker man: "Yeah, that's what I'm thinking."

Informant: "Sure, Johnson didn't go to California for nothing [Ollie had recently gone to Los Angeles], and Johnson gave you that . . . box of money that you took downstairs."

Locker man: "Uh, huh."

So the informant appeared to be telling the truth. The locker man, not knowing the FBI was listening in, seemed to confirm the basement episode.

This raised a tactical difficulty, because the locker man was an Ace Cab driver. The agents assumed that whenever they talked to an Ace employee, Costello would quickly hear about it. For a while, therefore, they made no effort to talk to the locker man. Instead, they continued to work with the informant, to see if he could find out anything else. But he was never able to add to his original story.

Finally, in February, the agents got in touch with the locker man and asked him to come in for questioning. He agreed to do so—but . . .

He said he didn't know Ollie Johnson and had never spoken to him except on one brief occasion in November—long after the money disappeared. He said he didn't even know who Ollie was until he saw his picture in the newspapers, and then he only remembered him vaguely as someone he had seen around the cab company.

He said further that he was not at Ace Cab at any time in the period between October 5 and October 8. During that time, he said, he was working somewhere else, although he later returned to Ace. And then he laid a hard fact directly in the path of the investigation: He said Ace Cab had no basement. The only thing remotely resembling one, he pointed out, was a grease pit where the cabs were serviced. The rest of what he said could have been lies—not knowing Ollie, not being at the cab company during the relevant period—but no basement! What became of the basement story in the absence of basement?

It had seemed to be a very promising lead, but it fluttered away. However, the FBI's interest in Ace Cab did not diminish; Costello's company continued to be a major target of inquiry. In the months that followed, the Grenap squad interviewed 150 Ace drivers, going through them methodically, filling scores of pages of reports. Nor did it stop with the cabbies; in many cases the agents also questioned their wives, girl friends, relatives and companions. They heard some more stories that led nowhere, but for the most part the Ace drivers were profoundly uncommunicative about Costello. He was just the boss, you know? They caught a glimpse of him now and then, but they really didn't know anything about him. And criminal activities? They didn't know from criminal activities. The huge interviewing effort turned out like most large enterprises: *Par-*

turiunt montes, nascetur ridiculus mus. The mountains labored, and brought forth a mouse.

There must be more to life than cab drivers. And there was; the Grenap squad was busy on many fronts:

1. The principal suspects were placed under surveillance. It wasn't round-the-clock shadowing—there weren't enough agents—but Costello was followed closely. In December, he had an FBI escort all the way to Florida and back; he said it was a nice vacation, but crowded. The others—Shoulders, Dolan and Johnson—were shadowed as often as possible, and agents spent long hours parked outside their homes, observing visitors and noting the license numbers of their cars. A capacity for boredom is required in most lines of work.

2. Agents interviewed the suspects' relatives, friends, associates and other people who came in contact with them. The net was spread wide; Costello grumbled that the FBI had "even talked to my mother-in-law in Chicago and my sister-in-law in Elgin, Illinois."

3. Some persons close to the suspects were "turned." The FBI persuaded them to become spies. They reported their conversations with Costello, Shoulders and the others, eavesdropped on telephone calls and generally snitched, picking up whatever information they could and passing it along.

4. As noted earlier, Costello's office phone was bugged, and the FBI reports strongly imply that there were wiretaps on Shoulders at various times. In addition, the agents obtained records of long-distance calls to and from the main suspects, to see whether there was a pattern of frequent calls to some city. If the money had left St. Louis, this might show where it had gone.

5. The suspects' financial transactions were examined for large bank deposits, lavish spending or other signs of sudden wealth, and "currency stops" were placed on them—the banks and stores they frequented were given the serial numbers of the missing money and asked to check each ten- and twenty-dollar bill they received from their suspects and their families.

6. Then the public was enlisted in the search. The FBI prepared a forty-four-page booklet listing the serial numbers of the missing bills, and distributed it to banks, law enforcement agencies, newspapers and business firms throughout the nation. Americans were urged to compare the tens and twenties in their wallets and purses with the serial numbers in the booklet.

213

One bill was discovered in Minot, North Dakota, by an airport employee who had "time on his hands" and checked his tens and twenties after cashing his paycheck at a local bank. Nothing else is known about the Minot incident. It was a different story, however, in Petoskey, Michigan.

Norman W. Clark, a twenty-one-year-old mail-truck driver in Petoskey, was planing to get married. He and his bride would need a place to live, and they had decided on a cottage owned by Mrs. Henry J. Krauser. On October 29, the young man gave his new landlady a rental deposit—a twenty-dollar bill and two tens. A few days later, in the mail, Mrs. Krauser received a copy of the FBI list. She checked her tens and twenties. The twenty-dollar bill Clark had given her was on the list.

Mrs. Krauser followed the instructions in the circular. She called the FBI office in Detroit. She figured they might send someone to look into it—an agent or two. What she got was the U.S. Cavalry, with bugles.

Dozens of FBI agents swarmed into Petoskey, trying to find out where Clark had got the twenty and whether there was any more of the ransom money in town. Some of them went door to door through the downtown area, checking the tens and twenties at banks, stores, hotels, restaurants and taverns, while others worked the outlying areas, inquiring at motels, gas stations—everywhere. But they found nothing.

Clark told the agents there were two places he might have got the twenty. On October 19, he had paid a gasoline bill at a Petoskey filling station operated by George Wilson. He had given Wilson a hundred-dollar bill and had received four twenties back. In the same week, he had cashed a check at a gas station in Manton, Michigan, and had received three twenties. He was pretty sure the twenty he gave Mrs. Krauser was from one of the gas stations, but he had no idea which one.

Over to Wilson's, quick. And there the agents heard an interesting story. On October 14 or 15, Wilson said, a car with Missouri license plates had pulled in. The driver bought gas and paid with a twenty. Between that time and October 19, when Clark paid his gas bill, Wilson had not banked any of the station's receipts, so one of the four twenties he gave Clark could have been from the Missouri man.

Wilson said the car was a big Oldsmobile and there were two men and a woman in it. He said they appeared to be thirty-five to forty years old, but he couldn't describe them beyond that. However, there was something else: The driver had inquired about the car ferry across the Straits of Mackinac, and when he drove away he headed north, toward the straits.

Crossing them would have taken him into the Upper Michigan Peninsula. He might have then turned west toward Wisconsin or Minnesota, or he might have continued north to Canada.

The incident at Wilson's station had occurred eight or nine days after the disappearance of the ransom money. Had the $300,000 been in the Oldsmobile? Had it been on its way to some destination on the Upper Peninsula or in Wisconsin, Minnesota or Canada? The agents worked their way up to Mackinaw City and across the straits, heading for Sault Ste. Marie. But they never found the car with Missouri license plates. North of Petoskey, boys, the trail is always cold.

Of course, the Oldsmobile may not have been involved in the case at all. The twenty that Clark gave Mrs. Krauser might have come from the other gas station—where the FBI got no leads at all—or from somewhere else altogether. And if it *had* come from the driver of the Olds, he might have obtained it entirely innocently and never known it was a ransom bill.

Nevertheless, the Oldsmobile incident stayed with the FBI. The agents continued to be interested in the car that had stopped in Petoskey that day—because the search for the missing money had begun to focus on the upper Middle West.

Early in November, a ten was found in Detroit; however, the FBI refused to give any details about it. Then a twenty was discovered in southern Indiana, somewhere between Evansville and Petersburg. Unlike Petoskey and Detroit, this was not in the upper Middle West, but Petersburg was not far from a major highway that led from St. Louis to Michigan. On November 6, FBI agents arrived at Petersburg's banks—the First National and the Citizens State Bank—and went through their tens and twenties, apparently without success. At the same time, newspapers reported that large numbers of FBI men had been seen in Indiana and Michigan. They were fanning out across the two states, looking for currency with telltale serial numbers.

For a while, there was a lot of activity—and then it tapered off. The problem was the genealogy of money.

It's easy to have money: Use a credit card. And it's easy not to have money: Use a credit card. But the ancestry of money is difficult. Who were its parents and grandparents? Most of the people who found a ransom ten or twenty couldn't remember where they got it. When someone did remember, then the person from whom he got it couldn't remember. And if he did, then the next person couldn't. It was sometimes possible to trace a bill back through two or three persons—but seldom more than that. The appeal to the public turned up only a few hundred dollars in ransom money.

215

Chapter **24**

H e was a *precarious* man. Each day was a struggle between rage
and composure. Anger was a huge lump inside him. Yet he lived and
functioned, owned a large, well-furnished house, drove a Cadillac, did
his daily work, had himself under control most of the time, was
outwardly steady. He could be loving, too. In prison, he painstakingly
constructed a replica of the Empire State Building for his young son,
using dice from Las Vegas casinos, and when he came home he bought
the boy an elaborate model train set, the largest the neighbors had ever
seen; it ran from the sunroom in the back of the house to the living room
in front.

But the rage was always there, just beneath the surface, in fearful
readiness. When it broke through, he screamed and cursed and, *in extremis,*
went for his gun. In 1962, he was indicted for second-degree murder,
accused of killing a man in a savage quarrel. Police cars and ambulances
came screeching to his house in the middle of the night; the neighbors
remember that, too. And there had been many arguments, brawls and
shootings before that; something violent happened each time he fell off the
taut rope of his life.

216

His name, like his temper, was uncertain. The St. Louis Bureau of Vital Statistics told the FBI that the name on his birth certificate was George J. Costello, and in the FBI files he is frequently referred to as George Joseph Costello. But a certified copy of the birth record, sent to the author by the same vital statistics office, gives his name as George G. Costello—no "J." or "Joseph." However, Costello himself said his name was Joseph George Costello, and in his death notice it was given as Joseph G. Costello. Regardless of whether "George" was his first or middle name, he seldom used it. He wanted to be known as Joe Costello.

He was born in St. Louis on May 31, 1908. His father was Paul Costello, a waiter, and his mother was Minnie West Costello. At the time of Joe's birth, they were living at 712 or 1712 North Broadway. Joe was their only child, but Minnie later remarried and had another son.

St. Louis starts at the Mississippi River on the east and spreads west for five miles, after which are shopping malls. However, the city also grew north and south, filling in the long, splendid curve that the river makes at this point, so there are several major north-south thoroughfares. Broadway is the oldest and longest of these, running the entire length of the city. Nowadays, it is overshadowed by the expressways that lope alongside it and then dash away to the suburbs, but in Joe Costello's youth . . . ah, ancient stories of life before shopping malls.

In 1909 or 1910, the near northside also produced John Joseph Vitale, who later became the leader of the St. Louis Mafia. Costello said he and Vitale had known each other all their lives, and it was more than a casual friendship: To some extent, Vitale was Costello's patron. Many St. Louis gangsters were not fond of Costello, but they knew the don had a liking for the hothead. The situation was described in an FBI report that quoted an informant who knew both men and was "well acquainted with all of the Italian hoodlum element."

"John Vitale keeps [other gangsters] from shoving Costello around," the report said. "In fact, Costello would be nothing were it not for the backing he receives from John Vitale. . . . Costello is intensely disliked by numerous St. Louis hoodlums, but they will not bother him because they are afraid of retaliation by Vitale."

But sentiment only murmurs; money talks. The informant also told the FBI that if Costello came into possession of a large sum of money and didn't tell Vitale about it, Costello "wouldn't last ten minutes, and he knows it."

And if the Greenlease ransom had passed into Vitale's hands, the informant added, "you might as well kiss it goodbye."

The near northside early in this century was conducted after the manner of Tony Weller. Its young people received the finest education their parents could afford; they were on the streets as soon as possible. Costello got only as far as the seventh grade "or thereabouts," a relative told the author. When he was about twelve years old, in other words, he made the acquaintance of the world and began hustling it.

Very little is known about his teens, except for one recollection that when he was fourteen or fifteen he hung around a garage where trucks were kept and managed to get occasional work there. And he may have still been in his teens when he married a girl named Bernice. That it might have been a teenage marriage can be deduced from the fact that they had two daughters and Costello was only twenty-three when he married for a second time. His second wife was named Marcella, and she was eighteen. That marriage also produced two daughters.

Sometime in the 1920's, Costello went to work for the Yellow Cab Company. Lou Shoulders said he met him sometime in the next three and a half years and Costello was driving a cab then. It was probably 1926 when he started, and he was eighteen years old. It was a matter of economics.

On March 4, 1936, he was sent to prison. He had been convicted of robbing a jewelry store in Farmington, Missouri. He was sentenced to four years in the Missouri penitentiary but was paroled ten months later. At his trial, he gave his name as George Costello; he said later that George was his middle name and he used it because he was ashamed.

He probably *was* ashamed, but he was also resolved. He was determined never to go to prison again—but that did not mean he would go straight. How, then, could he continue along criminal lines and still stay out of jail? He would rely on his intelligence. He knew he was smart. And, of course, the don was his friend.

For a long time, it worked. The St. Louis police picked him up frequently "on suspicion" of having committed a crime, or for "investigation," but nothing was ever proved. However, there were some close calls. In 1948, a messenger for the Krey Packing Company of St. Louis reported he had been robbed of almost $78,000 in company funds. The police investigated and found it had been a fake holdup. When the messenger was arrested, he said Costello had planned the phony heist. If that was true, it indicated Joe had moved into the executive suite; he was conceiving crimes now, and leaving it to underlings to carry them out. Costello was arrested, but he had an alibi. He said he had spent the day of the robbery with a woman named Pearl. Apparently Pearl said so, too, because there was no further action against Costello.

He was still driving a cab as late as 1939, but shortly before Pearl Harbor was attacked by somebody-or-other, he went briefly into the war effort. From September 1941 until February 1942, he was employed by the Fruin-Colnon Construction Company as an electrician, working at the St. Louis Small Arms Plant. By this time, according to the company's records, he was divorced from his second wife. At another point—the dates are not known—he drove a hearse for the Kutis funeral parlor. However, he did not remain a driver of cabs and hearses much longer.

In 1944 or 1945, Costello and a man named Leo Vincent Brothers acquired the Clover Club at 3501 Delmar Boulevard. It was described as a nightclub, but it had no liquor license. The customers brought their own whiskey with them, and the club sold "setups"—carbonated water, Coca-Cola and so forth—to mix with the booze. It's hard to see how there was any money in this, but there may have been other attractions, including the proprietors themselves.

Costello was becoming well known in the underworld, and his partner, Leo Brothers, was a celebrity. In 1930–31, Brothers had figured in one of the most sensational crimes of a high-crime era. He had been convicted of murdering Alfred "Jake" Lingle, a reporter for the *Chicago Tribune*. By the 1940's, he was out of jail and back in St. Louis, running the Clover Club with Joe Costello.

It was an unsavory place, due to its clientele. One night in January 1946, three men came into the club to celebrate. One of them had just been released from prison, where he had served a sentence for taking a woman across a state line for immoral purposes; he was known as "the much-married Romeo," and she had thought they were. Another of the revelers had also done time for a Mann Act violation, and the third stuck knives in people.

Costello said later that he knew these men by reputation, so "I went up to them and asked them to check their guns. . . ." This led to an argument, during which the knife man apparently decided he couldn't get to his favorite weapon in time. However, he had a gun in his pocket. He fired three shots at Costello, movie-style—through the coat. All three bullets missed Joe; instead they hit a cliché. An innocent bystander was taken to the hospital with wounds in the stomach, shoulder and hand. It was the first time Costello's name had appeared in the newspapers in connection with violence, but it was not the last.

In 1946, Costello and Brothers teamed up in a second business venture that proved to be notoriously profitable and profitably notorious: the Ace Cab Company. Its notoriety—prior to the Greenlease affair—was based on its reputation as the cab company of choice for men who wanted women. Ace Cab drivers were most likely to know where the action was and most willing to furnish it. When a customer wanted a girl, an informant told the FBI, Ace drivers had "strict orders" to call one of the supervisors, who would arrange it. His motto was ace service; if necessary, he would take the customer to the girl himself. The informant named the supervisor. He was a close, intimate friend of Costello, one of the three or four men he trusted most.

In the late 1940's, Costello married again, and this marriage lasted until his death in 1962. His third wife was from Chicago, and they had two children—a son and daughter. With the children from his previous marriages, Costello had five daughters and a son. The family lived on Gurney Court, in a solid, respectable South St. Louis neighborhood, than which there is no greater solidity or respectability on earth. The Costello home was a two-story brick house, substantial but not pretentious. It had about ten rooms, including four bedrooms, and a concrete front porch. The neighbors remember Joe as a proud homeowner who invested a lot of time and money in his house; among other things he had expensive stonework put around the fireplace. In the basement was a paneled recreation room that will come up again in this story.

A neighbor describes Costello as "a good family man—he loved his kids." His son was the envy of the other children on Gurney Court. The train set, a trampoline, a battery-operated replica of a Model T Ford—"that kid had everything," the neighbor recalls. For his daughter, Costello had a carpenter build an elaborate, two-story playhouse in the backyard. Nothing was too good for those kids of his; he doted on them.

Go and understand humankind, if you can. In his other self, the good family man was the furious man. The neighbors remember a lot of angry noise at the Costello house, much quarreling, many scenes. One of them says Joe could be passionately bad-tempered and "foul-mouthed." He recalls him shouting and cursing at a woman—"You dirty, filthy whore, you drink too goddamned much gin"—and at children too. One day, an older boy borrowed the Model T, drove it a while, and damaged it. Costello was livid with rage. He cursed the boy violently and shook his fist at him. The boy knew who Joe was, knew his reputation, but he shouted back: "You got a lot of money. You can get it fixed."

What did he look like, this precarious man? What was his outward appearance? To some of his neighbors, Costello looked Italian, and Phil King of the Grenap squad says he tried to give the impression that he was a power in the Italian underworld, a big-shot Mafioso—"very tough, don't fool with me." But a St. Louisan who knew him well says he doesn't think Costello was Italian at all—"I think he was 100 percent Irish." To the author, who saw him several times in the early 1950's, he looked Irish.

Physical description: ordinary. One neighbor says Costello was fairly tall—five eleven or six feet. But former FBI agent John Poelker says it was more like five eight or five ten. He was slender, weighing perhaps 160 or 165 pounds. His face was narrow, nose rather long, upper lip prominent— perhaps a slight overbite. The neighbor says his hair was gray and curly, but the author remembers a faded reddish-brown, as if it had been redder when he was young.

In his prime, when he was a grandee of the underworld, when the money was rolling in from the cabs, the whores and the burglars, Costello was a person of consequence on "the Strip." Every large city has one or more of these nightclub-bar-girlie-joint-porno-shop neon paradises, and in St. Louis in the 1940's and '50's it was an area around Delmar Boulevard and DeBaliviere Avenue, in the west end. To the Strip came tourists, teenagers and tired masses, bringing money, and hoods, harlots and hustlers, who took it. Here is the St. Louisan who knew Costello, talking about him in those confident days:

"I think he was the toughest guy on the Strip; nobody interfered with his rackets. He was a handsome man, very well-dressed, an immaculate man, always wore a great big diamond ring. He was very smooth, not like Shoulders in any way. Shoulders was crude."

The "great big diamond ring"? Costello, Brothers and another Ace Cab partner gave each other diamond rings to celebrate the company's success. Each was six carats. Then Costello gave his wife a nine-carat ring. The tender exchange totaled twenty-seven carats. Things were going well.

But the Greenlease case was the beginning of the end for Costello. Even though he was never charged with stealing the $300,000, the FBI was convinced he had masterminded the theft—again and again its reports refer to Costello as "the principal suspect in the disappearance of the . . . ransom money"—and the agents tried hard to prove it.

For months, they made his life miserable. He complained bitterly that the FBI was tailing him day and night, tapping his phones, questioning everyone who knew him or had even casual contact with him (including a man who had repaired the furnace at his home), investigating his finances, harassing his cab drivers. "They don't want to know the truth," he said, "they want to frame somebody." And he had no doubt who was going to be framed: "They want me for a fall guy." Furthermore, he was worried that they might succeed. In January 1954, he told someone, who passed it on to the FBI, that he thought Shoulders and Dolan were going to be indicted. Then he added, "They [the FBI] have enough on me to convict me on circumstantial evidence."

They didn't, but under the FBI pressure he started to go to pieces. He complained of frequent severe headaches, and he began to hit the bottle. Phil King says Costello had been a drinker when he was younger but had quit for a long time. Then, in his last years, "he started drinking heavily." The St. Louisan who knew him confirms this:

"He was buying Scotch by the case. Personally, I think he died of cirrhosis of the liver. He could have; I saw the color change in his skin. He was also having trouble sleeping. He was getting prescriptions for sleeping pills and taking them around to drugstores. He called me one time to invite me to play golf with him and Vitale. That was okay, but it was three in the morning when he called. I could see the decline in this man."

On January 17, 1954, a *Globe-Democrat* reporter called Costello to ask him about a story that had appeared in the *Post-Dispatch* that day.

"I've just taken eight sleeping pills, and I might not be able to talk very long," Joe said.

"Why did you take so many . . . ?" the reporter asked.

"I'm tired" was the reply. "Maybe I won't be around in the morning to find out."

There is no way to know whether this was a serious suicide attempt, but clearly he was, like Masha, in mourning for his life. Ten months later, on October 29, he was found in his bedroom, in blood-soaked pajamas. He had been shot in the chest, just above the heart.

His wife told the police he had awakened her about 3:30 in the morning, complaining that he didn't feel well. He asked her to go downstairs and get him a bowl of cereal. When she came back, he was on the floor by the bed, with a revolver in his hand. She called a doctor. He told her it was a serious wound and urged her to call the police and get Joe to the hospital.

The cops arrived a little after 5:30 A.M. Costello was still there. He told them he had been cleaning the gun and it had accidentally gone off. In America, according to what people tell the police, many guns accidentally go off at 3:30 in the morning.

An emergency operation saved Joe. But just before he was wheeled into the operating room, he told a reporter: "I wish it [the bullet] had gone three inches lower. I don't care what happens to me anymore."

He still cared enough, however, to fight hard against going to prison. When the FBI and St. Louis police finally nabbed him on a charge unrelated to the Greenlease case, he struggled for almost three years to stay out of jail. In a prolonged legal battle, he went all the way to the United States Supreme Court, not once but twice. Each time, the justices rejected his appeal.

It wasn't much of a charge. It rested on two rather technical points, one geographical, one legal. Geographically, some of St. Louis's suburbs are across the Mississippi River, in Illinois. Legally, it is a crime for persons previously convicted of a felony involving violence to transport or receive a firearm across a state line. Costello's 1936 burglary conviction had caught up with him—burglary is defined as a crime of violence.

Prosecution witnesses testified that Costello and another man, an Ace Cab supervisor, had gone to Granite City, Illinois, and had talked to a gun dealer about buying some weapons. Later, the supervisor bought three .38-caliber revolvers from the dealer and took them to St. Louis. One of them was found in the glove compartment of Costello's car.

He fought all the way. He had been arrested on the gun charge in February 1956, but the trial was not held until April 1957. The jury found both men guilty of violating the federal firearms law. Costello was sentenced to thirty months in prison, the supervisor to eighteen months. The appeals dragged things out for another year and a half, but in January 1959 Joe went to jail.

It had been a long run. He had wiggled out of so many arrests and investigations that he may have begun to think of himself as invincible, and he had the house, the Cadillacs, the diamond rings, the cab company—tangibles not of respectability but at least of success, and more important, the barriers he had erected against precariousness. He couldn't go behind bars. *This could not be happening to him.*

On January 5, 1959, he took an overdose of barbiturates. It was described as one and a half times the lethal amount—but his wife saved him.

Knowing he dreaded prison, she had been watching him closely, and she forced coffee into him, kept him awake, got him to a hospital. His stomach was pumped out. He survived.

A week later, after a final flurry of unsuccessful appeals, he was taken to the federal penitentiary at Terre Haute, Indiana. Later, he was transferred to Leavenworth, where he served the rest of his sentence, earning seven months off for good behavior. He was released on December 18, 1960.

Back in St. Louis, in end game, he began drinking heavily, gobbling sleeping pills, brooding, fighting. Rage, despondency and weariness contended for him.

In April 1961, after a furious argument, his wife went to the apartment of a woman friend to spend the night. Costello rushed after her and demanded to be let in. A familiar domestic scene: the drunken husband shouting, cursing and pounding on the door, filling the night with unholy noise and affrighting the neighbors, while the wife ponders what to do with him. Something, Christopher Fry observed, persuades women to the fallacy that men are desirable. Not long before, she had saved his life.

When his wife refused to let him in, Costello fired a shot through the glass panel in the front door. The bullet hit a wall inside, and shattered glass sprayed the apartment. Then he ran around to the back of the building and fired another shot through the bedroom window. No one was hurt, but Costello was arrested for discharging a firearm in the city, destroying property and disturbing everybody's peace. However, the charges were dismissed when a grand jury said it had been unable to obtain the full facts in the case.

It was different the next time. In February 1962, Costello was indicted for second-degree murder. He was accused of killing Edward G. Brown, co-owner of the Tic Toc Club, a nightclub on the Strip. Before he died, Brown named Costello as the man who shot him. But Joe told it another way. "I just went in there," he said, "and he [Brown] shot me." Costello had a bullet wound in his left arm.

A good witness nowadays is hard to find. When the cops arrived, there were bullet shells strewn here and there, a pungent smell of cordite in the air, barstools overturned upon their asses, and on the bar, nine empty glasses. But no people. They had drunk up, hastily, and left.

However, the police were able to piece together some of the story. Costello had gone to the club with two young women, and after considerable drinking, he and Brown got into an argument over taxicabs. Brown

224

told the cops Costello wanted his cabs to have the exclusive right to pick up fares at the Tic Toc, whereas Costello said Brown was angry because "I didn't produce the loads I was supposed to"—in other words, his drivers weren't bringing enough customers to the club.

There wasn't much information about the actual shooting, but two fourteen-year-old boys from Ladue, a high-income suburb, were on the Strip that night, still seeking life's meaning. As they were walking past the Tic Toc, they saw a man (Brown) stagger out, with another man supporting him, and try to get into a car. "I can't make it," the man gasped, and fell into the gutter. The other man disappeared. Aha, said the youths, life's meaning was that people got drunk.

Seconds later, they saw another man come out of the club, accompanied by two young women. They got into a car and drove away. The boys from Ladue said they wouldn't have paid any attention to this except that the man had blood on his shirt. No, life was more.

One of the women drove Joe home. Later he went to the hospital—this was the night the sirens screamed in Gurney Court. Reporters and photographers caught up with him there; they said he was drunk, incoherent and spattered with blood. A photograph taken in the emergency room—his last photo—shows an exhausted man, his eyes weary, his shoulders slumped.

He was scheduled to go on trial on the murder charge in September 1962. On June 28, however, he was found dead at his home. He was fifty-four years old. There were rumors he had taken another drug overdose, but a pathologist's report said the cause of death was disease of the heart arteries and congestive heart failure.

Chapter **25**

*C*arl and Bonnie were brought into the courtroom just before 10:00 A.M. on November 16, 1953. They were surrounded by so many guards that at first it was hard to pick them out. But Robert Greenlease wanted to see them. He leaned forward in his seat, staring at them intently. It was the first time he had seen the man and woman who had murdered his son.

Later in the morning, as they were being led from the room, Greenlease stood up. He looked at the prisoners for a long moment, seeming especially interested in Hall, the man he had known only as "M." Before sitting down, he shook his head slowly, just once.

During the trial, Carl wrote a short note to Bobby's parents. It was clear Greenlease didn't want to talk about it. All he would say was that Hall "begged forgiveness for this terrible crime" and said he hoped the missing ransom would be found and returned to the Greenleases. As if they cared about that—but Carl did.

From Death Row, however, Bonnie Heady wrote a longer letter:

Mr. and Mrs. Greenlease, I doubt if this letter will do much good, but there isn't anything we could do or say that would atone for our mistake. I do hope it helps a little.

I would give anything if I could go back to that Sunday in September and erase everything that has happened since. It all seems like a nightmare to me.

We have always known that we would have to pay, but that doesn't return Bobby, but if it gives you any satisfaction then we won't be giving our lives in vain.

I don't say I don't enjoy money, as everybody does, but that was not my motive. I could have been very, very happy with Carl living in my house as I had been, but he was used to more money. My case was loving not wisely, but too well. I wanted so much for him to be happy.

I never realized that Bobby would be such a sweet child until it was too late.

I am not trying in any way to make any excuse for my actions. As I don't have any, but I think anyone will find if you drink from one to two-fifths of whiskey a day for a year and a half that your brain doesn't function properly. Since I have been in jail is the first time I've been able to reason clearly for some time.

I would like for the sisters [at the Notre Dame de Sion school] to know I am sorry too, as their's [sic] is a wonderful faith.

I hope as time goes on it will help heal your hurt and that you find peace.

Yours resp. [respectfully]
Bonnie Heady.

The first step was the selection of a jury. From a venire of 125 persons, twelve white males were chosen. Minorities had been invented but not yet popularized; however, one of the two alternates was a woman. The jurors would hear the confessions Carl and Bonnie had given to the FBI, and some of the evidence. But because guilty pleas had been entered, they would decide only the punishment. A unanimous vote would be required for the death penalty. Each prospective juror was questioned by Judge Reeves. He concentrated on two points:

"Have you prejudged the case?"

"Are you opposed in principle to the death penalty?"

Both questions were crucial. On the issue of prejudgment, the lawyers for Carl and Bonnie sought to have the entire venire dismissed. They argued that an impartial jury could not be chosen from people who had been exposed to the massive news coverage and publicity of a notorious murder case in their home state. Judge Reeves overruled the motion.

On the death penalty, the defense did the best it could. Because there wasn't much doubt what the jury would recommend, the lawyers tried to prepare the way for an appeal on technical grounds. Twice they sought to halt the selection of the jury on the basis that the trial procedure was not valid. The jurors were not being asked to determine guilt or innocence, as juries have done since time immemorial, but only to decide the punishment. Judge Reeves overruled these motions, too.

There would be no insanity plea, either. As the trial began, it was indicated that Carl and Bonnie might try to escape death by claiming they were deranged, but Judge Reeves was having none of that. They hadn't pleaded insanity when they were arraigned, he said, so they couldn't now.

It struck a few people—not very many—as a little hasty. There was a flavor of frontier justice about it—rough, ready, rapid, and intensely satisfying. Since society could not cope with their offense, it simply made up its mind to rid itself of Carl and Bonnie, and to be as quick as possible about it. The solution wasn't very modern—they didn't sit on Death Row for years while legal writs shuffled from one court to another and Jarndyce haggled with Jarndyce. But that wasn't altogether society's doing; it was theirs as well. They decided not to appeal. They gave up.

U.S. Attorney Scheufler led for the prosecution. He outlined the circumstances of Bobby's abduction and murder and said the government would prove that it was a "carefully planned and pre-arranged scheme. . . ." This would demonstrate premeditation, which was necessary to sustain a charge of first-degree murder. That wasn't actually the charge against Carl and Bonnie (see Chapter 21), but this was a murder trial nevertheless.

Representing Hall was Roy Kaiser Dietrich, who at that time was president of the Kansas City Lawyers' Association. Judge Reeves said he selected Dietrich because he wanted Carl defended by "a man of . . . the highest legal ability and standing in his profession." Bonnie's defense was handled by Harold M. Hull, the attorney who had appeared for her at the arraignment.

Neither lawyer tried to portray Bobby's murder as anything but a profoundly vicious crime. Their only argument was that their clients had been destroyed—Carl by greed, Bonnie by marital sadnesses, both by alcoholism. They were incapable of acting rationally or decently. They could not resist a foul, ugly impulse. In essence, it was a plea of diminished responsibility.

"Money was everything to him," Dietrich said. ". . . With his money gone [after squandering the inheritance from his mother] . . . he planned and schemed for easy money. This was a terrible crime . . . but under those circumstances of drinking, any sense of decency . . . would be buried. . . . These are mitigating facts and . . . should be considered in determining whether his life should be taken or he should be given life imprisonment.''

Hull told the jury: ''I am not interested in sympathy for my client [but] I think after you hear the evidence for forty years of Mrs. Heady's life, you can realize that a recommendation of life imprisonment can be the outcome in this case.''

The chief witnesses against Carl and Bonnie were Carl and Bonnie themselves, in their confessions.

Bonnie's twenty-six-page statement was put in evidence first. Scheufler read it to the judge and jury, slowly, taking almost three quarters of an hour, making sure every word was clear. Bonnie listened impassively—one reporter wrote that she looked ''almost bored.''

Carl's confession was read by FBI agent Arthur S. Reeder. Hall sat quietly, resting his chin on his hand, his eyes closed most of the time, as Reeder read the thirty-seven-page statement. The voice in the courtroom was legalistic, dispassionate, drying out horror.

In the front row, Robert Greenlease's horror was not arid. His love supplied the fullness that the law drained away. He shook his head several times as his son's death was described, and once or twice he covered his eyes with his hand, but he said nothing.

The rest was anticlimax. Nothing more was really needed. The confessions, in their frightful detail, doomed Carl and Bonnie. Nevertheless, the prosecution presented a number of witnesses:

- John M. Gurley and Lloyd Parker, employees of the Sawyer Material Company in Kansas City, told of selling Hall a fifty-pound bag of lime eighteen days before the kidnapping, establishing premeditation.
- Mrs. Grace Hatfield, of the Hatfield Hardware Company in St. Joe, identified Hall as the man who bought a long-handled shovel from her, saying he was only going to use it once. Again, premeditation.
- Sister Morand, the receptionist at the Notre Dame de Sion school, was very pale, and her voice was so low the jury could barely hear it, but she identified Bonnie as the woman who came to the school, said she was Bobby's aunt, said his mother had had a heart attack, and took the

boy away with her. The nun said Bonnie told the child: "We're going to see Mama." Sister Morand's identification was positive; she looked directly at Bonnie and said she was the woman.

- FBI agent James Cadigan testified that two spent bullets were found in Bonnie's station wagon. Agent George A. Berley testified that ballistics tests proved both bullets had been fired from Hall's .38-caliber revolver.

Other physical evidence was described at the trial: the plastic sheet in which Hall had wrapped the body; interior photographs of Bonnie's house, showing the bloodstains that Hall had tried to scrub away, and Coroner Homer F. Mundy's description of the head wound that caused Bobby's death.

In addition, the FBI found bloodstains in the station wagon and on the ground and wheat stubble in the field where Bobby was killed. These stains and the stains in Bonnie's house were identified as human blood of type A. The remaining blood in Bobby's body was too decayed to permit a comparison, but it was determined that his blood type was A.

Three fragments of "a hard white substance" were found under the front seat of the station wagon. The FBI's microscopes showed they were human bone, and one of them had "a layered structure" similar to bone structure found only in the human skull. In this fragment, "minute quantities of lead" were discovered, indicating that a bullet had passed through the skull.

Bobby's parents testified at the trial, with their son's murderers sitting only a few feet away. Hall slumped in his chair, avoiding their eyes. Bonnie looked at them curiously once or twice, then averted her head. It must have been *hard* for the mother and father, beyond description *hard,* a supreme effort of anguish and will, but they did it; they went through the story from beginning to end, in the presence of friends who wept, strangers who stared, and two people who had come randomly into their lives one day, and torn them up like scrap paper.

Except for a few short absences, Robert Greenlease was present throughout the trial. He had heard everything, borne everything. Now, on the witness stand, his eyes filled with tears and his voice trembled. Once it seemed he couldn't go on; it was when he told of seeing Bobby for the last time as he let him off at school. But he *did* go on.

Virginia Greenlease saw her son's killers for the first and only time on

230

the afternoon of November 17, when she came to the courtroom to testify about her telephone conversations with "M"—how she tried to find out if Bobby was alive, and how "M" told her repeatedly: "I can assure you your son is alive and well." She gave her testimony in a low, firm voice. She did not falter, and she did not cry—the reporters wrote that she seemed "completely composed." But she was extremely pale. After Carl and Bonnie had been sentenced to death, a reporter telephoned her at home, and they talked for a few moments. She was still calm, but she said: "There isn't any form of death that can begin to compare with the suffering my husband and I have endured, much less what Bobby endured."

Since the facts could not be disputed, the defense had to delve into the intangibles. This is usually an affair of psychiatrists and psychologists, who make heavy work of it, but the defense did not summon the mental bureaucracy. Instead, Dietrich called a number of people from Carl's hometown, Pleasanton, Kansas, to talk about his childhood.

They described the stern, strict father who tried to do the right thing but didn't know how to raise a son; the father's death when Carl was twelve; the boy's loneliness after that (when Bonnie heard this testimony, she cried), and his erratic relationship with his mother—how she alternately spoiled him, ignored him and dominated him. Other witnesses told of his uncontrollable drinking and his obsession with money; one man said Carl "always tried to show off, with big bills in the front of his wallet" (hearing this, Bonnie grinned and nodded vigorously; she was doing all the emoting in this trial).

But it was a thin argument, and everyone knew it. Carl Hall had been a privileged child who had grown up in affluence and comfort. There had been no slum, no ghetto, no rural shack, no rats, roaches or dirt. His early ledger had only one major debit: He had been deprived of love. This, however, is a common entry.

Bonnie's lawyer, Harold Hull, called only one witness: her aunt, Mrs. Troy Baker. Once more, the elderly, ailing woman came to her niece's side, telling the jury that Bonnie had been "a very sweet little girl" who grew up to be "just a nice woman." Nellie Baker's world was in that word "nice." She went on to describe the Bonnie she had known—happy and normal until the breakup of her marriage; then a sad change, a downfall. And in reply to a question from Hull: "Yes, she was kind to children. She was a kind, lovable woman."

This talk of kindness and love troubled prosecuting attorney Scheufler.

231

He was worried it might get Bonnie off with life. In his closing argument to the jury, he dealt with it: ''Defense counsel said [Bonnie] loved children. But she was more interested in her dog than Bobby. . . . [She could have told Hall]: 'No, Carl, let us not do this. Let us not plan the death of a child like this.' She had a chance 50 times, 100 times, 1000 times to stop this thing . . . she could have said no. But she did not.''

Scheufler demanded the death penalty for Bonnie as well as for Carl. They had murdered for money, he said; they wanted ''murderous, filthy money to continue their greedy, destructive lives.'' They gave no mercy, Scheufler said, and they should receive none.

''Little Bobby Greenlease, defenseless, was trapped like an animal,'' the prosecutor declared. ''. . . It was one of the most heinous, brutal and cold-blooded crimes in the annals of American history. . . . If there was ever a case [in which] a jury [was] justified in taking a life, this is it.''

And as far as Hall was concerned, that *was* it. His lawyer said the expected things, spoke the predictable words. He alluded to the lack of parental love in Carl's childhood, and he ascribed the murder to Hall's ''constant drinking,'' which he said had deadened whatever ''finer things'' he might have had in him. But Dietrich's fire was somewhere else, not in this courtroom, not for this case. He said his client had ''a perverted, twisted nature'' and an ''overriding passion'' for money—''but Bobby Greenlease was worth more than all the money in the world.''

However, Harold Hull found in himself some fire for Bonnie. ''Whatever your decision,'' Hull told the jury, ''whether you send her to the gas chamber or to prison, she is walking into nothing but darkness. Our God is the only one who can punish the guilty. I'm pleading for mercy . . . death would be a popular decision, but cruelty, death and hatred breed only cruelty, death and hatred.''

The jury deliberated for an hour and eight minutes. First it decided Hall should be put to death; that took about eight minutes. Then it spent an hour persuading one juror that Bonnie Heady should also die; he said at first she should be given life imprisonment. At 11:52 A.M. on November 19, the jury came back into the courtroom and recommended the death penalty for both of them.

When the verdict was read, Bonnie did a strange thing. She smiled at the jurors. Then she turned and smiled at her lawyer, and then she looked at Carl and gave him a great big grin. No one ever knew why. For his part, Hall stared solemnly at the judge and jury as the clerk was reading. A reporter wrote that it was one of the few times during the trial that Carl's eyes were wide open.

Judge Reeves asked them if they had anything to say. "No, sir," Carl replied in a clear, firm voice. Bonnie shook her head no.

"I accept the recommendations of the jury," Judge Reeves said. Then he pronounced sentence:

"You, Carl Austin Hall, shall be transported by the United States marshal to Jefferson City, the state capital, where the sentence of death shall be imposed upon you in the lethal gas chamber during the day of December 18, 1953." He used the same words in sentencing Bonnie, substituting her name for Carl's.

The day after the trial ended, it was announced that Carl and Bonnie had decided not to appeal. Dietrich had said he was considering a motion for a new trial, followed by an appeal if that was overruled, but Judge Reeves said the defendants' decision meant "the matter is all over. . . . There will be no . . . delay in the executions. . . ."

That same day, Carl and Bonnie were taken to the state penitentiary in Jefferson City.

It was a terrible place. An old, ugly, dark prison. The cellblocks in tall buildings encrusted with grime, the ground between them bare and pitted. Broken windows everywhere, the lives behind them broken also. An overall sense of filth and despair, the whole enclosed by a dirty high wall.

Executions were carried out just after midnight. A short time before, the witnesses were led across the prison yard to the small building containing the gas chamber. In the dark, they picked their way nervously over the rough ground, barely able to see where they were going, while all around them arose a howling and shrieking, a ghastly clamor, a banging on windows and walls, the inmates saluting him who was to die, jeering those who were to watch, screaming their own misfortune, raving and raging in the night. There were thoughts of hell; there were speculations on madness and damnation.

The gas chamber was a round structure about eight feet in diameter and made of thick steel. The interior was entirely bare except for a heavy steel chair in the center (for Bonnie and Carl, a second chair was installed; they were to be executed together). A cup was suspended under the chair, and powdered potassium cyanide was poured into it. On the floor, directly beneath the cup, was a lead-lined bucket containing sulfuric acid.

The witnesses stood around the outside of the chamber, looking in through large windows. The condemned person was brought in, blind-folded, and strapped into the chair—thick leather straps around the chest, stomach, wrists, knees and ankles. When everything was ready, the heavy steel door was closed and locked with six large pressure wheels. A few moments later, the warden pulled a lever that tilted the cup, dropping the potassium cyanide into the sulfuric acid and creating cyanide gas. The witnesses saw a whitish-gray mist swirl up and fill the chamber. The victim was unconscious the moment he or she drew a breath.

It was a journey of terror that went faster and faster; the last weeks became days, became hours, became minutes. Then the iron door clanged shut, and it was moments. Now there was only a vast, immeasurable, suffocating fear, an unbearable fear, greater than anything ever known. The chest swelled and swelled until it seemed it must burst, the heart pounded violently, a nauseous bile rushed into the throat and mouth, the body trembled furiously, the bladder and bowels emptied, everything was out of control, spinning madly in a universe that had suddenly constricted to a single white-hot point of fear. An existence was racing toward that blinding point, would shatter against it, and be obliterated.

It was always rumored that it did not happen this way, that sedatives were administered beforehand and the condemned were merely drifting and dreaming in those last moments in the execution chamber. But Warden Ralph N. Eidson insisted Carl and Bonnie were given no drugs. "It may be done in some institutions," he said, "but it is definitely not done in ours."

Carl was in Cell 18 on Death Row, Bonnie in Cell 25. Each cell was seven by eight feet and had a metal cot, a toilet and a small washbasin, nothing else. The lights in the cellblock were never turned off, and a guard was stationed day and night outside Carl's cell and a matron outside Bonnie's.

In the month between the sentencing and the executions, a great deal was said and written about the condemned killers: what they ate, how they passed their time, how well or badly they slept, whether they repented their crime, whether they were prepared to die.

Bonnie spent most of the time lying on her bed reading magazines—any kind of magazine; she wasn't particular. Carl didn't read as much, but he got halfway through Bishop Fulton J. Sheen's *The World's First Love;* no one knows how. There were conflicting reports on whether he was repentant. All the clergymen who visited him said he was. One declared that

"Carl Hall died a tremendous witness for Christ." He quoted Carl as saying: "Tell the world. Tell them that only God is important. I know now." Another said Carl had "accepted spiritual counsel" and had achieved "an inward peace." But a prison official said Hall told him his only regret was that he had gone on a drunken spending spree in St. Louis that drew attention to him and led to his capture.

Inward peace is fine, but there were a lot of people out there who wanted to watch Bonnie and Carl die, die, die. U.S. Marshal William B. Tatman said he had received five thousand requests to witness the execution. However, only eighteen official witnesses and a few other persons were admitted. No member of the Greenlease family asked to be present, but Norbert S. O'Neill, one of the Greenlease business associates who had negotiated with the kidnappers, was a witness. Afterward he said: "I bucked myself up by thinking of little Bobby."

Little Bobby, yes. There was great interest in the execution, but not much sentiment for mercy. Missouri's governor, Phil M. Donnelly, said he had received only twenty or twenty-five appeals for clemency, most of them urging life imprisonment for Bonnie. Because it was a federal case, Donnelly pointed out, there was nothing he could do; only President Dwight D. Eisenhower could change the sentences. In Washington, the Justice Department said it had received only six pleas for clemency. Eisenhower took no action.

Eighty-one days after the kidnap-murder, Carl and Bonnie were executed. Bonnie's aunt, Mrs. Baker, came to the prison for a last visit, and then the condemned couple were permitted to talk to each other for about thirty minutes, with Bonnie sitting in a chair outside Hall's cell and speaking through the bars. No one listened in, but Marshal Tatman said "they appeared happy, and eager to see each other."

Shortly before midnight, they were driven to the building containing the gas chamber. As they started out, they could see the lights of Christmas trees and other holiday decorations in the prison. Before they got to the building, however, prison officials ordered the lights turned off. But it was a clear night; the stars remained.

In a small room next to the gas chamber, Bonnie and Carl recited the Lord's Prayer with two Episcopal priests—Reverend George L. Evans and Reverend Robert H. Bull II, both of St. Paul's Church in Kansas City, Kansas. Then Evans read the prayer for the condemned, from the Book of Common Prayer.

Just before they went into the gas chamber, Carl and Bonnie smiled at each other, held hands for a moment, and then kissed. Bonnie's lipstick was visible on Carl's mouth as he entered the chamber.

They were led in blindfolded. "Please be careful and don't let me fall," Bonnie said. Then, as they were being strapped in the chairs: "It's tight. I'm not going anywhere." Then: "Honey, do you have enough room?" Hall did not answer. Then: "Is my dress pulled down?" And finally, just before the warden pulled the lever:

"Are you doing all right, honey?"

"Yes, mama," said Hall.

Thus died the man known as "M." Money starts with an "m." So does mama.

Chapter **26**

*I*n mid-December, Lou Shoulders offered a slight revision, to see how it would play. He stuck to his basic story—that Hall's luggage was brought to the Newstead Avenue station with the kidnapper—but he changed the time element a little.

In the new version, Shoulders said he left the footlocker and suitcase in the police car while he was booking Hall, and then slipped the bags into the station *about ten minutes later*. He said this explained why none of the witnesses saw the luggage. It wasn't actually in the station at that point; it was outside, in the police car. After he finished booking the suspect, Shoulders said, he went out to the car, got the bags and tippy-toed in with them. He said he did this to keep things as quiet as possible until he could question Hall and find out why the bags were full of money.

It didn't play. It was too obvious. Shoulders was clearly trying to answer the Newstead Avenue Seven, whose recollections had become public by now. He was trying to show how he could have carried in the luggage without anyone seeing it. But the symmetry was fearfully against him. No one saw the bags brought in with Hall, and to balance this, no one saw them brought in ten minutes later. Instead, police clerk Walter McDowell testified that he saw Elmer Dolan bring in a footlocker *an hour and twenty minutes later*.

And there was something else. The new sequence called for Shoulders to be in two places at the same time. He is sneaking the bags into the station, but he has already left the station. This relativistic miracle, requiring a speed faster than light, was necessary because of Shoulders' previous testimony. He said he and Dolan left the station immediately after booking Hall, to deliver Shoulders' car to his girl friend. Immediately. So when did he bring in the bags?

The grand jury had been moving along. In October, it had questioned Shoulders, Dolan, Joe Costello, Oliver Johnson and Sandra O'Day. Then, in December, it summoned the seven police-station witnesses and Viola Freeny, the woman who had seen Hall brought out of the Town House without luggage. Several FBI agents also testified at this time.

On December 18, the jury indicted Dolan for perjury. On December 29, Shoulders was indicted on the same charge. The indictments said both men had lied in their sworn testimony about Hall's luggage.

"The aforesaid testimony of Louis Shoulders, as he then and there well knew . . . was untrue and false in that the suitcases . . . containing the ransom money were not taken into the police station at the time and in the manner alleged in the above-mentioned testimony of said Louis Shoulders," the grand jury charged. The wording was the same for Dolan.

Shoulders had done his plaintive best:

"Now for goodness sakes, ladies and gentlemen of this grand jury, I wish there had been 10,000 [people] seen me, or at least two or three policemen had been loafing around out there and seen me bring those suitcases in. Then I wouldn't have had all the trouble I have had. . . . Anyway, they didn't, and at the time I didn't want them to."

He hadn't worried about leaving all that wealth in the police car, unguarded, to hastening ills a prey. It was only for a moment or two, and "there were police around there," he told the jury, although he had just said there weren't. "Nobody was going to pick up suitcases right in front of a police station. Maybe they would, but I don't think so. . . .

"So we took Hall in. I took him over to the desk and booked him. In the meantime I think Elmer had one of them suitcases and went right straight back . . . to my office." As soon as Dolan came back, "I went outside and got that [other] suitcase in. . . . I got in the back of my office, and I done it purposely so nobody saw me with this suitcase, and they didn't."

238

Shoulders' stories were like laundry detergent: ever new, ever improved. Now he was saying he carried the footlocker around to the back of the station and went into his office by the rear entrance.

No matter. The grand jury said it was all a lie.

Shoulders and Dolan were not charged with *stealing* the $300,000, because the FBI hadn't been able to prove they had. Instead, they were accused of *lying* about it. They would go to jail, and people would conclude that some sort of approximate justice had been done—that they were actually serving time for theft as well as perjury—but they were never brought to trial for taking the Greenlease ransom.

The cup had other sour dregs for the FBI. The grand jury indicted only Shoulders and Dolan, not Oliver Johnson and not Joe Costello. And, as bitter as wormwood, almost three months had now passed and the money had not been found.

Ollie wasn't indicted because the U.S. Attorneys in Kansas City and St. Louis decided the perjury case against him wasn't strong enough. He had sworn Shoulders handed him one of the suitcases and told him to put it in the police car, which wasn't true, but that was really all they had on him. He hadn't lied about bringing the bags into the police station, because he never claimed he was part of that fictional operation. He had stayed in his car, outside the station, hadn't said he helped carry in the luggage, and hadn't said he saw Shoulders and Dolan do so. After much deliberation, the prosecutors reluctantly let him off the hook.

Costello took the Fifth. Both times he appeared before the grand jury, he refused to answer any questions about his activities on October 5 and 6, saying it might incriminate him. He simply clammed up completely about the day the kidnappers arrived in St. Louis and the day they were caught, and he challenged the FBI to prove he was involved in the disappearance of the $300,000, if it could.

Confronted with Joe's unyielding silence, and having no witnesses who would say what he was doing on October 5 and 6, the grand jury could only wait and see whether the Grenap squad came up with something. Costello himself said the FBI knew exactly where he was on those crucial days. He implied that he had alibis and that the agents knew what they were. He did, and they did.

For the most important time—the night of October 6—Costello had two alibis. When the first one failed, he fell back on the second.

The first alibi involved May Traynor. She said she was at Joe's house around 9:00 P.M.—when Hall was being arrested—and Joe was at home, not over at the Town House stealing $300,000. Moreover, she said she just happened to go down to the recreation room in Joe's basement and there wasn't any money down there. If this had been true, it would have been a big help to Costello, but May admitted subsequently that it was a lie—she wasn't at Joe's house at all. Much later, another person confirmed the importance of the rec room. But by then, May was as dead as Barabas's wench, and so was Joe.

The second alibi was sturdier. The Grenap squad had a terrible time with it; an entire seventy-page file is devoted to the question of whether Costello was polishing his golf game on the night of October 6. Joe was now saying he was at the Arena Golf Tee, a driving range near Forest Park, addressing the ball, head down, left arm straight, smooth backward swing, powerful drive, fluid follow-through, and watch that sucker go. People spend hours doing this.

An Ace Cab driver told the FBI that he drove Costello to the Arena Golf Tee at about 6:00 P.M. and left him there. The agents didn't like this at all; they questioned him again and again. Was he sure it was October 6? Well, he was "almost certain" but not "absolutely positive."

That wasn't too bad. Considering the loyalty of Joe's drivers, a jury might look skeptically at this part of the alibi. But then a man said he had seen and talked to Costello at the the Arena Golf Tee around 9:30 P.M. on October 6. That *was* bad.

The man said he had been at the golf range earlier in the evening and had left twice to run some errands. When he got back the second time, he said, Costello and his wife and young son were there. He said there wasn't any doubt about it: They were at the Arena Golf Tee, and the date was October 6 and the time was around 9:30.

Could it have happened that way? Shoulders and Dolan had arrested Hall around 8:15 or 8:30, and had booked him at 8:57. If Costello was the man Hall had seen in the corridor outside his room, then Joe would have had something like forty-five minutes—from approximately 8:45 to 9:30—to get the suitcases from Shoulders, take them somewhere, count out $300,000 and remove it, get the luggage back to Shoulders, possibly collect his wife and child, although Mrs. Costello could have driven her own car to the Arena Golf Tee, and get to the golf range. A damned close-run thing, but the implausibility wasn't really the problem.

The problem was what a defense attorney would do with it. Truth and justice are mighty, but when in trouble, go for reasonable doubt. With a witness who placed Costello at the golf range at 9:30 P.M., the defense could sow confusion and reap uncertainty.

Knowing this, the FBI decided to try for logic: Suppose it turned out that the Arena had closed early on October 6—long before Costello allegedly got there?

The agents found the Arena's cash register tape for October 6. It revealed total receipts of $2.40, representing the sale of four buckets of golf balls. They showed the tape to the employee who had been in charge of the driving range that day, and he said that with business that slow, he believed he would have closed early in the afternoon—no later than 2:00 P.M. But no record could be found that showed the actual time of closing. The defense would pounce on that.

So the weather was investigated. The agents obtained temperature readings for every hour of every day in October, and wind velocity records for October 6. The temperature at 2:00 P.M. on October 6 was 54 degrees, and the wind was fourteen miles an hour. For St. Louis, those were balmy conditions, but the Arena employee said they would have been "unfavorable" for hitting golf balls and he probably would have closed.

However, there was nothing in writing to prove he had—this was just a golf tee, not the National Security Council— so electricity was investigated next. If Costello had been correcting his slice at 9:30 at night, he would have needed lights. Unfortunately, the local utility, Union Electric Company, said there was no way to tell whether the power had been on or off at the driving range at that hour on October 6.

That took it back to human memory again. Another man, described as "a close associate" of Costello, told the Grenap agents he believed Joe was at the golf range that night; he said he remembered it because Costello bought him a hot dog and he didn't like hot dogs. He also said a woman at Arena told him Joe had bought ten or twelve buckets of balls, which he said would have kept Costello busy for four or five hours. However, the cash-register tape didn't agree with this, and after a while the man admitted he wasn't sure it was October 6 he was talking about.

A medical student at St. Louis University, serious about becoming a doctor, was taking golf lessons at the Arena. He told the FBI he went there about 7:30 P.M. on October 6 and found the driving range closed. He said he was certain of this. The place was "completely dark" and there was no sign anyone was there.

However, another man was equally sure the Arena was open. He said he and his thirteen-year-old son were there from about 7:15 to 8:30 P.M. on October 6 and at least five or six other people were also hitting balls. When the agents told him the cash register showed only four buckets of balls had been sold that night, he simply said he didn't believe it. Nothing much can be done with that attitude.

An FBI report said Costello was following the alibi investigation closely and had talked to several persons who had been interviewed by the Grenap squad. This happened frequently; the FBI would talk to someone about Costello, and then Costello would talk to the person to find out what he had told the FBI, and then the FBI would reinterview the person to find out what Costello had said. There was a certain situational looniness about it.

The alibi report said Costello indicated to some people that he was at the golf range that night, but the report added that he made no effort to influence what they told the FBI, or to intimidate them.

Apparently he didn't need to. He inspired loyalty in people, which was probably what an FBI source meant when he said Joe had leadership qualities. The Grenap squad questioned a woman employee of the Arena Golf Tee who could have been a key witness—she worked from 10:00 A.M. to midnight and she knew Costello. But when the agents asked her whether he had been there at the crucial times, she "absolutely refused" to talk.

"Do you remember the nights of October 5th, 6th and 7th?"

"Yes, I do," the woman said.

"Was Costello there on any of those nights?"

"I'm not going to tell you."

"Why not?"

"Because he's a friend of mine, and I regard him as a prince of a fellow. I'm not going to tell you anything unless he asks me to."

"What if we subpoena you for the grand jury?"

"Well, I'll tell them, but only if you do that, or Joe asks me to."

That was the risk. Under oath, she might tell the grand jury Joe wasn't there—or she might testify that he was.

It was a long and tedious investigation. The agents interviewed at least thirty-five persons for the sole purpose of finding out whether a golf range was open on a certain night. Some said yes, some said no, some said they weren't sure, and some said they didn't know, after which the Gallup poll asked them the location of Nicaragua. The music went round and round, and the defense could have made it come out reasonable doubt. So the alibi was never tested in court.

Costello had what could be loosely termed a gang. In his orbit were about a half-dozen men, most of whom worked for Ace Cab or had in the past. They were guys he had known for years and could trust. Some had done time, and all of them had rap sheets—criminal records—of greater or lesser magnitude. The old-fashioned word for them was hoodlums, later shortened to hoods. If they died violently, the newspaper headlines said, NOTORIOUS HOODLUM SLAIN IN GANGLAND STYLE, and readership improved.

When Costello emerged as the chief suspect in the ransom theft, his pals came under intense FBI scrutiny as possible accomplices. It was never proved that any of them helped him steal the $300,000, however, and it's possible none of them did. Nevertheless, they were prime suspects at the time, and foremost among them was Matthew Boyle (not his real name).

No one was more loyal to Costello and more trusted by him. If someone in the gang did help Costello get the money away from the Town House, says former agent Phil King, it would most probably have been Matt Boyle.

The FBI considered Boyle a suspect in the ransom theft mainly because of his close association with Costello. While unsavory, this was not indictable, but one FBI report was more specific. It said a "confidential informant" had noticed that Costello, Boyle and another member of Joe's gang were absent from the Ace Cab office at the time of Hall's arrest. However, this tip never led anywhere, and after a while, Phil King says, Boyle and the others in the gang were "more or less ruled out." But before that happened, the FBI had something in mind for Boyle. . . .

At the time of the Greenlease case, Matt was forty-three years old and had a criminal record that went back to his youth. While still in his teens, he was convicted of robbery and sent to a reformatory. He was seventeen when he got out, but when he was twenty he was behind bars again, this time in the St. Louis Workhouse. A year later, he was convicted of attempted robbery and carrying concealed weapons and was sentenced to two years in prison. Grade school, high school, college.

He once told the St. Louis cops he had known Costello "my entire life." So it was natural that he would go to work for Ace Cab, and ultimately he became a supervisor. He had been Joe's right-hand man at the cab company, he was godfather to Joe's son, and on one occasion, when Costello thought he was about to be arrested by the FBI, he hid out at Boyle's house. The FBI wiretaps show that the two men talked on the phone frequently, and even after Boyle ended his connection with Ace Cab, he continued to hang out there. Witnesses said he spent more time at the cab company than attending to the thirst of north St. Louis.

Costello had arranged a loan that helped Boyle and a relative buy a tavern on North Sixteenth Street, a few blocks from Ace Cab. The bar was called Club 16 and had formerly been owned by a counterfeiter. Matt was operating this dive, not energetically, when the FBI became interested in

243

him—and in the robberies at the Beatrice Foods Company and the Feld Chevrolet Company.

Both of these crimes had taken place before the Greenlease kidnapping, and they had been investigated by St. Louis and suburban cops, not the FBI. But the Grenap agents did not mock this useful toil; they were planning to do a number on Boyle, using the local material to pressure him. Before questioning Matt about the missing $300,000, they would look into "all his criminal activity," in order to put him at "the greatest possible disadvantage . . . in an interview." It was an ambitious idea. The FBI was going to try to turn Costello's closest pal.

On the morning of September 4, 1951, two men entered the office of Beatrice Foods and ordered the employees to lie down on the floor, which they did because the men were pointing guns at them. The robbers then took $5,385 in cash and checks, and went away.

Nine witnesses "positively identified" Boyle as one of the gunmen. He was arrested and charged with armed robbery. However, the charge was dismissed after some of the witnesses failed to appear and the rest changed their stories. They said they couldn't identify Boyle after all. The prosecutor asked one of them whether they would testify if he got the charge reinstated and put Matt on trial. The man reflected for a moment. Life was a problem. The problem was staying alive. "No," he said, "I don't think so. We're afraid we'd get our heads blown off."

On January 21, 1952, an employee of the Feld Chevrolet Company, in suburban Maplewood, was getting into his car in the company parking lot. A man came up to him, pointed a gun, and said: "Give me your money." He took $2,358 in cash and checks.

A few weeks later, the employee was called to the Maplewood police department to view a suspect: Boyle. He immediately identified him as the holdup man.

Later, however, the robbery victim was approached by another man—a big guy, six feet tall and weighing about 250 pounds.

"You should be completely sure of your identification," the big guy said. The employee then recanted. He said he was no longer sure it was Boyle. What with one thing and another, therefore, the case was dropped.

Two years later, the FBI reopened both investigations, trying to find a lever to use on Boyle. Agents checked the arrest records, talked to the cops who had handled the two cases, read the witnesses' statements and then reinterviewed them.

The agents had hoped to persuade Matt to inform on Costello. They would point out that the federal government had infused new vigor into the

Beatrice Foods and Feld Chevrolet investigations. They would warn him that he might be indicted after all, unless he cooperated.

But it didn't work. Everything depended on the witnesses—and they clung to life.

On New Year's Day in 1954, the newspapers got their chance: NOTORIOUS HOODLUM SLAIN IN GANGLAND STYLE. A member of Costello's gang met his end on a lonely road near Madison, Illinois, with two bullets in his head.

His name was John "Buddy" Lugar. He was not in Costello's inner circle, but he had been questioned about the missing $300,000 because for a while there was a theory that the money might have been hidden at a midtown hotel where Lugar lived (this phase of the investigation will be described in the next chapter).

Lugar had been arrested more than two hundred times, suspected of killings, bombings, robberies and beatings (some of them extremely vicious). His biggest score apparently was in 1930, when he and others got away with $1 million from a bank in St. Louis. Lugar's own uncle turned him in for that job, but later the uncle refused to testify against him, in the Beatrice Foods tradition. In 1932, however, Lugar was convicted of the attempted robbery of a bank in Des Moines, Iowa, and sentenced to fifteen years. But he was paroled in less than four, after some politicians interceded for him. Lugar returned to St. Louis, where he lived well despite an NVM (no visible means of support) rating. After his murder, it was discovered he was wearing a diamond stickpin, an expensive ring and two watches, and in his hotel room the cops found forty suits and a dozen hats.

On New Year's Eve 1953, he was celebrating in a bar, buying drinks for women, kissing them, having a fine time. He left the bar at 5:30 in the morning, in his Cadillac, saying he planned to continue his revelry on the East Side.

At 8:00 A.M. New Year's Day, a woman living near Madison saw three men get out of a car. Then she heard "a whole bunch of shots." Two of the men jumped back in the car and drove away, leaving Lugar's body by the side of the road. He had been shot twice in the head. His murder was never solved.

And that was that, except it wasn't. Lugar was dead but still useful. He made one more appearance in the Greenlease case, when Lou Shoulders offered the public a final revision.

In his grand jury and police board testimony, Shoulders had done

245

everything but give Joe Costello's Social Security number in identifying him as the second informant—the man who called him after Ollie Johnson's call. But Shoulders and Costello then staged the wiretapped charade recounted in Chapter 22, assuring each other solemnly, for the benefit of the FBI, that Costello had *not* been the second tipster.

Now, as his perjury trial approached, Shoulders talked to a *Post-Dispatch* reporter. No, he insisted, it hadn't been Costello, it really hadn't. It had been Buddy Lugar. He said he had mistaken Lugar's voice for Costello's.

"I plan to testify that it was Lugar, not Costello, who gave me this very important tip," Shoulders said. ". . . I had an urgent appeal from Costello, who called me today and said: 'Well, they've got me in it again on that tipster angle. . . . You ought to give the actual facts now.' In justice to Costello . . . I am giving this statement for what it is worth."

He did say, "for what it is worth."

Chapter **27**

*T*he missing $300,000 was at the Roosevelt Hotel, where Buddy Lugar lived.

It was at the Mobilfone Corporation, a company that installed two-way radios.

It was at the General Van and Storage Company, a large moving and storage firm.

It was at the Windsor Hotel, where Ace Cab reportedly rented a room.

It was at Costello's home on Gurney Court in South St. Louis.

Or none of the above.

When the search for the missing ransom turned from Carl Hall to Joe Costello, the FBI initially focused on Ace Cab, May Traynor's whorehouse and the Coral Court motel. All three places were investigated for many months (the Coral Court on the chance that Sandy and Ollie had rolled Hall after all), but they produced only a phantasmagoria of underworld speculation and dead-end tips. None of the three ever yielded anything concrete, anything that said flatly and definitely: Yes, the money was at Point A in the possession of Mr. X. Nor did they reveal the next step: Then it was taken to Point B and handed over to Mr. Y.

So the investigators had to check out the many other possible hiding places that rumor brought them:

1. The Roosevelt Hotel. An informant said the $600,000 ransom had been taken from the Town House to the Roosevelt Hotel, where it was divided, either in Lugar's room or in the room of an unnamed Lugar "associate."

The agents interviewed hotel employees, Lugar's friends and various other people. The most tangible information they got was that Buddy didn't make any phone calls from his room at any time on October 6 and that he apparently was in the room that night. This might indicate he wasn't at the Town House helping steal the money, but it didn't rule out his room as the place where it was split up. However, one of Lugar's friends, a gambler, told the agents he was with Buddy almost every night in the period just before his murder. He said he almost certainly would have known if Lugar had been involved in the ransom theft and had no reason to think he was. He also said Buddy was "a good burglar," which was as surprising as higher taxes. The Grenap squad finally decided there was nothing to the Roosevelt Hotel rumor.

2. The Mobilfone Corporation. This one was very tenuous. An informant said Costello and Matt Boyle had been seen at this company "on or about October 6." An FBI report said Mobilfone "may have been a meeting place, or a place where the missing ransom money could have been stored temporarily," but no evidence was ever found to support either possibility.

3. General Van and Storage. This rumor involved Shoulders, not Costello. It was reported that Shoulders or one of his friends might have hidden the $300,000 at General Van's warehouse on Delmar Boulevard, not far from the Town House.

It was the inventory scene in *Citizen Kane*. A vast expanse of furniture, sculpture, paintings and objets d'art, a sea of frescoes, tapestries, carvings, bronzes, brasses, bas reliefs, stained-glass windows, marble pillars, Greek vases, Roman murals, dismantled castles and crated cathedrals, an eternity of rare manuscripts, incunabula and sacred relics, the gold of the Incas, the jewels of Araby, Cellini's salt cellars, Dresden's milkmaids, Alexander's toothpick, Caesar's chamber pot. And somewhere among these treasures, somewhere in these acres of boxes, bales and cartons, was the missing Greenlease ransom? Hidden under Rosebud?

General Van gave the FBI the names of 103 customers who had deposited things at its warehouse between October 6, 1953, and January 1, 1954. The agents ruled out persons who had stored entire rooms of furniture and concentrated instead on boxes, trunks, lockers and suitcases. They scrutinized each storage slip, picked their way through the dusty accumulation to find the article, then examined it morosely for signs of ransom. Nothing.

4. The Windsor Hotel. This tip came from a man who had given the FBI some earlier information and then said he had forgotten to mention "a rumor." It was that the money had been divided at the Windsor Hotel, not the Roosevelt. But a hotel employee said he would have known if a group of men had met there on the night of October 6, because it was a very small hotel. He said there was "no unusual activity" at the Windsor that night.

There was also a rumor that Ace Cab maintained a room at the Windsor, but the employee said that wasn't so. An FBI report explained that this rumor may have started because a man involved in a cab strike had stayed at the hotel from September 3 to November 12. The agents took an interest in this man. They found he was "a sort of troubleshooter from New York who was in St. Louis in connection with the Yellow Cab strike."

The Yellow Cab strike? Why was a labor dispute involving another cab company mentioned in this report? The Yellow Cab fracas and out-of-town "troubleshooters" were to become important elements in the search for the missing $300,000. While attempting to identify Point A and Mr. X, it was also necessary to find Point B and Mr. Y. A St. Louis Mafioso, in a conversation with a man who turned FBI informant, alluded to this difficulty. "We have stuff that goes all over the country," he said.

5. Costello's house. The moment Costello became a suspect, the investigators assumed his residence would have served as well or better than Ace Cab as the initial destination for the money. Many businessmen bring work home from the office.

But how to prove it? The FBI never applied for a warrant to search the house—apparently it felt its case wasn't strong enough to persuade a judge to sign one. However, there was another possibility. . . .

Quis custodiet ipsos custodes? Did they have bag jobs in Rome? If the agents searched Costello's home illegally, there is no hint of it in the files; of course there wouldn't be. And if they did, what incriminations did they discover? Had Costello left the money lying around? They would have seen it. Did he hide it? They would have found it. Did he write a cryptic note: "$300,000 for me, rest to police station"? They would have deciphered it.

The agents believed Costello when he said, in one of the wiretapped conversations, that they could take his house apart brick by brick and wouldn't find the money. They may not have bothered with a bag job: too much risk with almost no chance of finding anything. Too much time had elapsed.

Hall confessed the kidnapping on the night of October 6, but it took *five more days* to get him to admit the murder—and only then did he say he had almost all the ransom when he was arrested. Until the night of October 11, the FBI thought *Hall* was the magician who had made the $300,000 disappear. During those five days, Costello didn't figure in the investigation at all, and actually it was longer than that—the FBI had to hear about the luggage that wasn't seen and the people who didn't see it, and then find them and talk to them, before it began to look at Shoulders and, after him, Costello. The agents lost precious time; Joe gained it. He had at least a week, probably more, in which to think of a foolproof hiding place—or turn the money over to another magician. Costello was slick and quick; he probably needed only a few hours. He would have whisked that money out of his house long before the FBI got in.

Since Costello might have kept the money or might have passed it to someone else, two lines of investigation had to be pursued simultaneously:

1. The first possibility was that Shoulders and Costello had pulled off the whole thing by themselves—perhaps with help from Matt Boyle or someone else in Joe's gang but without any major players from outside. In this scenario, Joe and Lou had not only stolen the $300,000, they had *held on to it,* hiding it somewhere known only to the two of them, or perhaps only to Costello. The FBI did not rule this out; it searched high and low for the place of concealment. In addition to the several already mentioned, dozens of others were investigated. The agents were everywhere, asking questions, checking stories, examining records, trying to pick up a trail that would lead them to the place where Costello had hidden the money.

2. But they had begun to think there might not *be* such a place, because Joe might not have kept the ransom. In that case, the loss of time would be even more damaging. If Costello had got rid of the money immediately, instead of hiding it, someone else had had a week or more to make it vanish, before the FBI even started to think about another magician.

Time was dominant now. Not sidereal time, absolute time or space-time, but Peter Lorre's time: You know what I think? I think time is a *crook.* The agents began to suspect time had been in the hands of some superior criminals, some people even more skilled and experienced than Joe Costello. They suspected they were chasing money that had been moved very rapidly and expertly. They thought it possible the ransom had been taken to another city altogether and laundered there, through an accommodating bank. They had begun to think it might have been a very *professional* operation. A John Vitale operation.

But they weren't *certain*. Costello could have done all that himself—sent the money out of town and had it hidden or laundered by his own criminal associates. Even now, Phil King says: "I really don't know whether Vitale was involved. . . . I just don't know about Vitale, one way or the other." And it was possible the FBI's sources had overstated Costello's closeness to Vitale, or even lied about it. Elmer Dolan, for instance, said it was "obvious" to him that Vitale "had a strong dislike for Costello." On the other hand, there was the underworld informant who told the FBI that Vitale was Costello's patron. Without the don's friendship, he said, "Costello would be nothing."

But neither friendship nor animosity was really the issue. The issue was $300,000. If Costello came into possession of a large amount of money and didn't tell Vitale, the same informant said, Joe "wouldn't last ten minutes, and he knows it."

And that, more than anything else, was the basis for the theory that half of the Greenlease ransom ended up in the pockets of the Mafia. If Costello had made a score of that magnitude, would he have dared to keep it from Vitale? Would he have run the risk? The don was certain to hear about it; the Mafia's intelligence apparatus equaled the government's in everything except cost. Vitale discovers Joe is holding out on him. Then what? Ten minutes.

On March 29, Elmer Dolan went on trial for perjury. The trial was held in Kansas City, with U.S. District Judge Albert A. Ridge presiding, and lasted three days.

Except for one thing, there weren't any surprises. Dolan repeated the testimony he had given to the police board and the grand jury—and the seven nemeses from the Newstead Avenue station repeated theirs.

Nevertheless, the FBI had taken pains. Its trial-exhibits section in Washington had constructed a scale model of the police station. The top lifted off to show the ground floor, and one wall was hinged so it would swing open. Using this model, the prosecution argued that the station's floor plan would have made it impossible for Dolan to bring in Hall's luggage without someone seeing him. The model was used again at Shoulders' trial.

Dolan was represented by a St. Louis lawyer named Mark M. Hennelly, who was considered a good man to have when you said something and seven witnesses said something else. Hennelly tried to plant as many doubts as he could. He asked police clerk Walter McDowell if he had been promised a promotion "for changing your story," and he challenged the testimony of Corporal Alexander Magee. He implied that Magee had gone along with the other no-luggage witnesses to cover up the fact that he was in the station when he should have been out on patrol.

However, McDowell said he had simply forgotten that he saw Dolan bring in a footlocker an hour and twenty minutes later, and when he remembered it, he came forward to amend his story. Magee explained that he came into the station to use the bathroom and stayed when Shoulders gestured to him to guard the door while Hall was being booked.

Doubt's meager harvest. The case against Dolan had not been shaken; the witnesses stuck to their stories. Then a thunderclap from the prosecution—the trial's only surprise, but a big one—in the testimony of FBI agent Frank F. Staab, a member of the Grenap squad.

Staab testified that he had questioned Dolan four times in November, after Dolan had appeared before the federal grand jury. The FBI was leaning hard on the young cop, figuring he and Ollie Johnson offered the best prospects for a breakthrough. And in November, it almost worked.

During an interrogation on November 3, Staab said, Dolan remarked that he "would be interested" in changing his grand jury testimony. Then on November 22, Staab asked him whether the suitcase and footlocker were brought into the Newstead station at the same time Hall was brought in. The FBI had asked Dolan this question again and again, and the answer had always been the same, but this time . . .

"No, afterwards," Dolan said.

For an instant, Dolan had let his guard down. But it was a chance remark by a tired and sorely beset young man. So the problem was: Could they make it stick?

Staab tried hard to clinch a breakthrough, but the missing-money investigation was like nailing gelatin to a wall. Dolan reverted to his original story. The moment passed—and with it, the best chance the FBI ever had to send Joe Costello to jail for stealing the $300,000.

Hennelly was on his feet, objecting, protesting, complaining, pleading, expostulating and remonstrating, as Staab sealed the case against his client. After listening to prosecution arguments that the agent's testimony should be allowed to stand, and the defense's insistence that it must be erased from human memory, Judge Ridge ordered the testimony stricken from the record and instructed the jury to disregard it. But the jurors had heard part of Staab's narrative—the most damaging part—and memory is often disobedient. On the other hand, Staab's contribution didn't determine the outcome. According to several jurors, the seven witnesses did that, the Seven Against Dolan.

Hennelly then stood on the burning deck, whence all but he had fled, to deliver his summation:

"Now, because of . . . a little inference here, a little inference there, Dolan is being tried for perjury," he told the jury. "If anything ever happened to one of my children and if anyone did what Dolan did [helping to capture Hall], I would get down on my knees every night and pray for him.

"There had to be a scapegoat when the government couldn't solve every phase of this matter," the lawyer continued. "There is no believable evidence against this man. He took the stand and told the truth. You are certainly not going to convict him on the kind of testimony you have heard."

But they did. After deliberating three and a half hours, the jury found Dolan guilty. Judge Ridge sentenced him to two years in prison.

Then it was Shoulders' turn. His trial began on April 12, also in Kansas City, before the same judge. The government called seventeen witnesses, but it was another rerun: The witnesses who counted were the Newstead Avenue Seven. Assistant U.S. Attorney Kenneth C. West asked each of them the same two questions:

"Did you see either Shoulders or Dolan bring in anything resembling a suitcase? Did you see any suitcases in the [police] station at any time that evening?"

Six of the seven answered "no" to both questions; with them it wasn't complicated. The seventh was Walter McDowell, back again so another defense attorney could rough him up. The young clerk repeated that he didn't see any luggage while Hall was being booked, but he saw Dolan wrestle in a footlocker an hour and twenty minutes later.

Shoulders' lawyer, Henry G. Morris, had a transcript of McDowell's first statement to the St. Louis police board, in which he said he didn't have a full view of the booking area and didn't see any luggage until the next day.

"Well, which story is true—the one you told then or the one you're telling now?" Morris demanded.

McDowell's explanation was the same he had given at Dolan's trial: After "further thought," he had remembered the footlocker. This did not satisfy Morris:

"Giving this matter further consideration—does that mean what you did to change your story after FBI agents, police officials and others talked to you?"

"No, sir."

Morris pounded away at him. Question after question about the conflicting versions—taking him through it again and again. Finally McDowell said: "If that's written down there [in the transcript], I guess I said it."

Morris: "Then is [it] true?"

McDowell: "Yes."

In other words, he didn't see a footlocker an hour and twenty minutes later. That's what Morris wanted. He wanted that footlocker out of there. Now all he had to worry about were the other six witnesses, and he had an idea about them, too.

Their testimony, he told Judge Ridge, "merely went to the proposition that they did not *see* the suitcases brought into the police station. None of the witnesses testified that it was *impossible* for the suitcases to have been moved or carried into the police station without their seeing them . . . [emphasis added]."

Shoulders took the stand in his own defense, and cried.

When Morris asked him to describe his education, the big cop began to weep, reaching up behind his glasses to wipe his eyes.

"I'm sorry to say I had very little education," he said.

"What was your education?" asked Morris softly.

"Fifth grade, second quarter," Shoulders replied.

At one point, he was crying so hard that Judge Ridge recessed the trial for fifteen minutes, to let him pull himself together. And when he wasn't blubbering, he was pugnacious, or his testimony would ramble off into irrelevancies. "Don't argue with the court," Judge Ridge would tell him, or, "Just answer the question."

After a while, he calmed down and testified about the events of October 6. His narrative wasn't very smooth—a couple of times he contradicted Dolan's version, for instance—but his fundamental position was fundamentalist, unaffected by the coaxings of sanity. He stuck unswervingly to his story. After that, it was up to Morris, also on the burning deck.

The government's witnesses, the defense attorney said in his closing argument, "have gone through brain-washing." Then he added: "Where is there direct evidence to dispute the testimony of Lieutenant Shoulders that he thought Patrolman Elmer Dolan brought one suitcase into the station, and that he [Shoulders] later brought the other suitcase in? . . ."

The jury deliberated for a little over two hours, and took two ballots. The first was eight to four for conviction; the second settled it. "This [was] the proper verdict to reach in this case," Judge Ridge told the jury, and later he said the evidence "conclusively proved the charge of perjury." He sentenced Shoulders to three years in prison.

Both Shoulders and Dolan appealed, but the judge refused to free them on bail while the appeals were pending. He ordered them to jail immediately. Dolan was sent to the federal prison at Texarkana, Texas, and Shoulders to the U.S. Medical Center in Springfield, Missouri, an institution for prisoners who require medical attention. He had a heart condition.

On January 21, 1955, while they were serving their sentences, the United States Court of Appeals for the Eighth Circuit rejected their appeals. In a decision written by Judge John B. Sanborn, with Judges Joseph W. Woodrough and Harvey M. Johnsen concurring, the appeals court said:

"Our examination of the entire record leaves us in no doubt that Dolan had a fair trial; that under the evidence and the applicable law, the question of his guilt or innocence was for the jury [to decide]; and that its verdict was conclusive." Shoulders' appeal was turned down in almost identical language.

It was the end of the line; they served out their sentences, although Dolan won some time off for good behavior. The court's decision also meant that an obstinate theme had been heard for the last time. At long, long last, the Greenlease case was rid of luggage. Everyone was—and is—sick and tired of luggage.

Chapter 28

*C*arnival! The carnival's coming! Weeks ago, signs and placards blossomed all over town: the famous show, the thrill of a lifetime, fun for young and old. Bring your best girl, bring the wife and kids, turn out the whole gang. In the hot sunshine, in the good old summertime, hand in hand, let's go to the carnival!

And now it's here! Tilt-a-Whirls and death defiers, Ferris wheels and merry-go-rounds, the Dodg'em cars, the sights and sounds! Hit a target for a doll with golden hair; ring a gong for a teddy bear. The fairgrounds are crowded with people, strolling, jostling, laughing, carefree: Hence, loathed Melancholy. The carnival workers are selling tickets, chances, trinkets, food, drinks, candy, sweating hard for dimes and dollars. Everything is noise and confusion.

Then it's over, and small boys have their first experience of Melancholy. The tents are struck, the booths dismantled, the show moves on.

And a few days later, the FBI finds ten- and twenty-dollar bills from the Greenlease ransom.

*   *   *

They were discovered in Sedalia and Springfield, Missouri; Norris City, Illinois; Lamoni, Iowa; Salt Lake City, and Denver. Each of these cities and towns had recently held a state or county fair that included a carnival. When the Grenap squad began looking into these touring shows, underworld informants said several of them were controlled by Chicago gangsters. The agents had a new investigative line to pursue: the possibility that the Mafia was using carnival workers to put the ransom money into circulation. In the casual atmosphere of a carnival, it would be easy to slip in a Greenlease ten or twenty when changing a larger bill for a merrymaker.

Therefore, the investigators took the Carnival Theory seriously when banks began turning in ransom bills not long after a traveling show had left town. Took it seriously although they knew it had several weaknesses:

1. Most transactions at carnivals involved small sums—a couple of bucks or a five or ten. A carny worker would get only an occasional twenty, fifty or hundred that would enable him to pass a Greenlease ten or twenty in change. On the other hand, there were a lot of people at a lot of carnivals; over a period of time, it could be done, and the Mafia had time.

2. Only a few bills were attributed to the Carnival Theory. Over the years, from all sources—banks, citizens, everybody—the FBI recovered only 115 Greenlease bills, totaling $2,250, and only a small number of these were from banks in carnival towns. Of course, this could have meant the banks or the Federal Reserve caught only a fraction of a much larger amount distributed by carnival workers—in which case the unusual laundering technique was an immense success.

3. Or the small number could have meant that the "carnival bills" had nothing to do with carnivals at all; they just showed up from someone.

But who? It's a large country, and impatient, too. A customer makes a deposit that includes some tens or twenties, or he has some that he wants changed into smaller denominations. The teller asks him to wait while the serial numbers are checked. Other customers complain of the delay, or there isn't enough staff for this time-consuming chore; the bank decides its routine cannot be disrupted. There were more than fourteen thousand banks in the United States in 1954, and innumerable transactions every day. It was impossible to check all the tens and twenties as they came in—but that would have been the only way to catch anyone.

Some banks did look at serial numbers at the end of the day or thereafter, but if a Greenlease bill turned up, its source by then was unknowable. All the bank could do was notify the FBI to come and get the money. And in many cases, not even this much happened. Their telltale numbers uninspected, the tens and twenties were simply bundled up and later sent to a

Federal Reserve bank. Nor would it have done any good to scrutinize deposit slips; serial numbers of cash deposits are not required.

Confronted with this local anonymity, the FBI turned to the Federal Reserve. It asked the Fed to check the tens and twenties in the shipments of cash that it received from member banks. Since computers had not yet perfected their master plan for mankind, the Federal Reserve banks used a quaint punch-card system that will be described later. This told the FBI which banks had sent in Greenlease money, but it provided no clues as to who had taken the cash to the banks in the first place. It might have been carnival workers or criminals or ordinary citizens.

4. The last weakness in the Carnival Theory was a lack of uniformity. The FBI found out that carnivals had also played recently in Philadelphia, Kansas City, Frederick, Maryland, East Palestine, Ohio, and Quincy and East St. Louis, Illinois—but no Greenlease bills had turned up in those places.

Under these handicaps, the Carnival Theory gradually faded away. Former agent Edward M. Moreland points out that it was never more than a possibility: "As we looked at a map showing where ransom bills had been recovered, it occurred to Herb Moss [Herbert K. Moss, the Grenap squad's supervisor] and others that it might involve some people who moved around a lot, and this led to the Carnival Theory. But it was just a theory. We never identified any carnival as being controlled by the mob or any that passed the money."

The FBI was investigating John Vitale, but it was keeping it as quiet as possible. A file was begun on his possible involvement in the theft of the ransom money, but a Grenap report said: "There still continues to be no open investigation, as such, of John Joseph Vitale [although] continuous inquiries are being made regarding his activities . . . because of his . . . relationship with suspect Joseph Costello. . . ."

The investigation was being kept "discreet," the report said, because if the FBI's interest in Vitale became known, information from "certain sources" would be "reduced substantially," and because if a deal was being arranged for Vitale to handle the $300,000, the agents didn't want to upset it; they wanted to know about it. They were probably too late, and they sensed this, but perseverance, dear my lord, keeps honor bright.

A third reason for the hush-hush, the report said, was Vitale's "numerous contacts outside St. Louis." This was not explained, but the author learned later what it meant: While the FBI was investigating Vitale in the Greenlease case, it was also looking into his ties with the Chicago crime syndicate. Specifically, it was interested in his dealings with Sam Giancana.

As part of the Chicago investigation, which also involved "people in Kansas City and Las Vegas," the FBI had bugged a Chicago dry-cleaning shop that Giancana used as a meeting place. Vitale and "other members of his gang" apparently were in and out of this shop also. The FBI was anxious to conceal the fact that it knew about the meeting place; it kept the Vitale-Greenlease inquiry as quiet as possible so as not to jeopardize the Chicago case.

The agents thought of Chicago and St. Louis as separate investigations; they had no way of knowing, at the time, that there would turn out to be a certain relationship between them. The Greenlease-ransom theft was never really solved—and yet it may have been; God was doing paradox again. And to some extent, Giancana would figure in the putative solution.

In big-time crime, nicknames are required: "Scarface Al" Capone, Jack "Legs" Diamond, George "Bugs" Moran, Jake "Greasy Thumb" Guzik, Anthony "Big Tony" Accardo. By this measurement—or any other criterion—Sam Giancana was a very important crook. He had *three* nicknames: "Mooney," "Mr. Mooney" and "Momo."

Before he was twenty years old, he had been arrested three times on suspicion of murder—in those days, no one was actually *convicted*. His ferocity and cunning marked him early for success, and he rose swiftly. In his prime, this small, sly man, with his feral smile and dark glasses, was believed to rank third—behind "Big Tony" Accardo and Paul "The Waiter" Ricca—in the huge crime organization that Al Capone had bequeathed to Chicago. Giancana controlled all gambling operations in northern Cook County, an immense fiefdom, and operated in Cicero, Illinois, as well.

He was already well known in 1954, and later events made him famous. A congressional committee discovered that he had plotted to murder Cuban leader Fidel Castro, at the direction of the Central Intelligence Agency. (Giancana's partner in this tax-supported venture, John Roselli, was later found in Biscayne Bay, in a barrel of concrete.) Castro easily foiled the various schemes, but the labyrinthine Cuban trail ultimately led to a suspicion that the CIA and the Mafia had been involved in the assassination of John F. Kennedy. For a while, this disturbed people.

259

*   *   *

The Mafia has always offered a varied product line: gambling, liquor, prostitution, hijacking, loan-sharking, labor racketeering, extortion, murder and theft. But Gresham's *real* law is that tremendous money drives out merely big money. Drugs, therefore, have become paramount. There never has been money to compare with drug money; a failing species will pay any price, bear any burden, support any cause that assists in its own destruction.

St. Louis was early in the field. In the 1940's and '50's, the city's Mafia operated an impressive drug ring that supplied heroin to a large part of the United States, including the biggest market of all, New York. The leader of the St. Louis Mafia at the time, Anthony Lopiparo, was said to be involved in the ring, but the driving force apparently was a younger mobster, Anthony G. "Tony G" Giordano. Another member of the drug ring, authorities said, was Giordano's longtime friend, John Vitale.

Although Vitale was arrested scores of times—suspected of murders, bombings, beatings, the usual litany—his only major conviction was in connection with drugs. Federal agents raided a tavern he was operating in downtown St. Louis and found a large amount of heroin. The government said later that Vitale and Giordano continued to traffic in heroin until at least 1955, buying it overseas through Charles "Lucky" Luciano, a renowned gangster who had been deported to Italy.

But there were hints that as Vitale grew older he may have turned away from drug dealing. In the 1970's and '80's investigative reports began to mention him more often in a Las Vegas context.

The long, silent rows of people feeding their hopes, forever, into the slot machines of Las Vegas are a paradigm of modern America, like the teenage girls wandering endlessly through shopping malls, or the talking toilet bowls in TV commercials. But the Mafia was not fanciful; nor was it concerned with life's emptiness. It saw money.

In 1971, a man named Primo F. Caudera went to the FBI with a business complaint. He said he was a promoter of gambling tours to Las Vegas—transporting the dreamers to the dream—and Vitale, Giordano and other St. Louis gangsters had been extorting $1,000 from him for each trip he organized. Recently, Caudera said, Vitale and the others had decided that his tours were cutting into their own tour profits and had notified him that henceforth he must pay $3,000 a trip. A few weeks after he talked to the FBI, Caudera's body was found in the trunk of his car.

In 1981, an FBI affidavit said the St. Louis and Denver mobs had secretly invested in a Las Vegas hotel and casino, and the St. Louis and Detroit

Mafia had bought another casino, also secretly. The affidavit said some of the gambling profits from both casinos were "skimmed"—illegally concealed to avoid taxes—and that as much as $50,000 in skim money from just one of the operations had been sent to St. Louis, with some of it going to Vitale.

It's not easy to draw up organizational charts for the Mafia. Minutes of meetings are not kept, and there are no press releases announcing personnel changes; these must be deduced from bullet holes. It is clear, however, that Giordano succeeded Tony Lopiparo as head of the St. Louis mob in the early 1960's. Vitale became Giordano's *consigliere*—counselor and second in command—but many cops and FBI agents considered them virtually interchangeable as don. When Giordano went to jail in 1974 for conspiracy, in connection with his secret ownership of a Las Vegas casino, Vitale came out of semi-retirement to take charge. Giordano was released in 1977 and resumed control, but when he died in 1980, Vitale again took over, until his own death in 1982.

They were very different personalities, and that may have been the key to their partnership; they complemented each other. Giordano was aggressive, belligerent and inclined to violent anger. Cops, reporters, the federal government's Organized Crime Strike Force and young women in tight jeans were among the greatest annoyances of his life; it was even worse if the girl wasn't wearing a bra. Vitale was a considerable contrast: calmer, less temperamental, more deliberate. He dressed well, was very fond of golf (playing golf, he once said, was vastly preferable to running a mob), had a certain urbanity about him, and was far more sociable. Unlike his colleague, he got along fairly well with federal agents, the media and other professional irritations. He was probably the most popular crook in town.

"I would call him and ask him to come down to the office," recalls former FBI agent John Poelker, "and he would say, 'Sure, I'll come down. I'm not going to tell you anything, but I'll come down.' He was a very accommodating guy, actually sort of gracious." Journalist Sally Bixby Defty, very knowledgeable about St. Louis and the first woman to become city editor of the *Post-Dispatch,* wrote that Vitale was sometimes called "the gentleman gangster" because of "his natty appearance and his civility to police and reporters."

Although Phil King says he isn't sure to this day whether Vitale was involved, the "Mafia theory" gradually came to dominate the investigation—the belief that the Mob had obtained the money from Joe Costello, had taken it somewhere and had either put it into circulation, by laundering it in some way, or had hidden it.

The Mafia investigation lasted longer—and was more frustrating—than any other aspect of the Greenlease case. For months the FBI tried to find out whether the Mob had taken the money, and if so, what it had done with it. For months, it probed and poked at this hard, silent criminal organization. And despite the uncertainty about Vitale, much of the investigation centered on him—because there really wasn't anyone else.

The possibility that Costello might have handled the whole thing himself had been debated ad infinitum, but like Omar Khayyám it always came out at the same place: Would he have dared freeze out Vitale? Moreover, Costello's connections with criminals in other cities, who might have helped him move the money, were nowhere near as extensive as Vitale's. Costello was essentially local; Vitale was national, when he needed to be. Had Costello nevertheless enlisted an out-of-town mob to help him? Why would he? He had Vitale right at hand. And using someone else would have risked the don's basilisk eye and swift, terrible vengeance.

Early in 1954 therefore, the investigation spread to five other locales: Kansas City, Chicago, Detroit, Colorado and central Wisconsin. In some cases, the FBI had received tips that gangsters in those areas might be involved; in others, their ties to Vitale made them targets.

In Kansas City, the investigation focused on two prominent gangsters who will be referred to pseudonymously as Joseph Ramone and Charles Travella. Both had long criminal records, and both had close ties to Vitale.

At the time of the Greenlease case, Ramone was thirty-nine years old. He had started out, the FBI said, as "a petty sneak thief," but he was upwardly mobile—he turned to stealing automobiles and auto parts, and he also did some whiskey hijacking and counterfeiting. By 1954, he had achieved "an expensive home," a Cadillac and "tailor-made clothes," according to an FBI report.

In 1946, an election was held in Kansas City. There was a controversy about it, and the ballots were impounded while the matter was investigated. On the night of May 28, 1947, the safe in the election commissioner's office was blown open and the ballots were stolen. A woman implicated Ramone and four other persons in the ballot theft. The woman was then murdered. Ramone was one of the chief suspects, but he furnished an alibi. It couldn't be broken, although it was unconvincing. He said he was with another gangster at the time.

262

The vote-fraud case, and many other things that were going on in Kansas City in those days, involved Charles Binaggio (his real name), a very powerful gang leader who had taken over most of the rackets and was a political force as well. After the ballots were stolen, Ramone "increased in stature [in] the underworld in Kansas City" and became one of "the strongarm lieutenants [in] the Binaggio group," the FBI said. He was a rising man in the organization.

And to help out, everyone kept getting murdered. In 1950, Binaggio was bumped off. An FBI report said there was "considerable speculation" that Ramone may have been one of the killers. In any event, he took over part of Binaggio's empire. By 1954, the FBI said, Ramone and another hood were running the rackets on Kansas City's north side.

In February of that year, he decided he needed a rest. He drove down to Florida, accompanied by his pal, Charles Travella. They stayed at a Miami motel from February 16 to March 6. Their vacation companion was John Vitale.

Learning of the reunion, the Grenap squad asked the FBI's Miami office to locate the gangsters "but not place them under physical surveillance." Miami agents found their cars at the motel, and apparently there was some surveillance after all, because the reports tell of several stakeouts, among them "a continuous surveillance" on February 20 and 21 at one residence that Vitale or Ramone apparently had called or visited, and "spot checks . . . several times daily" at another.

It was a standard operation. The agents obtained records of telephone calls by Vitale and Ramone and found out whom they had talked to, or tailed them to various places and found out who lived there. Then these persons were investigated.

That was the way it was going to be from now on: an ever-widening investigation of hundreds of persons who had any kind of contact with Vitale. It might be casual or suspicious, it might be an ordinary citizen or a crook, but it made no difference: The person contacted would be checked out. The FBI was a vacuum cleaner, sweeping up everything. The agents had done the same thing with Costello and were still doing it. And not only Vitale's contacts and Costello's contacts, but also the persons with whom their contacts associated, and sometimes the contacts of those contacts, unto the third generation. The reports filled up with names and then more names and then more. Someone kept track of them.

One tangible thing did come out of the Miami investigation. The agents got a look at some of the money Vitale, Ramone and Travella had spent during the vacation. None of it was Greenlease money.

*　　*　　*

Charles Travella was the other Kansas City hood who interested the FBI. One reason was that it suspected he had come to St. Louis on February 11, traveling under the name "E. Ross," to meet with Vitale and "a party from Detroit." The telephone number on E. Ross's plane reservation turned out to be the number at Travella's home; that wasn't very adroit.

In 1933, four men pulled off a series of truck hijackings in the Kansas City area. The drivers of the big interstate rigs were bound with adhesive tape and held prisoner while the contents of the trucks were sold. An FBI investigation led to charges against Travella and three other men, but a grand jury refused to indict them. While the hijackings were still being investigated, a group of men robbed a Kansas City bank messenger of more than $200,000, and murdered him. Travella was identified as one of the holdup men, the FBI said, but he slipped away. He was gone two years. When he was finally caught, there were "many delays" in bringing him to trial, and he was "never successfully prosecuted for this heinous crime."

The Kansas City police department gave the FBI the names of thirty-one gangsters who were known associates of Ramone or Travella. The FBI weeded out some of them on the grounds that they had left town, or life itself, and began investigating the rest.

It would be pointless to follow all these trails, since none of them led to the missing $300,000, but one has been selected as an illustration of federal thoroughness. It involved a gangster who will be called by a pseudonym, Tony Pino. With some additional name changes, the FBI report begins as follows:

"[An informant] of known reliability advised that Pino is apparently working for Joseph Ramone, operating the Bongo Club, and that Ramone apparently muscled Vincent Randazzo [not his real name] out of this club. . . .

"[Name deleted] stated that Pino has never had a bank account that he knows of and has always operated out of his hip pocket. He stated that Pino was at one time married and that his wife cleaned him out of everything. . . . He stated that Pino lives at the Weller Hotel [not its real name]. . . .

"[Name deleted] advised . . . that Pino had never paid the rent by check [and] for that reason he doesn't think he has a bank account. [He] stated that the lease for the Bongo Club and parking lot is in the name of Vincent Randazzo. It is a five-year lease effective January 6, 1951 to January 31, 1956, calling for a rental of $700 per month.

264

"[Name deleted] . . . advised that the license of the Bongo Club is in the name of Tony Pino for the year 1953; previously it had been in the name of Vincent Randazzo. He stated that this place had always been a source of trouble as it featured lewd and lascivious shows and are [sic] always in trouble with the vice squad. . . .

"[A member of the vice squad] advised Tony Pino and the Bongo Club had given him more trouble than any other place in Kansas City. He stated he has tried to close the place on numerous occasions but Pino is always able to get an injunction against him and remains open. [He] stated he doubts Pino has any money as he is a big spender and whenever he makes $100 immediately spends $150."

The FBI was trying to find out whether Pino had a bank account in which he might have deposited some of the Greenlease money. No luck. It was trying to determine whether he displayed any signs of sudden wealth. No luck. It found out where he lived, inquired about his reputation, traced the license, lease and rental at his place of occupation, talked to all kinds of people about him. Considering that Pino was only a suspect at third remove—an associate of two suspects (Ramone and Travella) who were suspects because they knew a prime suspect (Vitale)—it was a very thorough job. But no luck.

It will do no good to seek out the lewd and lascivious entertainment at the Bongo Club. That wasn't its real name, and the girls are now much older.

Chapter 29

*7*he possibility that Kansas City gangsters had helped Vitale dispose of the ransom money was investigated "intensively," Phil King recalls, but "nothing was ever proved."

Some Detroit mobsters were also under suspicion for a while. "There was a guy in Detroit who was close to Giardano and Vitale," King says, "but that turned out to be a dead end." A Grenap report said Detroit banks had put currency stops on the accounts of "several known Detroit hoodlums," meaning the banks checked tens and twenties deposited by these persons against the serial numbers of the Greenlease bills, but the stops were canceled at the end of 1953; they had yielded nothing.

The Detroit investigation may have been prompted, too, by the rumor that Ollie Johnson had given an Ace Cab driver $10,000 in ransom money, with instructions to take it to Detroit and "peddle" it there. But mostly "we were just looking at Mafia people who might have been connected with the money," King explained. The Kansas City mob was a hot prospect for quite a while, but Detroit seems to have cooled off early.

*　　*　　*

Then a reputed crime family in Colorado entered the picture. The Bonasera clan (not their real name) came under scrutiny on a backtrack from an investigation in Wisconsin, and also because of suspected Mafia associations. "Somewhere along the line," King says, "we got some information that because of their Mob connections they may have had something to do with handling the money."

The Grenap files do not indicate that the Bonaseras had any link to Vitale, and their Mafia identity in general was ambiguous; some of them apparently were respectable, hardworking Italian-Americans. A source who apparently was a local law enforcement officer told the FBI that as far as he knew, none of the four Bonasera brothers had any "criminal connections."

But in years past, Angelo Bonasera had been "head of the Mafia or 'Black Handers' " in southern Colorado, according to a "confidential informant of known reliability." He must have been the FBI's oldest informant; the Black Hand, as a name for the Mafia, went out with price stability.

Angelo had four sons. A Grenap report said three of them "have in the past had connections with former gamblers and racketeers in Pueblo and Denver."

The FBI amassed other information about the large Bonasera family—wives, widows, uncles, nephews and cousins—but some of it was so old it was genealogical. So the question was: What did it have to do with the Greenlease case? The answer may have been goat cheese.

One of the brothers, Philip Bonasera, had engaged in various business enterprises in Colorado, including a cattle-feeding lot and a goat-cheese factory. In 1953, he moved to Wisconsin, where he became overseer of a four-thousand-acre cattle ranch. The FBI thought it was possible he got the job because he had Mob connections, but it could have been his expertise with cows and goats. At any rate, it apparently was Bonasera's job in Wisconsin that sent agents backtracking to Colorado to investigate him. Then, when Angelo's ancient Mafia reputation came to light, the entire family was investigated. No evidence was ever found implicating any of them in the theft of the Greenlease ransom—but the FBI was intensely interested in anyone who had dealings with the owner of the Wisconsin ranch.

In this book, he has been given a fictitious name, Thomas Genova. A succession of mystery men and women had strutted and fretted their way through the long Greenlease drama, and now came one of the most mysterious of them all: an enigmatic figure living on a heavily guarded ranch in central Wisconsin.

With Genova, the Greenlease case began to narrow down at last. After Wisconsin, only Chicago would remain—and Genova had connections there as well. It is even possible the FBI had finally found someone who had been involved with the missing $300,000 after it left St. Louis. However, this was only conjecture. Many things about Genova were conjectural.

In 1958, the U.S. Attorney in Chicago, Robert Tieken, drew up an organizational chart, bullet holes and all, for the city's crime syndicate. He listed Anthony Accardo as the top man and Paul Ricca as second in command. The next in line, according to Tieken's diagram, was Thomas Genova.

The Chicago police were vastly experienced when it came to the Mob, although their knowledge tended to the same conclusion as studies of human folly: Nothing could be done about it. Their experience made the cops skeptical about the high rating given to Genova. But this may have been because they admittedly didn't know much about him. Genova had kept a much lower profile than Big Tony, The Waiter, "Mooney" Giancana, "Milwaukee Phil" Alderisio, Murray "The Camel" Humphreys and the rest of the nicknames. For a long time, he was uncommonly successful in keeping his name out of the newspapers. He stayed at his ranch in the far reaches of Wisconsin, and no one really knew what went on up there.

Law enforcement officers in Wisconsin were equally mystified. "Genova fits into the rackets in Wisconsin," one of them told the *Chicago Tribune*, "but we haven't been able to find out exactly what he's doing. [He's] sitting up on his ranch in sand hill country [and he's] losing thousands of dollars each year."

This was sarcasm at the grass roots. It referred to Genova's Wisconsin income-tax returns, which were examined by state investigators. From 1951 through 1959, he reported total income of $90,408—an average of about $10,000 a year. But in the same period, he reported $201,000 in losses on his ranch. Yet he seemed prosperous. He had a fleet of large trucks that drove in and out of the ranch, carrying Black Angus cattle, which are expensive. During the 1950's, when he seemed to qualify for food stamps, he was buying more and more land for his ranch; ultimately he had between four thousand and five thousand acres.

The Wisconsin investigators said their information showed links between Genova and "scores" of gangsters, including the Chicago boss, Accardo. In 1955, Big Tony headed a large delegation of hoods at the funeral of Genova's first wife, and the next year Genova attended the Fourth of July party that Accardo hosted annually on the lawn of his home. The Mob saw nothing remarkable about this celebration; it was the highlight of the criminal year. When Accardo's daughter was married in 1961, Genova was among the guests.

However, his social appearances were rare. He was almost never photographed, and the newspapers called him the invisible mobster. Although he had a home in Chicago, he spent most of his time at the ranch. But the state investigators said Genova ran the gambling and prostitution in Gary, Hammond and East Chicago, Indiana.

Yes, but how did he make a *living*? According to his Wisconsin tax returns and state agents, it was macaroni. A Chicago macaroni company paid him $138.50 a week as "a specialty salesman, promotional expert and sales supervisor." Other pittances came in from insurance commissions (he was a licensed insurance broker), an association of grape distributors, and a sewer-cleaning company. Cleaning them, from a Mafia standpoint, was an oxymoron.

Pinball machines were better. Between 1954 and 1958, according to later testimony before the Senate Rackets Committee, the Chicago Mob made $12,707,570 from pinball operations in Gary, Hammond and the rest of Lake County. Not all of this went to Genova—the Mafia has many Swiss bank accounts to feed—but neither was his share macaroni. The Senate committee described Genova as a "top syndicate person," and the *Chicago Daily News,* after conducting its own investigation, said "an invisible hoodlum baron"—Genova—"runs the Lake County rackets from a 4000-acre ranch [in Wisconsin]."

In 1954, however, none of this had come to light. Tieken hadn't listed him as one of Chicago's top gangsters, the Wisconsin authorities hadn't looked into his activities, and Robert F. Kennedy and Pierre Salinger hadn't investigated him for the Senate Rackets Committee. All the FBI had was a shadowy figure who might or might not have been involved in the missing Greenlease ransom.

So it's something of a mystery how they got on to Genova. There is no indication in the Grenap files that he had any connection with Vitale, and Phil King doesn't remember whether he did or not. One possibility is that a tip pointed to Genova. Or it may be that he was investigated simply because the FBI was combing through the Mafia—anywhere and everywhere—looking for leads. The final possibility has to do with the fact that a little of the ransom money was found in the upper Middle West. Not in Wisconsin itself, but not far away.

Chapter 23 told of a car with Missouri license plates that pulled into

George Wilson's gas station in Petoskey, Michigan, on October 14 or 15—eight or nine days after the ransom money disappeared. The driver bought gas and gave Wilson a twenty-dollar bill that could have been the Greenlease twenty discovered later by Mrs. Henry Krauser. The car then headed north, toward the Upper Michigan Peninsula. From there, it could have gone on to Canada or it might have turned west—to Wisconsin. And Genova was the FBI's only suspect in Wisconsin.

It was thin stuff—very thin, as slender as a presidential explanation. It was speculation pure and simple, but the Grenap squad couldn't ignore it. Suppose the missing $300,000 had been in that car, on its way to Genova's secluded, heavily guarded ranch? And suppose the driver, inadvertently or consciously, had used one of the Greenlease twenties to buy gas?

It has to be remembered that only a few ransom bills ever showed up. When they did, the FBI had to concentrate on the areas where they were found. It couldn't do as the drunk did when he lost his wallet on a dark street. He looked for it under a lamppost a hundred feet away because there was more light there. But the FBI had to go where the money appeared. So it focused on instances like Petoskey and suspects (or coincidences) like Genova—and, finally, on Chicago.

To the extent that the case was ever solved, the Federal Reserve's punch-card machines solved it. The machines turned up fairly strong evidence that the missing ransom had been taken from St. Louis to Chicago, and indications that it may have been laundered through a Mafia-linked bank—the Southmoor Bank & Trust Company of Chicago.

It had become clear, the FBI said later, that the list of ransom serial numbers "was so voluminous that banks and other institutions handling money did not have the time or manpower to check each $10 and $20 bill coming into their possession against the list." So the investigators turned to the Federal Reserve.

The Fed had punch-card machines. These were old-fashioned devices operated by old-fashioned human beings. In the FBI–Federal Reserve procedure, the punch-card operators were given ten- and twenty-dollar bills that had come in from member banks. They punched the serial number, Federal Reserve letter and series year of each bill into a card.

Then the card was fed into a collating machine that had a master punch card with the serial numbers, Federal Reserve letters and series years of the missing Greenlease money. If a punch card matched the master card, a ransom bill had been discovered. And the FBI knew which bank it had come from, because the tens and twenties were in packages with the name of the bank that had sent them in, and even the name of the teller who had packaged them for shipment to the Fed. Money was talking.

But it wasn't saying enough. The procedure was slow, and because it was slow, it was inevitably incomplete. The Federal Reserve Bank of Chicago, for example, received an average of 100,000 twenties each day from banks in its district, but it had only four punch-card machines, and the operators could make cards for only 20,000 bills a day.

This was a crucial point. The FBI had come up with a classic example of real-world investigation—hard, tedious routine, not glamorous at all, movie potential nil—but the Chicago Fed was able to process only about one fifth of the tens and twenties that came in. The rest went back into circulation without being checked. It will never be known how many of these were Greenlease bills. If the missing $300,000 was laundered into the spending stream, virtually all of it simply circulated until it wore out and was destroyed, without ever being detected. This is almost certainly what happened; it is doubtful to the point of impossibility that the vanished treasure still exists, hidden away somewhere. But unpersuaded optimists should start their search in Chicago.

The missing money consisted of 16,971 bills. Only 115 were ever recovered. The punch-card procedure traced 58 of these—almost exactly half—to banks in the Chicago area. The rest showed up from banks and private citizens in "widely scattered parts of the United States," the FBI said. There was a pattern only in Chicago, nowhere else. "We began finding [Greenlease] twenties coming in from Chicago banks to the Chicago Fed," Phil King says. "The Chicago banks got more of them than any other banks—we never got more than a few from banks in other Federal Reserve districts." And, he adds, more of them came from the Southmoor Bank & Trust Company than from any other Chicago bank.

Fifty-eight bills out of almost 17,000 is not an impressive sample. Dallas Anderson and other leading statisticians would demolish anyone who drew conclusions from that kind of data. But as small as the number was, it was half the total of recovered bills, and no other part of the country yielded anything close to that. What are patterns for? The 58 bills persuaded the FBI that the stolen $300,000 was most likely taken from St. Louis to Chicago.

The Southmoor Bank was more speculative. Someone *might* have brought the Greenlease money to this bank. Someone might even have

271

stored it first at Genova's ranch and then taken it to Southmoor. However, no concrete evidence was ever found to support either of these surmises, and there were other equally possible scenarios. In a 1966 memo, for instance, the FBI pointed out that Joe Costello "had contacts in Chicago, and . . . made trips to that city on many occasions." If Costello had handled the whole thing himself, it probably ruled out the Wisconsin ranch, since he had no known connection with Genova. It didn't necessarily eliminate the Southmoor Bank, but Costello could just as well have laundered the money at another Chicago bank. Of course, the Costello scenario encountered the Vitale objection.

As far as Genova's ranch was concerned, all the FBI had were his Chicago connections, so the ranch as a possible storage place was only a guess. But when it came to the Southmoor Bank, the investigators had a little more. First there was the fact that more of the Greenlease bills were traced to this bank than any another, and then there was the background of the bank itself.

"We found it had gang connections," says Phil King.

The bank's co-founder and chief stockholder was a man named Leon Marcus. He was "a very close friend" of one of Al Capone's henchmen, his bank was used by "all south side bookmakers," it was prominently involved in the $2.5 million looting of the Illinois treasury by State Auditor Orville E. Hodge, and its subsidiary, Southmoor Securities Company, loaned $150,000 to Sam Giancana.

Marcus was a Latvian immigrant with financial talent. During the Depression, he began buying real estate and, according to the Chicago and Miami crime commissions, associating with gangsters. In 1946, Marcus and another man, a bookmaker, founded the Southmoor Bank on Chicago's south side. The bookmakers quickly got the idea. "In order to operate a book on the south side," an investigative report said, "it was necessary to see someone in the Southmoor Bank."

At the bank itself, President Edward A. Hintz was cashing fraudulent state warrants (payments) for Orville Hodge; always get to know the president. The Southmoor Bank played a key role in Hodge's thefts; reporter George Thiem wrote later that the state auditor "couldn't have succeeded in looting" a state trust fund and money appropriated to pay contractors "without the aid of the top officers [of] the Southmoor Bank and Trust Company."

There isn't space in this book for a detailed description of the massive defalcations of Orville Hodge. Readers are referred to Thiem's fine account, *The Hodge Scandal* (St. Martin's Press, 1963). Hodge and Hintz went to prison in a scandal that, as they used to say, rocked the nation; familiarity has dulled this phrase.

One aspect of the Hodge case would have been of greater interest to the FBI if it had known Hodge would be revealed later as a world-class swindler, and the Southmoor Bank as his accomplice. The aspect was Hodge's financial interest in a hotel in Fort Lauderdale, Florida.

Hodge bought a half-interest in this hotel in January 1953. The Southmoor Bank loaned him the money. In December, Joe Costello went to Florida for a vacation, accompanied by his wife and May Traynor and tailed every step of the way by relays of agents from FBI offices along his route. (Costello spotted them every time; a Grenap report said he waved to them as the cars cruised down the highway.) The Costellos and May were in Fort Lauderdale for four days. They stayed at Hodge's hotel.

If the agents had known Hodge was a crook and had connections with the Southmoor Bank, and that Southmoor might have laundered the Greenlease ransom . . . but they didn't learn these things until later. It meant the FBI didn't look into a possible connection between Joe Costello and Orville Hodge. In itself, that wasn't a serious omission, because there was never any indication that Hodge had anything to do with the Greenlease money— but a Hodge-Costello investigation might have discovered whether Costello knew about the Southmoor Bank.

George Thiem's book is about the Hodge scandal, not the Greenlease case. But at one point he mentions that Hodge's insurance agency in Granite City wrote the liability insurance for the Ace Cab Company of St. Louis. It's likely, therefore, that Costello knew Hodge, and it's possible the underworld grapevine told him things about Hodge that the FBI didn't yet know. If so, he may have known what kind of bank the Southmoor Bank was. Did he handle the laundering by himself after all, using Southmoor? Without telling Vitale?

On the night of March 31, 1957, two men grabbed Leon Marcus, shot him in the head and dumped his body in a vacant lot. A piece of paper was found in his pocket. It said:

"Recieved [sic] from Mr. Sam Giancana, $100,000.00 to apply on mortgage in the amount of $150,000.00 on the property located at [address and name of a suburban Chicago motel]." The receipt was signed "Southmoor Securities Company." Southmoor Bank's subsidiary had loaned Giancana $150,000 to buy a motel.

So it was, almost certainly, a Mafia bank. Who would have been more likely to arrange for a Mafia bank to handle the Greenlease money: Costello or Vitale? That isn't to say Joe couldn't have done it, but except for his relationship with Vitale, he had no known ties to La Cosa Nostra. While Vitale on the other hand was a *member*. The chain of circumstances that had started in a Chicago dry-cleaning shop and had gone on to the Southmoor Bank seemed to lead not to Costello but to Vitale. Of course, that's all it was: circumstantial.

Viewed one way, it mattered who did it. Only the guilty should be punished and their reputations dishonored; many avoid this, but the world endorses the principle. Viewed another way, however, it didn't matter. Because *no one* was ever punished for taking the money to Chicago and cleansing it—possibly—at the Southmoor Bank. No one was even arrested, much less indicted, and the missing ransom was never found.

Someone had beaten the FBI. Was it Costello or was it the Mafia? Perhaps the question would be answered by the last mystery man.

Chapter 30

There ought to be a literary device to indicate the passage of time. Something better than the prosaic words, time passed.

But it did. The 1950's went on, and the Greenlease case began to fade away. Carl and Bonnie had been executed, the FBI had been unable to prove Joe Costello had a part in stealing the $300,000, Lou Shoulders and Elmer Dolan were serving prison sentences, ostensibly for perjury but actually for their roles in the theft, Oliver Johnson had gone to Los Angeles, where he wasn't talking and never would, Sandra June O'Day was continuing her turbulent pilgrimage, and a long, hard investigation had not recovered the money.

And time defeated the FBI. It was at least five days—probably more—before the investigation switched from Carl Hall to Joe Costello as the most likely suspect in the disappearance of the $300,000. Costello or the Mafia thus had plenty of time to take the money to the Southmoor Bank—or some other willing institution—before the Grenap squad got on the right trail.

When the punch-card arrangement went into operation, Phil King points out, the FBI found it was tracing tens and twenties that were coming back to the Federal Reserve Bank of Chicago for the second or third time. The bills had come in from Chicago banks at least once and gone out again before the punch-card system was set up. The laundering bank had lost no time putting the ransom money into circulation. It thereupon became anonymous.

Presumably there was discounting all along the line. Elmer Dolan said later that Costello and Shoulders offered him $50,000 as his share, but he turned it down. Afterward, he said, Costello informed him that he had sold Dolan's share for either 10 or 20 percent (on one occasion, he told Elmer he got $5,000 for it, another time, $10,000).

If the same 10 or 20 percent held for the entire $300,000, then it was sold for either $30,000 or $60,000—a meager return for the risk involved, but on the other hand, it was gravy; they hadn't *worked* for it. Since Dolan rejected his share, Costello and Shoulders got all of the $30,000 or $60,000. It is not known how they divided it; perhaps half and half.

Of course, Costello could have been lying to Dolan; he may have cut a more advantageous deal. But if it *was* 10 or 20 percent, then Lou Shoulders got only $15,000 or $30,000 (or less if it wasn't half and half) for a crime that ruined his career, wrecked his life and sent him to prison. Others have done better, usually on the lecture circuit.

Costello prospered—for a while. He got at least $15,000 or $30,000 and didn't go to jail, not then. But his role in the Greenlease case was the beginning of his downfall. From then on, the FBI never let up on him, made his life miserable, and finally put him behind bars on another charge.

There were, however, two winners:

1. The bank. If Costello acted alone, selling the ransom to the bank for 10 or 20 cents on the dollar, the bank's profit was $240,000 or $270,000. The corrupt executives of a corrupt bank bought $300,000 in stolen currency and channeled it into ordinary bank transactions, replacing $300,000 in regular bank funds. They then pocketed the regular funds, minus the $30,000 or $60,000 they had paid Costello.

2. The Mafia. If Costello sold the ransom to Vitale for the same 10 or 20 percent, the Mafia's first net was the same $240,000 or $270,000. It then sold the $300,000 to the bank, and the same laundering operation took place. But modern corporate practices required the Mafia to maximize its profit, so the bank's share would have been much less. However, it was a Mafia bank after all; a family matter, so to speak. If the Mob allowed it the same 10 or 20 percent it had given Costello, then the bankers also got $30,000 or $60,000. Or perhaps they demanded more for the risk they were taking.

276

Thus, when all the discounting was finished, when everyone had been paid, the Mafia's final net may have been between $180,000 and $240,000. How much of this did Vitale get? $100,000? $150,000? It's impossible to say. The Chicago Mob would have wanted a hefty cut, but the St. Louis don presumably got the largest share.

All the figures given here are suppositions; the entire edifice has been erected on a couple of remarks by Joe Costello to Elmer Dolan. The reality depends on what percentages were actually paid to Costello and the bank, and on the negotiations between Vitale and his associates in Chicago. They were very businesslike negotiations, it can be assumed. *Les affaires sont les affaires,* as Al Capone used to say.

And there is a final supposition: that it all happened that way—that Shoulders and Costello stole the $300,000, that Costello then sold it to Vitale, and that Vitale arranged to have the money taken to Chicago and laundered there, most likely at the Southmoor Bank. Was this the reality? Was this what happened to half of the ransom that Robert Greenlease had paid in a doomed effort to save his son? Was this the solution to a crime that was never solved?

In August 1958, there was a reprise. For a few days, the Greenlease case was the subject of national attention again. It was back in the headlines, briefly, as part of an investigation of the Teamsters Union. Several of the Grenap suspects came unwillingly to Washington to be questioned by the Senate Select Committee on Improper Activities in the Labor or Management Fields, popularly known as the Labor Rackets Committee or the Senate Rackets Committee.

The committee was headed by a grim old senator named John L. McClellan, a Democrat from Arkansas. The other Democratic members were Senators John F. Kennedy of Massachusetts, Sam J. Ervin, Jr., of North Carolina and Frank Church of Idaho. The Republican members were Senators Irving M. Ives of New York, Karl E. Mundt of South Dakota, Barry Goldwater of Arizona and Carl T. Curtis of Nebraska.

The labor racketeering probe brought prominence to the committee's chief counsel, Robert F. Kennedy, later attorney general and his brother's chief lieutenant; assistant counsel P. Kenneth "Kenny" O'Donnell, who became a White House aide to John F. Kennedy; staff investigator Pierre Salinger, who became presidential press secretary; investigator Walter J. Sheridan, and the committee's chief accountant, the formidable Carmine S. Bellino.

The McClellan committee's principal targets were the huge International

Brotherhood of Teamsters and its president, James R. Hoffa. In a long, sensational and often-stormy investigation, the senators charged that the Teamsters under Hoffa were a deeply corrupt organization with extensive and intimate ties to the underworld. The committee looked into literally hundreds of murders, beatings, pension-fund thefts, rigged elections, under-the-table deals, unsavory financial transactions and other illicit activities allegedly involving the Teamsters. And then in August 1958, the investigation worked its way to the missing Greenlease ransom.

Vitale and Costello were subpoenaed. They showed up at the appointed time, gave their names, took the oath and sat down in the witness chair, after which they seemed to disappear; there was no further communication with them. By coincidence, they were each asked forty-nine questions. Both of them refused to answer forty-nine times. They invoked the Fifth Amendment, saying responsiveness might incriminate them.

"Well," McClellan told Costello, "you ought to know."

However, the committee had other witnesses who *did* talk. One was a man who will be called Herman Brown (not his real name), an organizer for the Teamsters Union. Another was his former wife, Peggy (also a pseudonym). She testified that Brown had told her, "Joe Costello got the Greenlease money." Brown said he hadn't told her any such thing: "Absolutely not."

"Organize" is one of those words, like "patriotism," that language hides behind. Many people have been organized into the hospital. Herman Brown had been in St. Louis in the autumn of 1953, when the Teamsters were trying to organize the Yellow Cab Company. Robert Kennedy questioned him about this.

Kennedy: "Were you . . . beating people up in St. Louis?"

Brown: "No, sir."

Kennedy: "Was that part of your job in St. Louis?"

Brown: ". . . doing what?"

Kennedy: "To beat people up."

Brown: "My job was to organize unorganized workers [the cab drivers]."

Kennedy: "Was it part of your job to beat people up, intimidate them, and to cause damage to the taxicabs?"

Brown: "That is no part of no organizer's job, Mr. Kennedy, and it was not [part of] mine; no, sir."

Kennedy: ". . . It is just a coincidence that every place you go, there happens to be violence; is that right, Mr. Brown?"

Brown: "Every place I go there was no violence. . . ."

278

Against this background, Brown's former wife testified. She told the committee her husband went to St. Louis in November 1952 to work for a Teamster local there, and became a close friend of Costello and Vitale.

Kennedy: ". . . These were two of his close personal friends in St. Louis?"

Mrs. Brown: "Yes."

Kennedy then referred to the episode in October 1954, when Costello was found wounded at his home. He asked the witness: "Did Mr. Brown ever tell you why Joe Costello shot himself?"

Mrs. Brown: "Do I have to answer that?"

Kennedy: "Yes, you have to answer it."

Mrs. Brown: "Well, I don't want to answer it. After all, I have a little girl to raise [her daughter by Brown], and I know what I am dealing with. You may not know these people, but I do."

Chairman McClellan suggested the committee could hear her answer behind closed doors, but Kennedy objected: "It is extremely important . . . in connection with showing the tie-in of Mr. Brown with some of the most notorious gangsters and hoodlums in the United States . . . people who were [involved in] the most reprehensible kind of crimes."

Kennedy's insistence brought an anguished reply from Peggy Brown—a long, agonized cry from the depths:

". . . I may get killed for telling. But I want to tell these people and all of you, and the whole United States, that they don't even know, that since 1955 and 1956, the FBI in St. Louis have been sweating me about the Greenlease money. I didn't get a penny, and Brown knows that, from the Greenlease money. I didn't get a thing. But the man that got it must have prospered from it. But I have all the trouble with the FBI. I think it would be fair—I don't want to hurt or implicate anybody, that is a big, big thing—[but] I feel in my heart that I should be left alone by the FBI.

"You see, Mr. Brown does not know what he left me in. I hope he is here to listen to it. They tell me that I must have the Greenlease money. Well, he [Brown] did tell me who got it, and why the man shot himself, and I don't feel the FBI should sweat me any more. I think they should clear me. That is the only reason I want to make a true statement today. I feel the United States and the FBI should stop coming to me and trying to pressure me and annoying me and sweating me for the Greenlease money."

Then she answered the question: "Brown told me, 'Joe Costello got the Greenlease money,' and that is why he tried to kill himself. I should never

279

tell a soul, he said, but if I was ever questioned by the FBI, I should immediately warn Mr. Costello, which I did in 1956.''

McClellan asked her if she ever told the FBI what Brown had told her. No, she said, she told the agents she didn't know who took the Greenlease ransom—didn't know anything about the case at all.

McClellan: ''[But] you are now telling the truth about it?''

Mrs. Brown: ''Yes, I am, so help me God. . . .''

Money is an artist. It paints pictures. Such pretty pictures:

Two men steal a large sum of money, thinking it is from an embezzlement and then learning, too late, that it has the blood of a child on it. One of the men goes to prison and spends the remainder of his life hauling out trash cans. The other takes to drink, fires a bullet into his chest, is sent to prison later, and then dies. A woman lives in fear of her life, is tormented by investigators, and is finally driven to tell her story, wondering all the while if she will be killed for it. Yet we all wish to be artists. What pictures we will paint! Such pretty pictures!

Herman Brown denied the whole thing. He insisted he had never told his wife that Costello took the $300,000.

Kennedy: ''You didn't say anything [like] that?''

Brown: ''Absolutely not.''

Kennedy: ''This is all a figment of her imagination?''

Brown: ''Yes, sir.''

Then Kennedy pointed out that Brown had checked into a sanitarium in Battle Creek, Michigan, on October 8, 1953—two days after the money vanished. Brown said he went there ''to lose some weight, brother. I was a sick man.'' It did no good, however, to bring a medical excuse to Robert F. Kennedy.

Kennedy: ''Isn't it correct that you went there [to the sanitarium] because of the Greenlease money disappearing, Mr. Brown?''

Brown: ''Absolutely not, Mr. Kennedy.''

Kennedy: ''[Didn't the FBI suspect] that you handled some of the money from Mr. Costello?''

Brown: ''Absolutely not, Mr. Kennedy. Absolutely not.''

Kennedy probably did not think Brown had taken part in the actual theft. He was looking for the *courier*. He was implying that it may have been Brown who transported the $300,000 from St. Louis to Chicago to be laundered, and then checked into the sanitarium to get out of sight.

Many years later, Phil King told the author he believed the courier was either Brown or another Teamster official who will be called William Simpson. The Senate committee also questioned this man, but he wasn't asked about the Greenlease case. Simpson had been a bargaining agent for a Teamster local in St. Louis but had moved to a local in Indianapolis in 1951.

Committee investigator Walter Sheridan believes the courier may have been a man who will be called Russ Jones, a Teamster business agent who was also associated with non-Teamster unions in Indianapolis and Chicago. He was also a jewel thief. Without mentioning the Greenlease case by name, Kennedy questioned Jones about money:

Kennedy: ''Have you ever gone to anyone and asked them to get rid of some money for a few cents on the dollar?''

Jones: ''Absolutely not.''

Kennedy: ''Some hot money that you had?''

Jones: ''Absolutely not.''

Kennedy: ''Did you ever handle any . . . hot money or kidnap money, stolen money?''

Jones: ''No, sir.''

The Senate investigation had one important result, however. It led Walter Sheridan to Elmer Dolan. And this brought the missing-money investigation as close to finality as it ever got.

Before that, however, there were other finalities. One of them was the death of May Traynor.

They don't make madams like May anymore. A mehitabel, that's what she was. Toujours gai, there's life in the old gal yet. Here she is, telling the Senate committee about the time $17,500 was taken from her safe-deposit boxes. She says some FBI agents come to her house and ask her if she had cash in the boxes. ''I sure did,'' she says. Well, they say, ''You haven't got it any more.''

The agents take her to the banks, and $17,500 is gone. She says Joe Costello took it—he had access to the boxes—and she complains to his wife:

''. . . I tell her what happened. She said, 'What right did you have to let the FBI in your house?' I said, 'If anybody should ask you, that is my house, you so-and-so.' Then the fun started.''

But it isn't fun at all. It's the angry end of an old, close friendship. May files suit against Joe, saying he owes her $35,000 in unpaid loans and money he obtained from her ''improperly.'' She loses the suit—the judge says she didn't present enough evidence that Joe took the money without her permission. The old friendship turns into bitterness and enmity.

On September 20, 1961, at three o'clock in the morning, a man calls the police and says something seems to be wrong at May's house. When the cops get there, the front door is open and a burglar alarm is ringing inside the house.

May is in the front hall. Her hands are bound with tape. She is dazed and confused—an old woman staggering around the hall in her nightgown, hardly knowing where she is. And there is blood all over her. Her gray hair is streaked with it, her hands are covered with blood, there are splotches of blood on her nightgown. She has been beaten with a baseball bat and shot five times. There are two bullet wounds in her back, two in her left thigh and one in her left hand. One of the bullets has damaged her liver and she will die of peritonitis.

May was alone that night. She had retired from business, or at least semi-retired, and there were no girls in the house. But habit was strong. When the doorbell rang at midnight, she thought instinctively of customers; it had always meant customers. She opened the door.

Two men forced their way in. They shoved her into the kitchen, tied her hands, and began hitting her with the baseball bat. Wham, wham, wham on an old woman. Beating her cruelly, battering her. A fine species; it calls itself *Homo sapiens*. Then they shot her five times.

May told the police, ''Joe Costello sent them.'' But she couldn't identify the men who beat and shot her, she gave the cops nothing to support her claim that Costello was responsible, and she was rambling and disoriented. Two days later, she died. She was seventy-one years old.

The police arrested Costello, but he said he had nothing to do with May's death. At the time of the attack, he said, he was at the cab company, arguing with ''a drunken cab driver.'' He said the argument ended when he got a gun and fired a shot in the air; he was still doing it his way. No charges were brought against him in May's murder, and her killers were never found.

In 1958, Walter Sheridan was in St. Louis for the McClellan committee, checking some information that he thought might tie the Teamsters Union to the missing Greenlease money. It didn't lead to anything conclusive, but in the course of his investigation Sheridan got to know Elmer Dolan. Gradually, a friendship developed.

Dolan was wary, of course. He was one of the walking wounded—a man who had gone to prison essentially for someone else's crime—but when

Sheridan talks about him, it is evident that he liked him and felt sorry for him, and this must have communicated itself to Dolan. Over the next four years, Sheridan made a point of seeing Dolan whenever he was in St. Louis, and he talked to him long distance now and then.

In those four years, however, Dolan never opened up to Sheridan—never told him the true story. "I knew he wanted to tell me," Sheridan says, "but he never did."

Phil King was also in touch with Dolan and got the same impression. On July 30, 1962, he advised Washington that he believed Dolan was "on the brink of 'coming over.' '' But Dolan wanted his confession kept secret; he was worried about the effect publicity would have on his family. The FBI assured him that any information he gave would be kept confidential.

It was the finalities that had freed him. On May 11, 1962, Lou Shoulders had a heart attack and died, at the age of sixty-three. A little more than a month later, on June 28, Joe Costello died. Dolan had a wife, and at that time, six children. His fear of Costello and Shoulders had kept him silent. After they died, he told Sheridan he wanted to talk.

On September 11, 1962, Dolan flew to Washington. Sheridan met him at the airport and took him to FBI headquarters, where Phil King was waiting. . . .

Dolan's confession ran six and a half single-spaced pages, supplemented later by several lengthy interviews in which he gave additional details. A number of points have to be mentioned before the confession itself is described:

1. Dolan never signed his statement. He refused to. He didn't say why, but it may have been a last, lingering reluctance to commit himself completely. He may have thought that if the confession came to light, despite the FBI's assurances, he could take refuge in a technicality. He could say he never *signed* a confession. But there isn't any doubt that it is Dolan speaking. Phil King and Richard J. Gallagher, an FBI supervisor, were present when he made his statement, and he repeated the main points to Walter Sheridan immediately afterward.

2. The FBI kept its promise. The confession stayed in the files for twenty years, with never a hint to the news media, the public or anyone else that Elmer Dolan, two decades before, had told part of the true story of the Greenlease money.

3. Twenty years. And then on October 8, 1982, a front-page story appeared in the *St. Louis Globe-Democrat:* FBI FILES UNLOCK MYS-

283

TERY OF GREENLEASE RANSOM. The story was based on Dolan's confession. It was written by two *Globe-Democrat* reporters, Sue Ann Wood and Edward W. O'Brien. They had found the confession in a mass of Grenap material that they had obtained through the Freedom of Information Act.

4. In a general sense, however, Dolan's confession was not new. It actually only confirmed what had been widely believed at the time: that Shoulders and Costello stole the $300,000. It changed belief to certainty—but the belief had been there all along.

5. And the confession took the solution only part of the way. It did not reveal what happened to the money *after* Shoulders and Costello got it. It didn't tell where the ransom went after it left Costello's house.

The confession begins prosaically: "I would like at this time to advise that on October 6, 1953, I was working the 3 P.M. to 11 P.M. watch as a member of the St. Louis Police Department."

Then Dolan told of being Shoulders' driver that night and having dinner with him at June George's home. About 7:30 (after the third phone call from Costello), Shoulders said, "Let's go," and they drove to the meeting place. Costello was already there—Dolan had seen him before and recognized him. In another car was a man he didn't know but later learned was Ollie Johnson. Shoulders and Costello talked for a few minutes, out of Dolan's hearing, and then all of them drove to the Town House.

"Steve, this is Ollie." Dolan gave the password, and the two cops went in and arrested Carl Hall. This part of the confession was the same as Dolan's previous testimony, but then he added something new:

As he stood over Hall, guarding him, Dolan heard Shoulders open the apartment door and go out. He was gone about ten or fifteen minutes. Dolan didn't see him go out—only heard him—and didn't know where he went, but in one of the subsequent interviews he said he believed what happened was that Shoulders stepped out into the corridor and handed Hall's suitcase and footlocker to Costello. It was a sound assumption.

When they left the apartment, Dolan started toward the front of the building, but Shoulders said: "Don't take him down the elevator. Take him down the back way." Dolan turned the prisoner around and headed for the rear exit. Then another new detail:

As he started toward the back, "I observed Shoulders and Costello standing in the hallway near Hall's apartment, and *another individual* who I could not identify at that time and whom I still cannot identify. The best

284

I can recall concerning the unknown man was that I could see a hat brim and an arm. It appeared to me [that] he was partially concealed behind a drape. It appeared that he was purposely trying to conceal himself.''

Who was the third man in the corridor? It wasn't Ollie Johnson—Dolan was sure of that, and anyway, Ollie had retreated to his car by that time—so who was standing there with Shoulders and Costello? The Polonius behind the arras, hiding himself from view. The last mystery man.

Almost incidentally, Dolan's confession validated the guilty verdicts in the perjury trials: ''I wish to state . . . that neither Hall, Shoulders or myself were carrying any suitcases or trunks [when they left the Town House].''

They took Hall to the police station, booked him and put him in a cell—all as described previously. Then they left the station—but they didn't go to June George's house to deliver Shoulders' car. They drove to Costello's house.

Shoulders went in, leaving Dolan outside in the police car. After about twenty minutes, Costello or Shoulders (Dolan couldn't remember which) came out and told Dolan to come inside. And then:

''When I entered the house, it was dark [but] I saw someone else in the house, who appeared to be a male, whom I could not recognize.''

It was almost certainly the same man he had seen at the Town House, but Dolan still couldn't identify him. In one of the subsequent interviews, however, he said he didn't think the man at Costello's house was Joe's lieutenant, Matt Boyle. By implication, this would mean it wasn't Boyle at the apartment, either.

The confession continued: ''I followed Costello or Shoulders down some stairs to a rathskeller in the basement. On . . . a coffee table I observed two large trunks, one black and one green, which were opened and contained a large sum of currency. In addition, there were large stacks of currency on the table. . . .''

The FBI had finally located Point A: the rec room in Costello's basement. Shoulders had handed Hall's luggage to Costello and someone else at the Town House, Costello and someone else had taken it to Costello's home, and when Shoulders and Dolan got there, Costello and someone else had just finished counting the ransom and dividing it.

''We made some money today,'' Shoulders told Dolan. He was gloating. He was jubilant. He pointed to the money. ''Half of that is ours,'' he said. Then he told Dolan his share would be $50,000. ''What are you going to do with it?'' he asked jovially.

Dolan said he didn't want it. He didn't yet know that it was the Greenlease ransom; he just knew something was terribly wrong and he had

285

got mixed up in it by accident and he wished to God he hadn't. Later he told FBI agent Edward Moreland that his words to Shoulders were: "I don't want anything to do with that crap."

"You really don't have anything to say about it," Shoulders said coldly. And suddenly the young cop was very frightened.

Nevertheless, he said he refused to take the $50,000. In December 1955, however, newly out of prison and hard up for money, he met Costello at a restaurant, and Joe told him he had sold his share for $10,000. He offered it to him. Dolan said he turned down the $10,000 but finally agreed to take $1,500 "because it was Christmas time and he did not have a job." He said he spent part of it on presents for his family and the rest went for living expenses. Elmer Dolan's merry Christmas.

When they left Costello's house, they took Hall's suitcase and footlocker with them, leaving half of the ransom behind. On the way to the police station, Dolan said, he tried to convince Shoulders that they were making an awful mistake—that they would never get away with it, never get away with taking all that money.

He said he was scared stiff—scared they would be caught, scared Costello and Shoulders would kill him if he didn't go along, wishing he had had the nerve to pull his gun on them down there in the rec room and arrest them and stop the whole thing, but he couldn't do it because he was afraid of them. Instead he tried to talk Shoulders out of it, but the big cop just looked "happy over making some money" and wouldn't listen to him.

They got back to the Newstead Avenue station and carried in the luggage containing half of the ransom. It was an hour and twenty minutes since they had booked Carl Hall.

Shoulders went back to the holdover and started talking to the prisoner. About forty-five minutes later, he came into his office, where Dolan was guarding the footlocker and suitcase. He told Dolan the man they had arrested was the kidnapper of Bobby Greenlease.

God, with His paradoxes, will not leave us alone.

The story was over.

But it was not over.

What happened to the $300,000 after Shoulders and Dolan left Joe Costello's house?

Who was the third man in the corridor?

Was it John Vitale?

Or was it some other mystery man?

On March 25, 1970, the FBI closed the Greenlease case.

286

Acknowledgments

The following persons helped me with this book, in interviews or in other research, and I am grateful to them: Phillip M. King, I. A. Long, Sandra June O'Day, Bruce S. Shoulders, Selwyn Pepper, Carl R. Baldwin, James A. Kearns, Jr., John H. Poelker, Edward M. Moreland, Walter J. Sheridan, Mrs. June Michael, Mrs. Mary Kay Eifert, James L. McMullin, James C. Millstone, Thomas J. Deakin, Harvey Shoulders, Raymond F. Pisney, Richard J. Gallagher, Michelle Brown, William J. Scott, Kenneth W. DeMent, John J. Hynes II, Larry Brockelsby, Mrs. William Barnes III, William H. Bryan, Gerald Brown, Patrick F. Healy, Lee Norrgard, Lawrence J. King, James Vermeersch, John Gammon, Jack A. French, Gerard M. Weisbrod, John Pelly, J. D. Kirschten, Lois Kuhl, and a number of others who preferred to remain anonymous. I am also grateful to Bruce Lee, Douglas Stumpf, Jared Stamm, John Harrison and Joan Amico of William Morrow and Company, and my agent, Robert Lescher.

The principal sources for the book were 2,530 pages of FBI reports, 1,100 pages of St. Louis Police Department reports, hundreds of news stories from the *St. Louis Post-Dispatch,* the *St. Louis Globe-Democrat,* the *Kansas City Star,* the *Chicago Sun-Times,* and the *Chicago Tribune,* and personal interviews. Other material came from court decisions, transcripts of trials, congressional testimony, and other official documents. Conversations and other quoted material are based on interviews or official records and reports.

To J.P.

Fathers Day - 1990

All my love, forever n' ever,

Susie